D0952162

Reinventing Professional Services

Reinventing Professional Services

Services

BUILDING YOUR BUSINESS IN THE DIGITAL MARKETPLACE

Ari Kaplan

WILEY

John Wiley & Sons, Inc.

Published by John Wiley & Sons, Inc., Hoboken, New Jersey.

Published simultaneously in Canada.

For general information on our other products and services or for technical support, please contact our Customer Care Department within the United States at (800) 762-2974, outside the United States at (317) 572-3993, or fax (317) 572-4002.

Wiley also publishes its books in a variety of electronic formats. Some content that appears in print may not be available in electronic books. For more information about Wiley products, visit our web site at www.wiley.com.

Library of Congress Cataloging-in-Publication Data:
Kaplan, Ari, 1973-
    Reinventing professional services : building your business in the digital marketplace / Ari Kaplan.
       p. cm.
    Includes index.
    ISBN 978-1-118-00190-5 (hardback); 978-1-118-09750-2 (ebk);
    978-1-118-09751-9 (ebk); 978-1-118-09752-6 (ebk)
      1. Professions—Marketing.   2. Information technology—Management.
   3. Technological innovations—Management.   I. Title.
    HD8038.A1K35 2011
    658.4'063—dc22

                                    2011011001

Printed in the United States of America
13

For Lauren, for inspiring me and always having my back.
And, of course, for Emory & Hannah

Contents

Introduction: **The Rise of the White Collar Hustler and Your Path**
to Practical Innovation **xi**
Getting Started xiii
What's in This Book xvii

Chapter 1: **Finding Your Way in a More Informal, Instant World** **1**
Create Opportunity by Becoming a Visible Enthusiastic Expert 5
Increase Your Visibility and Realize Your Potential 6
Enthusiasm Is the Hallmark of the Modern Hustler 11
Expertise Is Easier to Convey Than Ever Before 14

Chapter 2: **Innovators Adapt, and You Should Too** **17**
Set Goals for Social Media 19
Begin Cultivating Offline Relationships Online 21
Embrace Transparency Because Everybody Knows Everything Anyway 24
Grass Roots Medicine 26

Chapter 3: **Recognize the Resiliency Revolution and Join It to Grow**
Your Practice **33**
Seize Opportunity Whenever Possible 35
Flexible Fees Make Cost Conversations More Cheerful 36
Alignment Is the Answer to Better Client Relationships 39
Technology Offers Better Communication All Around 43

Chapter 4: **Students Have Everything to Gain from the White Collar Hustle** **47**
Busting Myths About Networking 50
Be Disciplined and Accountable 51

Share Your Successes and Your Failures   54
Be Prolific and Fast   55
Be a Resource, Focus on Others   56
Follow Up   58

Chapter 5:   **Know Your Clients and Patients Because They Expect You To**   **61**
Accountants and Technology Are a Good Match   63
Leverage a Variety of Tools to Promote Your Practice   65
Answer the Question the Client Should Have Asked   66
Merge Talents Wherever Possible   70

Chapter 6:   **Putting Your Practice through a Wind Tunnel Will**
             Blow You Away   **73**
Even Small Elements of Inefficiency Can Have a Large Impact on
    the Bottom Line   75
Define Your Value Proposition to Focus Your Future   78
Finding True Worth Is Wiser Than You Realize   80
Become a Chameleon to Kick Start Your Initiatives   81

Chapter 7:   **It's a Small Street, So Befriend Your Neighbors**   **89**
Know Yourself to Better Understand Others   91
From SWOT to Sales Is a Path to Prosperity   93
Change But Don't Change Who You Are   95
Tie Profits to Success to Build Trust and Motivate   97
Trust and Respect Now Matter More Than Ever   99

Chapter 8:   **Networking Is Dead; Long Live Networking**   **101**
Go Where Your Audience Goes   102
Use Tools that Your Audience Uses   103
Find a Geek to Help You Get LinkedIn   104
Integrate Your Efforts to Save Time and Sanity   105
Explore Facebook for Fun and Professional Potential   107
How to Decide Whether You Should Blog   107
Spend Time with Your Audience and the Members Will Spend Time with You   110

Chapter 9:   **Proactive Professionals Pay Attention to Progress**   **111**
Sales and Marketing Have Evolved So You Should Too   116
Medical Records Are Right on the Money   119

Chapter 10: **When You're Allergic to Wool, Wear Cotton or Suffer for Your Entire Career**   **125**

Passion, Time, and Luck—Plus Relationships   127

The "Yes" Business   129

Make Every Client a Secret Shopper   131

Global Roots in Virtual Spaces   132

Set Expectations   133

The Art of the Referral   135

Chapter 11: **Meet Your Clients and Patients Directly**   **141**

An Accelerant of Change   145

Displacement Anxiety   149

Chapter 12: **Mailing Lists, the Media, and Making Mistakes**   **153**

Become an Umbrella Salesman   154

Benefits, Business Development, and Beyond   158

Meeting the Media   159

Make Mini Muffins with the Media   160

Being the Media   164

You, Too, Can YouTube   165

Chapter 13: **Forget Technology, Remember Others to Build True Relationships**   **169**

Use Technology to Say Thanks and More   174

Pay Attention to the Pitfalls of Participation   176

Confidentiality Is Critical, So Know When to Keep Quiet   177

Be Careful Creating Professional Relationships Online   179

Advantages of the Cautious Approach   180

Chapter 14: **The Foundation for Follow-Up Is Easy to Establish**   **183**

Timing Your Tidings to Connect with Colleagues   185

Hosting Events Is for Everyone   188

Thoughtful Follow-Up Is Favorable   189

Writing and Its Spinoffs as Marketing Are Remarkably Effective   190

Conclusion: **Cultivating Community**   **195**

Resources   199

Acknowledgments   205

About the Author   207

Index   209

Introduction

The Rise of the White Collar Hustler and Your Path to Practical Innovation

Between my college graduation and my first semester of law school, I spent a year living in Kobe, Japan, working for the Japanese government through the Japan Exchange and Teaching Program of the Council of Local Authorities for International Relations. During one of my vacations, I made a last-minute decision to visit Nepal and flew into Kathmandu late one spring evening in 1994. I was alone, with only a backpack and a *Lonely Planet* guidebook. I recall a single telephone in the airport and I waited in what seemed like a very long line for an opportunity to call a few guesthouses in the city.

As I waited, I paid little attention to the travelers around me or to their systematic usage of the phone. I periodically looked up from my book and noticed that each subsequent person on the line lifted the receiver, dialed, and waited for almost the exact same amount of time as the preceding individual. As one walked away, another stepped forward, lifted the receiver, and executed the routine. It was very mechanical and efficient.

There was, however, one problem that went unsaid until I had an opportunity to play the game.

The phone was broken!

Each person took the same steps and realized the same result—failure. They thought those steps worked for their predecessor and simply followed his or her lead. They were unaware of the earlier results so they left in confusion without saying a word to their fellow travelers.

Upon realizing the trouble, like a courteous Eagle Scout, I turned to the person behind me and informed him that the handset did not work. He smiled and waved as I walked away to either find another pay phone or some other type of travel assistance. When I looked back, I was surprised to see him holding the receiver attempting to make a call. Even more startling was that despite my advisory to him and a few others within earshot in the line, not a single person left. Not one.

Today, providers of a broad range of professional services find themselves waiting in a proverbial line to use tools and techniques that are of waning utility. It is harder for them to build relationships with the same longevity and, therefore, they face greater challenges in developing business. Although most had been following a similar path for years with a fair amount of success, the recession and the impact of technology on information-oriented advisory careers are forcing them to become more entrepreneurial. A well-respected education, industry experience, and a book of contacts are no longer enough. There is a renewed focus on practical innovation.

The trends have, in a word, forced each professional to become a *hustler.*

This book is designed to provide readers with authentic insights on charting an accessible course for making small changes that have the potential to achieve identifiable results. It offers concrete ideas for engaging more fully with clients and prospects, raising your profile and that of your practice by contributing to the growth of your professional community, and creating additional opportunities to interact with your core audience.

Each chapter features an overall message, for example, Chapter 5 is about profiling and understanding your customers, clients, patients, and so on. Commentary from experts in various industries supports that message and there are often references to online resources that will help you execute this idea.

Ultimately, that is my goal. I want you to read this book, select a single idea that you believe can work in your practice, and act. Period.

To that end, I make you two promises. First, you are likely to fail at some point. Second, you are unlikely to succeed if you are not willing to fail, even in some small way. Of course, every step forward involves some risk. As professionals, we abhor risk. It is antithetical to our training. In fact, we seek out advanced education and licensed skills to eliminate as much risk as possible.

The reality is, however, that success in today's highly populated professional communities requires both skill and style. Technology can help you hone both. New tools allow you to showcase your talent to a much broader audience. They empower you to interact with that audience in a more organic fashion. And, they create meaningful opportunities to follow up in a seamless and effective manner.

Everyone has a story about his or her first client or first job. It always seems like serendipity in hindsight, where the stars aligned and someone caught a very lucky break. In fact, there is often additional detail that reveals the coordinated long-term effort required to create that opportunity and others like it.

"The challenge is that people want the silver bullet, the formula, the magic potion," says Bruce Jones, Programming Director at the Disney Institute in Orlando, Florida, which trains executives worldwide on adopting the Disney model of creating an emotional connection to their brands. "It is not magic; it is day in and day out commitment," he adds.

That commitment might come in the form of networking or it might manifest itself in one's dedication to improving his or her community. Ultimately, it is demonstrated in ways that individuals can easily tailor to their own strengths and personalities. It is the modern hustle for longevity and client service recognition.

Everyone can take a common sense approach with their own branding, which reflects their character and capability. "We are not perfect," says Jones. "We strive for perfection and we'll settle for excellence, but we won't settle for anything less."

> The challenge is that people want the silver bullet, the formula, the magic potion. It is not magic; it is day in and day out commitment.
>
> *Bruce Jones, Programming Director at the Disney Institute in Orlando, Florida*

Getting Started

The central focus of today's white-collar hustler is a well-crafted plan and a dedication to a routine set of activities that contributes to the professional's success, as well as that of those he or she serves. Throughout this book we'll explore how to make a plan that draws on individual strengths and needs. Having a plan, though, is not enough. Being accountable is essential. It is also important to bring others into the process; by telling someone about your goals, those in your support circle can help you with encouragement and reinforcement. In these pages, we'll also explore the roles of proactive listening and introspection, as well as the importance of being true to yourself.

The first step comes with understanding that professionals can change the manner in which they get from point A to point B in achieving business goals, without fundamentally changing their identity as doctors, lawyers, dentists, veterinarians, accountants, and the like.

Consider my experience as a swimmer: I have always loved swimming and, of course, hated it at the same time. As hard as I tried, I never seemed to get better or faster, but it has been my primary workout since following up on a New Year's resolution in 2007 and joining a local masters swimming team. After a frustrating practice session, a fellow teammate suggested that I read *Total Immersion: The Revolutionary Way to Swim Better, Faster, and Easier* by Terry Laughlin and John Delves (Fireside, 1996) to focus on my stroke, rather than my strength.

As soon as I began reading it, I realized that I had for years been concentrating on spinning my arms around as quickly as possible instead of streamlining my body to move through the water more aerodynamically like a fish. I asked my coach, Ultraman Canada finisher Melanie Fink, to help me implement the changes to my stroke and formation. Fink, the owner of Personal Training of Short Hills LLC, challenged me to dismantle my existing notions of swimming and reform my entire perspective on the sport. And, as you might imagine, I resisted.

For months, I struggled with learning new techniques and swam slower than ever before. But then it started to get easier and I began swimming faster, but more efficiently. Instead of using 24 strokes to make it across a 25-yard pool, I was across in 20, then 18, and now, depending on how tired I am, even 16 or 14. I am not stronger, but I am more economical with my energy and effort.

While the professional community is not necessarily struggling to make it across the pool, licensed experts in every discipline are sensing a revolution in how they deliver their services to a more empowered audience of clients in a dynamic economic environment.

Advancements in technology have commoditized many of the services professionals once offered for a fee. Now, they are giving that information away and searching for higher-value revenue streams. Social media has completely shifted the landscape from commentary to conversation. While experts once informed individuals about key issues in their field, they are now responding to queries and discussing those issues in an open forum. That transparency has completely reconfigured the setting.

Lawyers, accountants, doctors, bankers, architects, veterinarians, dentists, and others who used to focus solely on their craft are now reconsidering their "stroke count," having come to realize they are making inefficient efforts. Just as importantly, many realize they hamper themselves by avoiding calculated risks that are likely to produce results.

I actually avoided this risk on behalf of my then-seven-year-old son, whom I coached in Little League. I didn't play baseball as a child; the thought of getting hit by the ball always scared me. That, and a complete lack of coordination. But my son can play. And, he loves it. So I coach.

All of the kids who pitched were eight, almost nine. For weeks, he kept asking me for permission to pitch and I quietly suggested that he keep practicing. The truth was that I was afraid that a batter would return one of his pitches right into his head or chest. Toward the end of the season, another coach offered him a chance and I acquiesced.

He walked the first and second batters. To be honest I was relieved because he didn't get hit with the ball. Then he struck out the third and fourth batters. Every kid in the dugout was on his feet. Two on, two outs, and he struck out the last batter retiring the side with no runs scored. Amazing! Like it was no problem. Like failure was not an option.

In fact, failure is always an option, often a very real one. Complacency can be a smooth road on which to travel. It might be safe. But, where will it take you? And, of course, there are risks. After all, I'm glad my son pitched, but it took us a while to get him to stop sleeping with his baseball glove.

"Success today requires the willingness to take a risk and to put your stake in the sand," says Nancy Fox, founder of The Business Fox, a coaching and training company. "You really can't afford to treat your practice like a practice anymore; you have to be an entrepreneur and view it as a business," she advises.

While it was once an advantage to have a personal brand, it is now essential. Without one, you often limit your value within your organization and the community. Hoping the phone rings is an exercise in wasting energy because, among other reasons, fewer people are using the phone to interact with their counselors. The marketplace is competitive; only those who target their audience and find ways to creatively interact with its members will continue to thrive.

Expectations, both internal and external, are higher. Decades ago, junior associates had seven or eight years to prove themselves. Today, they have three. And, one must be proactive now or face the consequences later. Those that are often reap rewards.

Two days after my son's baseball game, I received this e-mail from a student at a law school where I had spoken a while back, who viewed his job search this way:

> Ari,
>
> You do not remember me, but I met you when you spoke at [our] Law School last year. I just wanted to email you to let you know that I followed your advice and got a job as a result of it. I won't bore you with the details but basically I became a networking whore/junky. I just wanted to e-mail you to say thank you for your assistance.

Like this student, professionals must shift from being reactive to industry change to proactively incorporating new ideas into their practices. And, of course: *hustling*.

Over the past few years, I have had the opportunity to interact with thousands of professionals. Whenever I asked one about the key to success in his or her field, the response was typically: "I am a hustler."

Aside from all of the gadgetry and Internet-based solutions, or the calls for value-billing and improved customer service, many of the professionals with whom I have spoken attributed their success in one method or another to leveraging a cocktail of efforts that helped them fuel the hustle and create possibility. Fox paraphrases a quote that captures the essence of the new hustler's revolution: "If you're interested in success, you'll do what is convenient. If you are committed to success, you will do whatever the hell is necessary."

Each professional can find parallel challenges that colleagues in other disciplines are facing, as well as strategies that are helping them reshape their efforts. We must engage in a broader conversation that enables providers of services to reinvent instead of simply repeat past exercises. Most are steeped in tradition in terms of how they develop and cultivate client relationships, interact with peers, and collaborate. They continue to operate within models of hourly billing and base earnings solely on the time spent. Each profession also views its own protocols in isolation, but there are more universal similarities than many realize. From accountants to architects and bankers to barristers, there is a dynamic approach that could work for you.

Whatever name we give it, however we described the process, one thing is clear: the path to growing a professional business has changed. This book explores how to get on the new track, a process that needn't be painful and could even be fun.

What's in This Book

The transformation of professional services has been characterized by a more proactive base of clients/patients, who are empowered with information and heightened expectations. Each chapter is designed to help you navigate the evolution of this interdisciplinary phenomenon.

This introduction contrasts the urgent need for change with the approachable manner in which one can make subtle adjustments to remain on pace with progress.

The first three chapters highlight the characteristics that professionals should incorporate to properly position themselves for change. Chapter 1 suggests that in order to navigate today's more informal and instant environment, licensed practitioners should seek to become visible enthusiastic experts. Doing so will allow them to realize their potential. Chapter 2 justifies the need for innovation and encourages individuals to embrace new ideas in a traditional culture. Chapter 3 cites specific trends related to pricing, partnerships, and correspondence that will help professionals thrive.

The next three chapters are meant to establish a generational understanding of how to practically approach goal-setting. Chapter 4 is designed for students to understand how to see the foundation for a future in a fiercely competitive market. Chapter 5 prompts professionals to learn more about their clients and patients, while Chapter 6 provides guidance on reshaping their practices based on the needs of those clients and patients.

The next four chapters are designed to help individuals and organizations adapt to new methods of communication and encourage experimentation with technology. Chapter 7 suggests that streamlining operations can revitalize revenue streams. Chapter 8 focuses on the updated art of networking in a digital world. It addresses the social media landscape and offers suggestions for acclimating to this new environment. Chapter 9 sets forth the advantages of taking a proactive and direct approach to connecting with clients or patients. And, Chapter 10 promotes the idea of customizing each approach to suit one's particular circumstances. It recognizes the critical nature of referral sources and strategic techniques for creating opportunity.

The remaining sections are designed to spark new ideas and inspire calculated risk-taking with a full understanding of the potential consequences. Chapter 11 prompts professionals to seek out specific contacts, rather than hope to make their acquaintance in the future. Chapter 12 provides concrete examples of how to execute and achieve those goals. Chapter 13 reminds readers that the ultimate goal is not to become adept at using a tool, but to enhance your ability to form genuine relationships. It also provides certain points of caution in creating those relationships online. Chapter 14 offers creative ideas for following up with those you meet and for remaining in touch with them.

Finally, the conclusion conveys the ultimate goal of cultivating community. It highlights that doing so creates opportunity and enables one to more effectively hone his or her message.

The suggestions and conclusions are based on proven efforts, as well as the experience, of those featured in the book. They are leaders in their fields and recognized as much for their accomplishments as the manner in which they achieved them.

The chapters are designed to form a cohesive journey from theory to reality, but can also be read selectively. Just as the book encourages customization of your approach in your practice, I have written it to allow you that same flexibility in the way you interact with the material. I hope that you find the content thought-provoking, action-oriented, and empowering.

CHAPTER 1

Finding Your Way in a More Informal, Instant World

The new formula for prosperity among most professionals is to become a visible enthusiastic expert. This chapter will discuss how increasing his or her visibility can help a professional realize business-development potential, why modern hustlers are known for their enthusiasm, and the relative ease with which one can showcase expertise in a digital marketplace.

■ ■ ■

Important changes in marketing are already taking place. In fact, we are in a new era that values momentum over perfection.

For decades, personal marketing was time consuming and challenging because nothing could be released into the public domain until it was perfect. There was no tolerance for mistakes or inconsistencies.

Today, we are in the environment of perpetual beta, where technology has created a climate of perfect imperfection. The culture is more accepting of shortcomings. In fact, there is a certain authenticity in being almost cool. It is more relatable. It conveys sincerity. It builds trust.

There is also a certain freedom in not worrying about flawlessness and instead concentrating on commencement. Professionals are now liberated to start more initiatives just like the entrepreneurs they admire. They simply need to look to themselves for ideas.

"I think personal responsibility and accountability is the answer," says Nancy Fox. "We are our own mirrors for everything else."

When that mirror is unclear, there are so many more voices available today to provide another perspective. The conversation is taking place. There is a choice of when, how, and even if you will participate.

Mark Britton and his team are pushing professionals to progress whether they like it or not. He once took his four- and six-year-old sons skiing down the backside of the 11,166-foot Lone Peak, purportedly some of the most difficult terrain in Big Sky, Montana. It was a challenge (for all three of them), but the sons, now a few years older, are virtual experts. Soon after their trip, Britton founded Avvo, an online service for finding and rating doctors and lawyers. Avvo has become one of the most popular ratings services and is proverbially taking both professions on a similar adventure down the digital slope of Web 2.0 interactivity.

No stranger to industry transformations, Britton was the first general counsel of Internet-based travel reservation web site Expedia.com, and helped take the company public in 1999. In the spring of 2004, he moved to Italy to serve as an adjunct professor of finance for Gonzaga University in Florence, where he conceived of a service to replace the phone book. He notes that lawyers and doctors spend more than \$1 billion and more than \$500 million, respectively, per year on advertising in the telephone directory. "Anytime the Yellow Pages is a primary resource for consumers, something is broken," he says.

Avvo represents the rise of community interaction between consumers and professionals. In addition, "There is a broader understanding and acceptance of ratings systems if you are a professional interested in transparency," he says. People have been rating books, movies, food, and other items for years. Their opinions have helped shape future generations of those items and producers continue to pay close attention to the feedback of their customers.

Today, most service providers, from dry cleaners to doctors, realize that customers/patients/clients will offer feedback. Professionals want them to share that feedback responsibly and based on honest data. "Word of mouth is valuable, but when choosing a doctor or lawyer, it is also helpful to have someone increase your comfort level that the professional can handle the matter well," Britton says.

Despite the availability of free information to answer complicated questions, consumers still need professional advice. One might be able to draft a contract or design minor architectural changes to a small room at home, but once there are variables to that initial effort, an individual will want a trusted resource. Specialization of those resources has resulted in an unchallenged reverence, but not all professionals are created equal. Modern transparency tells a more detailed story, to which each professional is permitted to contribute.

Restaurants, for example, operate in volumes that are much greater than doctors or lawyers. As a result, there are fewer overall people with experience, coupled with the notion that they are less likely to discuss their ophthalmologist than their local baker. "People are interested in offering commentary, and in that way Avvo has stoked the conversation," says Britton. In addition, Google is fostering a culture of professional open awareness. Most public records include at least minimal details about the backgrounds of one practitioner over another.

The increased digitization of documents is leading to one universal truth: your background will be publicly available. Choose to shape that public impression because once it is out there, prospective clients will judge your achievements. "Anything that we find value in will be rated," predicts Britton. "In fact, the more money and emotion that are involved, the greater the likelihood that if it is not being rated today, it will be rated shortly," he adds.

As a culture, investment in the Internet continues, and it is, therefore, becoming more valuable. As a consequence, the Internet is becoming a greater part of life. "It is not your choice not to participate anymore," cautions Britton. "Your life is on parade in the ether and it is only going to increase."

There is a dramatic convergence occurring where the public and private aspects of an individual are developing into a single personality. There is no longer an easy distinction between one's professional profile and his or her personal background. People who started tweeting for business inevitably use it for personal use (even if just to wish a professional contact a happy birthday). And, that is, of course, the point.

The goal is to develop relationships over contacts. To produce substance, as well as exude style. My United States Supreme Court gift shop tie reminds me of this balance every time I look at it.

On December 5, 2007, I had the privilege of covering the oral arguments in the consolidated Guantanamo Bay detainee cases of *Boumediene v. Bush* and *Al Odah v. United States* at the Supreme Court as part of the official press corps. I arrived at the steps of the grand courthouse at 2 A.M. on a 20-degree almost-winter morning to experience the pre-rock concert-like atmosphere with more than 50 other people in the line hoping to secure a seat in the public gallery. Although my editor assured me that I would receive a press pass, I did not want to take any chances. I also wanted to really appreciate the magnitude of the case at issue.

To collect footage in advance of the event for a documentary project on which I was working, I brought my tripod and video camera in a backpack. I started interviewing people waiting in line who were kind enough to leave the comfort of their sleeping bags to share their reasons for risking frostbite at the foot of the famous steps to listen to a court case. It was inspiring. I was a hard-core investigative journalist—in my own mind, at least. Ari Kaplan, Supreme Court reporter. I envisioned the Academy Award for the footage, the Pulitzer Prize for the commentary. It would be a professional milestone.

There was just one tiny miscalculation.

Before I left for the trip, my wife, the smartest person I know, suggested I wear a suit. I vehemently resisted, noting that I was a one-man camera crew and needed the freedom to practice my craft. I did not need a suit, I was a journalist! She wisely persuaded me to at least take a pair of slacks and a collared shirt.

At about 6 A.M., it started snowing. By 8 A.M., I was the first in line outside the public affairs office to obtain my press pass. A few minutes later, standing before the public affairs officer in my slacks, hardtop Adidas sneakers (I did not bring shoes either), and layers of frostbite-fighting thermal wear, I realized that there was a problem. I was not wearing a tie—an apparent prerequisite for a male journalist to sit in the press gallery (I ignored the hardtop sneakers, correctly figuring that no one would notice).

One of the reporters joked that former Chief Justice Warren Burger used to personally ask reporters improperly dressed to leave their seats after the justices took the bench. So I ran to the gift shop and bought a $40 blue striped silk tie adorned with the scales of justice. I could almost hear my wife laughing as I was running.

The press officer approved of my outfit and assigned me to seat E-1, next to Pulitzer Prize-winning reporter Charlie Savage of the *New York Times*, then covering the event for the *Boston Globe*. One of the court's massive interior columns blocked part of my view, which was lucky because Chief Justice Roberts did not have a good line of sight to my souvenir tie, which now hangs proudly in my closet (though sadly gets little use).

The tie reminds me of the balance between style, substance, and tradition. It highlights that professional services do differ from other consumer-oriented industries in certain ways. There are protocols and practices that were once unique to lawyers or doctors or accountants. Today, however, the universal benefit of raising your visibility, even in a limited fashion, is more compelling than certain nuances that may or may not exist.

Create Opportunity by Becoming a Visible Enthusiastic Expert

I was attending an annual industry conference and a person with whom I was not familiar waved at me from a distance as we approached one another. He smiled as our paths crossed and we made momentary small talk. He thanked me for my recent advice and asked me to continue sending him my newsletter. I really did not know him, but he was well aware of my work and passion for sharing practical guidance with my audience.

It is easier to learn about that audience and tailor information for its members than it has ever been. As people select experts, they are no longer looking only for those who are well-educated and capable—that much is assumed. They want to see public validation of their work in the professional community. As a result, professionals who can showcase their talent directly to their target audience are perceived as more visible and, therefore, become more marketable.

The success strategy for licensed professionals has always involved hard work, long hours, extensive resumes and long-term client relationships. The nature of those relationships, however, has changed as the pool of potential opportunities has shifted. Technology now permits access to more people in diverse areas who have traditionally been difficult to reach.

The increased number of choices and the prevalence of tools that enable potential clients and customers to do some of the work themselves is causing commoditization. Taxes can be filed online, simple illnesses can be diagnosed via medical web sites, basic room additions can be designed with self-service CAAD (computer-aided architectural design) programs, and, of course, a variety of legal documents can be drafted for free. People are now much freer to eliminate or reduce the need for licensed resources that once held a monopoly on trusted information. This shift requires those experts to convey basic knowledge, but in a way that tailors their understanding to the issues with which their existing or future clients are struggling. They are required to routinely engage in conversation on issues about which their clients or patients have acquired some knowledge and may have preexisting ideas.

Increase Your Visibility and Realize Your Potential

As a child, Chris Reimer worked for his grandfather, an entrepreneur who started a company manufacturing windows in 1949. "Being around that type of environment gave me the first taste of entrepreneurial work," he says. After graduating from Marquette University in Milwaukee with an accounting degree, he became a certified public accountant (CPA) and held a variety of finance-related roles, including one as the chief financial officer of a small business in St. Louis. Like many professionals, "I always made a good living, but can't say that I identified with what I was doing," he recalls.

After eliminating the idea of starting a mobile shredding business because of its prohibitive start-up costs, he considered developing a line of humorous t-shirts, similar to the popular items sold on SnorgTees.com or BustedTees.com. He thought that he would enjoy the exercise of designing the shirts and that he could run the business out of his home as it would be completely online. "For a year, I dreamed about ways that it would explode on impact," recalls Reimer of his new company, Rizzo Tees LLC.

Of course, as is common with start ups, by the time the site—RizzoTees.com—went live on October 30, 2008, he had no money left for marketing or advertising. So, five days later, Reimer registered for an account on Twitter and began telling people about his shirts.

"I was not an early Twitter adopter, but Twitter was a perfect fit for me," he says. Although he started growing t-shirt revenues from his Twitter audience, his presence as a social media authority was rising even more quickly. "As my personal brand grew, it started pulling me away from accounting," he recalls. "I was increasingly disenchanted with my day job because I was enjoying Rizzo Tees so much," he adds.

As the shirts continued selling through Twitter and later Facebook, Reimer began discussing social media more publicly, but he was still trying to maintain a separate existence from his traditional job. "The idea of making funny t-shirts and being a social media devotee did not mix with the role of a chief financial officer," he notes. "I wanted to keep that job and did not want anyone to ask any questions."

By 2010, his audience members encouraged him to engage in social media consulting full time. He even considered creating Rizzo Media Works to perform advertising and digital marketing. "That business plan was not pleasing to my wife because there was no guarantee of income," he jokes, but the CEO of Scorch Agency soon offered him the opportunity to become the company's Chief Marketing Officer. "That was my dream fulfilled and Rizzo Tees ended up being the springboard." In early 2011, he accepted a new position as Vice President of Social Media with Falk Harrison, a St. Louis-based brand communications agency.

Some professionals are comfortable experimenting with public forms of social media, but many fear the potential consequences of engagement. As a result, they pay no attention to the conversation and fail to participate in any meaningful way. Reimer decided to simply begin by listening, which is often how natural discussions occur. The individual, who is unfamiliar with a particular topic or those speaking, simply stands by to learn more about the context of the discussion before providing additional commentary. In Twitter parlance, Reimer began by "following" the "tweets" of certain individuals and organizations.

"When you meet people in person, typically someone has to make the first move," he says. "There is no such thing on Twitter." You simply click "follow" on their Twitter page and you are now privy to everything they say—voila! People actually appreciate when you follow them. "You are spending a little bit of your social currency when you follow and you get some in return," adds Reimer, who started following more people and they began following him in return. Of course, he made some mistakes along the way; he admits that his auto-response thanking people for following him turned out to be a nuisance, which he quickly removed.

In a technological environment, people tend to be more forgiving in marketing. They are used to hiccups. Cell phones drop calls often enough that people understand when you lose the signal. Everyone with a computer has rebooted at some point in his or her life. And, of course, there are countless examples of viruses invading someone's phone book and spamming everyone he or she knows. Minor mistakes are part of progress.

I launched a webinar series called 30-Minute Thursdays in October of 2009. The webinars have offered creative ideas to hundreds of professionals nationwide. My first presentation, *Five Easy Ways to Create Opportunities in a Down Market*, was a great success both in terms of the high rate of attendance and the number of people who followed up with my sponsor. So, when planning for the second date, *Five Ways to Use the Holiday Season to Raise Your Profile*, I felt confident that I had mastered the webinar model.

Unfortunately, I had essentially double-booked myself during the second program. I was scheduled to speak live in Philadelphia at 2:30 P.M. ET and my webinar was scheduled for 1 P.M. No problem. I secured wireless Internet access and found an empty ballroom in the basement of the hotel where I was presenting. Subscribers started logging into the session before 1 P.M. and I began promptly. It was about 20 minutes after I started delivering my presentation that I noticed the "START WEBINAR" button at the top of the page.

> Your life is on parade in the ether and it is only going to increase.
>
> Mark Britton, founder, CEO, and president of Seattle-based Avvo

I pushed the button, heard the announcement that "the webinar is now beginning," and faced the reality that I had been talking to myself for quite some time. It was a dramatic public error. I immediately ended the webinar and within minutes, I sent an e-mail acknowledging the mistake. The number of kind responses from the attendees assured me that all was not lost and they indeed returned for the make-up session. I have a feeling they called in just for the adventure. Some even sent humorous reminders to press the "start" button.

Anyone who tries to leave his or her comfort zone falters at some point in a marketing or networking endeavor. That does not mean, however, that the effort is wasted. When you ask someone to meet and they decline, you have still set the foundation for a follow-up request. When you engage in social media and do not feel like you are reaching a substantial audience or efficiently utilizing your time, you are, at a minimum, listening to a conversation that will help you direct your efforts in the future. It is about communicating your message and letting that message reflect your character.

Reimer started to contribute to the conversation by sharing news links. Period. Only after his listeners began to reciprocate did he start mentioning his passion for t-shirts, red wine, and the National Basketball Association (NBA). "You are letting people get to know you," he advises. But he set boundaries because as tens of thousands of people started following him, he realized that they were not all friends. As such, he has chosen not to reveal any family-related information.

That said, "What I did with Twitter is to be an open book of transparency and let people know who I am," he recalls. And, of course, that simple act of engagement produced results. "I realized that it helped sell t-shirts because people are more apt to buy products from those they know, like, and trust."

As one of the most traditional principles in business, there is nothing exciting about the "know, like, and trust" formula. When you combine it with the "visible enthusiastic expert" concept, you begin to realize that you can empower yourself and your practice to build professional relationships that are more likely to yield the outcome toward which you are working.

As the Vice President of Social Media with Falk Harrison, Reimer encourages professionals to blog, but goes beyond that traditional advice. Understanding that many experts support personal charitable endeavors, he suggests, for example, recording participation in such efforts using a Flip video recorder and sharing clips online to reflect the character of the organization. A blog is just one potential distribution source. The video can be uploaded to a YouTube account (which can be created upon simple registration at the site) or sharing the link to the video with followers on Twitter.

Google will also index any keywords associated with the video and enrich its search results to reflect your dynamic use of content.

"Most people have the same web site with the same outbound message, headshots, and contact page," highlights Reimer. "There is generally no compelling message that entices people to spend more time on their site," he adds. Those who veer ever so slightly from this mold can distinguish themselves from their peers.

For generations, licensed professionals grew business by demonstrating their knowledge and cultivating referrals. Today, they must use their basic knowledge to establish relationships and, therefore, need to consider giving it away for free. It is unnatural, but increasingly effective. "Even if you share a little bit for free, when you do it in a more authentic way, people will trust you and see your value," says Reimer, who offers the example of a friend who is a health insurance broker in St. Louis.

Reimer advised him to generate inbound marketing leads by demonstrating his expertise instead of making routine cold calls. He suggested that he create a portal to showcase his expertise in various ways, including on a blog. He compared it to a printed newsletter that his audience can share more easily. That said, "Even an e-mail is not quite as sharable as a re-tweet or pressing a Facebook 'like' button."

He never started the blog.

Coincidentally, another contact of his mentioned that she had found her health insurance broker by entering a variety of search terms into Google. Her efforts led her to an individual's blog hosted by Blogger, Google's completely free tool that offers basic features to enable writers to begin experimenting with the medium. Reimer visited the site and noted that despite his opinion that the blog contained basic information and was not well designed, it was better than anything else his colleague found online. It gave that broker a visibility advantage. The broker did not cold call this particular prospect, but she felt as if she knew him anyway. "The bullhorn was turned around," says Reimer.

Reimer himself once had a trademark problem with one of his Rizzo Tees T-shirts. After receiving a cease-and-desist letter, he noted his concern on Twitter. A random attorney in Indiana was "listening" and contacted him. He offered to assist on a flat-fee basis and very quickly retained a new client. Instead of a giant bullhorn, the lawyer in Indiana used a similarly sized eavesdropping tool to successfully raise his visibility.

Even if you share a little bit for free, when you do it in a more authentic way, people will trust you and see your value.

Chris Reimer, Vice President of Social Media with Falk Harrison,
a St. Louis brand communications agency

Enthusiasm Is the Hallmark of the Modern Hustler

In the same way that Chris Reimer was able to find a career, or in many ways create a career that showcased his passion, professionals today must do the very same thing. They must find what it is about their work that captures the essence of that excitement.

Only the renowned experts in a particular field can engage clients and attract referral sources merely by being the singular expert on that topic. The market is so competitive that people often view their counselors in one area or another as fungible. They believe that there are likely to be multiple individuals or organizations that can successfully navigate a particular issue.

For example, there are first-rate hospitals around the world that can often handle a complex health matter, even one that has a significant idiosyncrasy. There are now hospital advertisements on television, the Internet, and even highway billboards. From fertility clinics to cancer centers, medical institutions are vying for patients.

Law firms are increasingly trying to figure out the formula for not only attracting a premium corporate client, but maintaining that relationship over the long term. They are willing to bill differently, change staffing patterns, and cede control to their clients or a client's outside advisors in an effort to demonstrate their commitment to efficiency.

All of these initiatives spotlight the level of interest an individual or an organization has in collaborating with a potential client, but what highlights the necessary level of enthusiasm is the individual story. That provides the essence of why a customer would choose one practitioner over another practitioner with similar skills.

It is often said in veterinary circles "People don't care how much you know, until they know how much you care," reports Graham Milligan, the Director of Clinical Services Division at the Royal Veterinary College at the University of London, in Hatfield,

England. He notes that while pet owners rarely question the technical ability of a veterinarian, they are very sensitive to the professional's demeanor.

Traditional veterinary instruction focused on rote memorization of factual information. Yet the client often determines the nature of the treatment. "The emphasis on preventive measures is becoming more important on small animal work," Milligan says, highlighting that weight management, older pet clinics, and puppy training, among others factors, are increasingly popular.

In addition, he advises that pet owners most often select their vet based on location, unless they receive a personal recommendation from another pet owner (even a stranger they might meet in the park). As such, it is even more critical for animal doctors to demonstrate their caring nature to clients than it is for most other professionals. "Vets who care more differentiate themselves, but they generally make pretty poor marketers," says Milligan. "That is not what motivates them and it is not why they went to veterinary school," he adds. While that fact is probably true of most professionals, the new reality is that professional services firms are like many other businesses.

> It is often said in veterinary circles: "People don't care how much you know, until they know how much you care."
>
> Graham Milligan, the Director of Clinical Services Division at the Royal Veterinary College at the University of London, in Hatfield, England

Ultimately, it is not just because a medical facility cured a patient or that a law firm won a case, it is that its human talent is so excited about the success of the patient or client that the facility or firm wants to tell as many people about the journey, rather than solely the destination.

Today, in order to convey the level of enthusiasm that potential business associates require to consider a professional's work, there needs to be a unique level of interaction. And that interaction must convey the human aspect of the relationship. It must provide insight into who you are, as much as what you can do. If traditional business is transacted between parties that know, like, and trust one another, there is a remarkable opportunity to develop that familiarity and sincerity in a richer way. A great personal story doesn't hurt.

Tejas Kapadia is a New Jersey lawyer. He was always interested in charitable giving and believed that businesses should give directly to the communities in which they generate their revenues. His brother, Hemish Kapadia, a New Jersey accountant and a bone marrow donor, agreed.

Raised by parents who grew up in India, the duo hoped to open a small business in Mumbai and then donate a percentage of their profits to support local charitable endeavors. Recognizing the increased interest in fast food there (Pizza Hut and Subway are among a number of restaurants with a presence throughout the city), they focused on the donut market. They moved across the world in October of 2006 and self-funded the opening of the American Donut Shoppe in the food court of an urban shopping mall in March, 2007. After more than four years, the business has five locations throughout Mumbai.

"It has been an adventure since doing business in India has almost nothing to do with legal practice in New Jersey," says Tejas Kapadia.

Neither brother is particularly passionate about donuts, yet both are excited about their charitable goals—to support local education and bone marrow programs—that the donut business can help them achieve. "Donuts are simply a product that I felt that we could make with some degree of quality without using chefs," he said.

Ironically, the Kapadia brothers originally anticipated training employees to make the donuts, but to improve efficiency they ultimately imported a donut-making machine from the United States. Even in an endeavor where contributing to the local economy is a primary concern of the business, efficiency remains paramount.

To continue to grow, the duo expects to add India-based partners and eventually franchise the business throughout the country. Once they confirm those plans, Tejas Kapadia will return to a general legal practice back in New Jersey, though he likely will spend a lot of time counseling start-ups, particularly since he has lived the experience his future clients will face.

Kapadia not only built a franchise, but actually created a market for something that did not exist. In fact, many people confused his donuts for an Indian look-alike called a Medu Vada, which is a deep-fried and spicy treat. At about $1 each, the donuts are increasing in popularity, and their mini-donuts, at about 50 cents each, are also gaining market share. The American Donut Shoppe has grown from a retail outfit into an office and wedding catering business as well.

Kapadia highlights that "In the last 5 years, the entire culture of India seems like it is going through a transition." He cites the rising number of shopping malls and western influences. The American Donut Shoppe is experimenting in a client-centered shift in taste the same way that professionals throughout the United States are adapting their businesses to a client-focused method of communicating. They too are reversing the bullhorn, but not without learning a few lessons along the way. "To pull something like this off, you need a large degree of patience and willingness to sacrifice your time," says Kapadia.

Expertise Is Easier to Convey Than Ever Before

In addition to visibility and enthusiasm, one needs demonstrable expertise. Reimer figured out how to raise his visibility in a genuine way, while Kapadia has leveraged his enthusiasm to bring about positive change in a shifting cultural landscape.

In the modern technological environment, however, demonstrating expertise is often the easiest of the three factors. Reimer took time to raise his visibility and Kapadia has sacrificed a great deal to showcase his enthusiasm (though there are easier ways to do so).

Expertise is often considered elusive. It evokes images of a wall filled with framed certificates and plaques interspersed with shelves featuring medals and gifts of gratitude. Experts themselves are bespectacled, with salt-and-pepper hair standing in front of a bookcase lined with scholarly material. That, in many ways, is traditional, long-form expertise. In a nontraditional era, however, expertise is not just experiential but referential.

One is able to easily convey expertise by associating with other experts and by demonstrating an understanding of key issues. It worked for the health insurance broker, and continues to be an effective technique.

I once wrote a guest blog post for the local section of the *New York Times* and mentioned Fashion's Night Out, an event created to promote excitement for fashion during the recession. The international event encourages various stores to hold shopping celebrations. The article was not necessarily about the occasion, it simply used the occasion as a lead-in to the story about a local business. The very next day, I received an e-mail from the public relations firm representing an area department store asking if I would be interested in other fashion-related resources. The person who contacted me perceived me as an expert in fashion after reading my blog post.

If an accountant, doctor, or lawyer wanted to convey his or her expertise in a particular subject, but did not have the time to write a detailed article with 300 footnotes and teams of research assistants, or even publish a shorter article in a newspaper, there is an alternative.

He or she could draft a short, two-to-three-paragraph description of an issue and interview one or two experts on the matter. He or she could then share that content as a guest contributor for an influential blog or online publication. That effort will enable one to spotlight expertise as well as provide an opportunity to meet other experts in the field.

Hayes Hunt is a Philadelphia-based partner with Cozen O'Connor, a law firm with 550 attorneys in 24 offices. He represents individuals, corporations, and executives in criminal and civil litigation, ranging from health care and tax fraud to professional licensing and federal investigations. Hunt is a former public defender and is the director for the firm's Prisoner Civil Rights Panel Program for the United States District Court for the Eastern District of Pennsylvania. He also created the Cozen O'Connor Trial Academy and the Cozen O'Connor Deposition Program.

Add to that background his recognition as a "Pennsylvania Super Lawyer" in 2010, a *Legal Intelligencer* "Lawyer on the Fast Track," in 2007, and a Pennsylvania "Rising Star" by *Law & Politics* in 2005 and 2006. Hayes is a bona fide expert, yet he still struggles with how to most effectively convey that expertise.

He once spent a lot of his marketing efforts presenting continuing legal education programs to other lawyers and business professionals about white-collar criminal defense and trial advocacy. "But I got zero work from it because people were not picking up the phone to call me for work related to that," Hunt recalls. He was also told to write long articles in his areas of practice; that was similarly unsuccessful.

After a law firm coach suggested that the partners begin to carefully experiment with LinkedIn, Facebook, and Twitter, he was still suspicious, but knew that he needed to market more aggressively. "I always viewed that type of brief communication as non-professional speak using emoticons and abbreviations," he says. "I saw it as a social mechanism for dating or communication as opposed to a professional way of marketing to clients and referral sources," he adds.

Then he started to share links to articles that he had read with contacts and began to change his attitude about what he considered unconventional forms of marketing. He created a LinkedIn account and reached out to a few contacts. Within a few months, he accumulated almost 500. He shares the posts he writes for his blog, From the Sidebar, with those LinkedIn connections, among others. They combine his personality with his practical perspectives on the law. He described the online journal as a collection of practical tips about trials and litigation.

Hunt questions whether professionals tend to rely too much on their firm's name and less on their own promotional prowess. "How we market ourselves tends to get lost," he says. Admitting that his first blog post was very intimidating and a mental hurdle, he enjoys the interaction with his readers. "I view the practice of law as problem solving, which is why I love it," he notes. "The dialogue helps me learn and become a better lawyer."

RECAP

- Raising your visibility allows your audience to get to know you. As they do so, they will come to appreciate your perspective. Make it easier for them by reversing the bullhorn so that your audience members can address you in the same way that you speak to them. Twitter is an interesting example of this practice.
- Enthusiasm requires a unique level of interaction, as well as a compelling personal story. Proficiency and demeanor are often influenced by a professional's overall level of excitement.
- Practically demonstrate your expertise by blogging or guest blogging.

CHAPTER

2

Innovators Adapt, and You Should Too

As different markets change, those who remain successful through each transition adapt by innovating to continue to reach their audience. This chapter will provide concrete examples of that innovation using the real estate and medical professions as background. Those professionals who embrace transparency as a tool to reach out to others, and apply grass roots principles in a return to the basics to connect, will more easily navigate the changing landscape.

■ ■ ■

Take the Candito Group for example. It has operated a luxury real estate brokerage firm for 30 years in Naples, Florida, and once held the record for selling the highest priced estate in the area. While it placed small ads in local newspapers with listings, its marketing was generally by word of mouth. At some point over the past few years, the company's positioning in the luxury market changed. The economy certainly impacted business, but the company's communication pattern did so as well. "There is a shift in the way marketers are sending messages out to consumers and how they hear them," says Lauren Candito, the co-founder of Orlando, Florida-based Social Media Solutions, a social media marketing agency that helps companies leverage social media platforms to better connect with their audiences.

The increased use of sites like Zillow, Active Rain, Trulia, and Zolve, as well as a dramatic roller coaster ride in property values, has irreversibly transformed the real estate industry. Like other professionals, real estate agents are facing intense competition, but unlike the others, there are lower barriers to entry. You don't need three years of law school or to endure the CPA exam to become a real estate agent. As a result, the industry is crowded with savvy marketers and experienced salespeople. Despite their talent, however, they are still operating in a traditional environment that is experiencing a shift away from tradition.

The Candito Group's business suffered from the conversion from word of mouth to an online dialogue that gives clients direct access to property information and broker contacts. Agents were once the gatekeepers of listings, but today that information is so accessible that the agents are counselors rather than guardians of data. Their evolution parallels that of most professionals. Patients have already found a preliminary diagnosis based on symptoms entered in a Google search before even coming into the office. Clients routinely research legal issues and even ask questions of prospective lawyers online before having a live conversation with a new attorney.

For real estate agents, it comes down to learning how to build your brand presence online. "It used to be that people recognized your face in a meeting, but now they are looking for you on Facebook and Twitter," says Lauren Candito, daughter of the Candito Group's owners. "We are trying to be a voice for the southwest Florida community," she adds. Prior to its recent efforts, the Candito Group was not discussed online.

Recently, however, the company created a blog that Lauren Candito arranged to have linked to the web site of the Naples Florida Chamber of Commerce. With that positioning, the company is engaging in direct communication with prospects. "Social media marketing and related technologies empower us to connect with new people or groups that we wouldn't have been able to meet before," she says. "They allow us to penetrate the online realm and the Candito Group now reaches 10 times more people than it did with traditional advertising."

> Social media marketing and related technologies empower us to connect with new people or groups that we wouldn't have been able to meet before.
>
> *Lauren Candito, co-founder of Orlando, Florida-based*
> *Social Media Solutions*

Set Goals for Social Media

To avoid becoming stagnant in the modern marketplace, the Candito Group set specific goals for its social media campaign. It wanted its brand to be both the subject of discussion in the community and to serve as a voice in the south Florida luxury real estate market. And, it sought to be distinct from other agents. "You are not going to talk about work for an entire personal conversation, so don't do that online," advises Candito.

As a result, the company does not use its social media presence to simply offer virtual tours or residential listings. Instead, it focuses on the community aspects of the information. For example, its brokers only follow local individuals on Twitter. They also study local issues on which they can share the benefit of their experience. In Naples, for example, it is increasingly difficult to sell a home so many owners are considering renovations. When the Candito Group sees tweets about contractor or architect recommendations, its principals follow up directly and create a positive line of communication. "It makes the conversation a lot more natural," Candito says.

In fact, just as few people like being bombarded with real estate listings and virtual tours, they may not want excessive amounts of information about legal reforms, accounting regulations, or Medicare updates either. They are interested in how a professional can help solve a problem in the initial stages. The details will come later depending on the depth of the relationship. "The core concepts that we apply to the Candito Group can be applied to any personal sales role," she says.

Use social media to increase the reach of your networking capabilities. Given her residence in Orlando, Candito suggests searching the terms "Orlando Accountant" on Facebook to determine the local professionals that are leveraging social media in their businesses. At the time this book went to print, that search only returned 14 results, which is a small universe of potential contacts.

Of course, there are different techniques that can be used to build a relationship established online. You can listen to your audience members and get to know them. Or, you can simply send them as much information as possible about your services. "Focus on engaging conversations and building value," says Candito. "It gets more results in the long run."

The Candito Group, for example, invests less in its traditional marketing and focuses more of its efforts online. As it studies the lifestyles and industries of its target clientele, it tries to organically reach lawyers, big business owners, and entrepreneurs, who are either local or interested in a presence in the local market. "It comes down to knowing your audience, and the days of mass mailing are gone," Candito adds. "Spend more time on finding those you are targeting." The real estate business is, after all, a local endeavor. Property is stationary and is sold most often based on location. There is a premium that most people pay based on that factor so the concentration of the property representative is critical, and his or her ability to highlight that knowledge is increasingly important in an information age.

Rodney Johnson is a broker associate with Prudential California Realty in Los Angeles and has been focusing on property in the San Fernando Valley, northwest of downtown Los Angeles, for more than two decades. He moved to the city in 1981 for the same reasons that many flock to the west coast. He had a degree in radio and television, and from 1983 to 1986 worked for ABC Entertainment reading scripts for the network's prime time programs. After a downsizing left him unemployed in 1986 and with few opportunities to continue in television, he started working in real estate on February 5, 1987. That day he met someone who completed four transactions with him worth in excess of one million dollars. His success continued until a dramatic market correction in 1992. "I realized that what was driving the market at the time was foreclosures, so I went after them," he recalls.

Johnson hired a part-time assistant despite having no income at all. He set a goal of convincing three lenders to trust him with their bank-owned property portfolios. Over the next five months, he and his assistant only closed two transactions and did not acquire any bank-related listings. He was on the verge of declaring bankruptcy in May of 1993 when a major mortgage lender hired him. They began listing the bank's foreclosed properties and by July of 1993, he had secured approval to work with a second lender. "That snowballed and we ended up representing a lot of smaller banks that year," he says. From 1993 to 1997, his group grew despite the calamitous Northridge earthquake in 1994. "It devastated the real estate landscape and nothing sold," he says. As buyers returned to the market, he sought their business and almost doubled his income by the end of 1994.

By 1997, foreclosures were on the wane because of the rapidly inflating real estate market. Despite his success with banks, he continued to build his traditional brokerage practice so that when the first major lender scaled down, it did not affect him. He took advantage of the prosperous market over the next decade, but by 2007, he was managing foreclosures for the same banks that retained him in 1993 and 1994.

In order to battle a punishing market, Johnson was able to leverage some of his listings to provide a sales advantage. For example, he had a listing for a 15,000 square foot home that dropped its asking price from $8.9 million to $5.9 million and was still not selling. Given the lack of interest, he proposed that a prospective buyer consider purchasing the vacant land next door and build a mansion for much less money. With the client already interested, he approached the landowner and helped sell the property for $2.5 million. In 2009, his team had the highest number of sales and gross commissions in southern California, ranking first out of 1,600 agents. It averaged almost one sale per week.

Then the government ended its first-time homebuyer credit, which made the market even more challenging for home sales. To face this directly, as the Candito Group is doing in south Florida, Johnson is improving his presence on the Web so that people can find his group. "What we're seeing is that 90 percent of the buyers are starting their search online," he says. "We are also seeing that they don't want to talk to realtors yet," he adds.

That realization is something that many professionals are facing. With an array of sites capable of providing answers to questions that were once reserved only for free consultations in person with an expert, many of those authorities need to reconsider their business models. "In the old days, we would get a call from a sign in front of the house," says Johnson. The Internet has replaced that sign just as it has replaced the basic answer to the legal question or the quick accounting concern.

Begin Cultivating Offline Relationships Online

Real estate buyers want to spend the least amount of time gaining the maximum amount of exposure to an area, including a visual depiction of the listing. When they do make actual contact, they expect to be able to do it seamlessly. Since the first impulse is to conduct research alone, rather than to ask the broker a question, once a prospective buyer actually makes contact, that interaction must be flawless. "You have to develop a relationship via the Internet," highlights Johnson. "It is on their terms, not our terms anymore."

While he and the members of his team were once concerned with needing to show too many homes to a potential client, they are now sensitive to showing the smallest number of appropriate homes. In fact, clients narrow down the search pool for them. Web sites like Zillow and tools like Google Earth give people a chance to identify surrounding areas and tax records without ever paying a visit. "It has been better in terms of time, but we have had to nurture the relationship online to get to it," he says.

From a seller's perspective, he wants them to act in ways that will inspire action by, for example, pricing their property right. "In this market, buyers are not making offers if it is not priced right," he reports. That said, "we can't go back to the old models of just lowering the price; you must have your house in great condition as well." To do so, Johnson says that brokers need to be more truthful with clients given the market realities, particularly in a new culture of open communication that is often very public.

The Candito Group is seeing public communication via Twitter and Facebook about individuals seeking to renovate rather than sell their homes. Their response needs to be sensitive to that query and understand the motivation behind it. It requires a level of emotional intelligence that fewer needed in the past to secure client trust. Today, trust is an essential component of that relationship.

Part of that nurturing process is providing as much useful information to demonstrate how a professional respects the time of his or her client. Johnson, for instance, offers visitors to his many web sites an opportunity to create their own ListingBook.com accounts, which allows them to search potential properties in real time the same way a realtor searches on the Multiple Listing Service. He uses the Web both to get to know his clients as well as to attract them. For instance, Johnson created search-engine friendly web sites like "SearchSanFernandoValley.com" and "Searchwestsideproperties. com." By optimizing important keywords in the domain name, he is enhancing his competitiveness.

While this strategy seems a perfect fit for real estate agents, it is just as effective for lawyers and medical professionals. Dr. Ira Klemons, who is discussed in chapters 3 and 10, leverages the power of Headaches.com and MovementDisordersUSA.com. Prominent Seattle-based Harris & Moure successfully promotes its maritime practice through, among other sites, CruiseInjury.com.

Since people frequently search by term, rather than individual, one can powerfully leverage the Internet for a particular profession (within acceptable ethical standards, of course). One may not know that Harris & Moure represents victims of cruise ship accidents, but when he or she types "cruise injury" into Google, that person will see that "CruiseInjury.com" is a top-ranked destination, called "Cruise Ship Injury Law." The site contains a host of resources for a prospective client, including a frequently asked questions section and an e-book on cruise-related injuries.

The volume of information available requires professionals to proliferate their message in various targeted formats throughout the Web to reach the widest-possible audience. "When I list a property for sale, we put it out on 42 different major web sites," says Johnson. Since most of his potential customers are initially on the Web, rather than calling him after seeing a sign on the street or an ad in the phone book, he wants to be in as many places on the Web as possible. In addition, like the Candito Group, he is engaging his clients in a chat and developing a relationship.

He is simply going where the discussion is taking place, rather than forcing the people with whom he would like to speak to come to him. That is the key component of the modern trend in professional services. Skilled experts are finding ways to engage their audience wherever that audience is most comfortable, rather than solely in the professional's office. The core component of this reinvention is listening to a client and delivering what he or she wants instead of what one sells. It requires an ability to adapt, customize, and collaborate.

When I list a property for sale, we put it out on 42 different major web sites.

Rodney Johnson, broker associate,
Prudential California Realty in Los Angeles

Embrace Transparency Because Everybody Knows Everything Anyway

San Diego-based software developers Lawrence Duffin and Sam Metri of Taza Corporation began marketing software for the real estate industry in 2006, during the last year of the great boom. The duo created an application to help real estate developers building condos track and market their units.

As the economy began to spiral downward, there was a decreasing need for the tool. Fewer condos, if any, were selling and developers had a much greater challenge managing their inventory, rather than monitoring sales and marketing. "Taza Corp. needed to adapt because clients were feeling the pain of the recession," says Metri. Taza then reissued its software and characterized it as a product that could support the default service industry.

The duo recognized that they were always trying to facilitate transactions, and while the market shifted, they were still seeking to make the same impact. They also created a variety of different ways that their 120,000 current users could access the program depending on their respective roles in the process. For example Tazacorp. com and TazaREO.com are for brokers while Tazavox.com is for asset managers and banks.

Migrating information to the Web offers many advantages for the real estate industry, since it has always been document-heavy given the nature of the conveyance and the number of filings required to certify the transaction. It is a highly regulated field involving multiple parties such as lenders and local governments, each with their own restrictions.

Traditionally, clients and brokers transfer their documents to one another by fax. But when a bank has hundreds of thousands of homes in foreclosure, faxing is not an option. "This is a fundamental change for agents and escrow companies," says Metri. It took Taza three years to train 70,000 real estate agents to use software instead of hard copies of documents to close a transaction. Instead of large files that track correspondence and paperwork, each property has a virtually paperless record. Investors, banks, and agents can now receive real time access to data and status details.

Software is not only revolutionizing the nature of basic transactions, but it is also streamlining valuation issues. A decade ago, homebuyers needed to hire a licensed appraiser to value their home. As the number of unsold properties rose exponentially, this became increasingly inefficient. "When it comes to hundreds of thousands of properties, the appraisal process was not fast or cheap enough," says Metri.

Each property now has a Broker Price Opinion, or BPO, indicating its value, which is an acceptable amount for the bank that owns the property. "The whole middle man is gone," adds Metri. In fact, the entire culture of selling default-oriented real estate has changed. The government has even encouraged short sales of property in lieu of foreclosure due to the negative impact such a sale may have on an owner's future credit.

"The government does not want banks to foreclose; they will give you a chance to sell at market value," Metri explains. "A short sale means that the bank is going to lose less because it does not have to take ownership, change utilities, pay commissions, as well as other expenses." The volume has changed the industry in other ways as well. The focus on real estate now and in the future will likely be greater transparency, particularly given the medium through which parties exchange information and execute transactions. Buyers could know how many offers an agent has and sends to the seller. A decade ago, software developers like Taza had difficulty penetrating the closed real estate market; today the technology is replacing the agent in some cases as a filtering path to the seller, given the greater availability of knowledge.

In the same way that many individuals would never purchase a book without checking reviews on Amazon.com, they will want to understand the transparent nature of an agent and other parties to a transaction. "Now all professionals are a little more cautious about the decisions they make and actions they take because those details will be public," says Metri. "That was never the case before."

To facilitate this exchange, Taza established a social forum to enable networking between all of the users on its network. Just as Johnson and his team are developing their relationships online, Taza is creating a similar environment. The ability to maintain these connections is what often creates a competitive advantage. The Candito Group is sharing referrals for home renovation experts and Johnson is offering tools for multiple listing searches.

Every industry is facing this reality. Even within real estate, escrow companies and title issuers are becoming increasingly digital. They are able to process orders in mass quantities seamlessly. This is eliminating the unnecessary relationships. It is redefining the nature of those relationships. And, it is proving that the only way to address change is to change with it.

Grass Roots Medicine

Innovation is about adaptation, but it is not always easily incorporated. For instance, medicine is sick. That is the diagnosis of Dr. Bryan Vartabedian, a pediatric gastroenterologist at the Texas Children's Hospital and the author of *Colic Solved: the Essential Guide to Infant Acid Reflux and the Care of Your Crying, Difficult-to-Soothe Baby* (Ballantine Books, 2007). "Doctors have really grown apart from their patients," he says. Visits are getting shorter, the communication is often minimal, and the experience of seeing a provider has changed. He attributes this shift to lower insurance reimbursements to physicians. That drop is limiting the amount of time a doctor can spend with a patient, which is leading to less satisfaction on the part of the patient. "Physicians have become disconnected from our core role of being healers," says Vartabedian.

Some doctors are trying to create boutique practices by charging patients a subscription fee (e.g., $2,000 per year) for a more service-oriented experience. He believes that social media can bridge the divide that health care restrictions have created.

While doctors and existing patients are not connected on Twitter and Facebook, for example, because they cannot discuss protected health information, he predicts the growth of secure Facebook-style platforms and the integration of single electronic records.

In addition, Sermo.com is purportedly the largest online community of physicians, where they can discuss drugs and devices, treatment plans, and collaboration. It claims to encompass professionals from 68 specialties and all 50 states. "Doctors don't want to spend a lot of time talking about medicine," he admits, noting that most physicians with whom he interacts online discuss personal issues like divorce and administrative professional concerns like health care restrictions, tort reform, or malpractice. "I would like to see social media use evolve to a point where I am interfacing directly with patients," he says.

As an example, he offers HelloHealth.com as an indication of future direction. Jay Parkinson founded Hello Health in Brooklyn, New York, in 2008 to offer Web-based healthcare delivery.

In collaboration with Quebec, Canada-based Myca Health, it is endeavoring to help doctors treat patients using video, voice, and data on a variety of platforms, including cell phones.

Vartabedian is not new to characterizing industry changes. His book on colic questioned the notion of a condition plaguing infants that pediatricians had universally accepted for more than 50 years. It prompted him to begin blogging in the fall of 2006, and he is an active user of Twitter. "I am constantly impressed with the fact that there are so few doctors in the social media space; it says a lot about the medical profession right now," he notes. "Doctors have a lot on their plates, so it stands to reason that they don't want to go out and share information on Twitter either doctor to doctor or doctor to patient."

Vartabedian notes that since more doctors are employees than ever before, they haven't been as focused on networking as their more senior peers. "The medical profession is being redefined and a lot of physicians don't even realize that," he says. Pharmacy benefits and insurance companies determine the types of drugs doctors can prescribe, patients are more empowered with information, and technology is eliminating the need for certain types of medical care.

To participate in the redefinition, physicians, like all professionals, must understand their digital footprints. Identify what patients or clients will find when they inevitably Google your name and your practice. "As time goes by, those of us who are creating content in the online space will have a marked advantage," says Vartabedian. In fact, he believes that doctors have an ethical responsibility to participate in the online conversation to offer prospective patients the highest quality medical information.

Medical experiences are not always positive and Vartabedian has a solution: Fight criticism with content. The rise of services like Yelp and Avvo has given patients a forum to express their opinions about their medical experiences. Just as lawyers have had to address these issues, medical professionals are now facing similar concerns. Some doctors even require patients to sign a form certifying that they will not publicly criticize their physician. "Rather than stop people from saying things, doctors should be creating content that will take higher priority," recommends Vartabedian.

To create that content, he suggests that practitioners budget their time for social media efforts. Select tools and types of content that are most accessible to you. Some may prefer Twitter over LinkedIn, and blogging over both. "While good social media doesn't make up for being a bad physician, get out there, create content, and engage in the conversation."

The banter will drive the interaction and the increased inter-action will foster stronger dialogue. As professionals interact with peers and prospects, they will raise their visibility, as well as their promise. "It is almost as if social media has the potential to save medicine," says Vartabedian.

It might even save lives as well.

Dr. Anas Younes, a medical oncologist with Houston-based MD Anderson Cancer Center, one of the world's leading cancer insti-tutes, is interested in increasing patient awareness and participa-tion in clinical trials for lymphoma treatments. "My efforts have no financial impact whatsoever; it is an academic and public service," he says. "My goal is to establish a dedicated virtual group of follow-ers of families and caregivers of patients, as well as doctors, nurses, and professional foundations interested in lymphoma research with whom I can share news on clinical trials to encourage patients to participate at MD Anderson and elsewhere, so we can speed prog-ress in improving the cure rate."

> It is almost as if social media has the potential to save medicine.
>
> *Dr. Bryan Vartabedian, pediatric gastroenterologist, Texas Children's Hospital and the author of* Colic Solved: the Essential Guide to Infant Acid Reflux and the Care of Your Crying, Difficult-to-Soothe Baby *(Ballantine Books, 2007)*

Younes highlights that there has been a shift in cancer research needs over the past decade. "About 15 years ago the challenge was the lack of new drugs, but in the last 5 years, several new drugs have been developed for cancer therapy that need to be tested in patients to determine their efficacy," he advises. "We have too many drugs and too few patients willing to participate in a clinical trial." In fact, he notes that about 3 percent of cancer patients in the United States participate in clinical trials due in part to a lack of trust and a misperception of the "guinea pig" profile, he says. "Patients need to be educated that the purpose of clinical trials is not to experiment on them but rather to help them through experimental therapy" he added.

Younes stated that doctors in the United States diagnose approximately 74,000 patients with lymphoma every year and there are more than 350 active clinical trials. (Visit clinicaltrials.gov to learn more.) A 3 percent participation rate equates to about nine patients per study. "As a result, half of the trials close before they enroll the adequate number of patients and it is basically a wasted effort," he says.

In response, he promotes high-priority clinical trials directly to those who follow him on Twitter and his "fans" on Facebook. "You need to provide reliable information and awareness to patients and caregivers directly, but you also have to provide a trustful relationship," he notes. He believes that this type of communication will persuade individuals to consider participation in clinical trials.

Younes also occasionally submits guest blog posts to Cancerwise. com, MD Anderson's main blog, shares pharmaceutical data on Facebook, arranges for interviews of patients on YouTube, and participates as a guest on an MD Anderson Cancer Center podcast series. He shares all of these links via Twitter and Facebook. There is evidence that his efforts are working. Following a recent series of interviews about a Hodgkins lymphoma trial, his team received referrals from YouTube viewers in Russia, Spain, and Argentina. "There is no limit to who you can reach through Facebook and Twitter, particularly since their contents are searchable through Google," he reports.

> You need to provide reliable information and awareness to patients and caregivers directly, but you also have to provide a trustful relationship.
>
> *Dr. Anas Younes, a medical oncologist, Houston-based MD Anderson Cancer Center, who promotes high priority clinical trials directly to his "fans" on Facebook and those who follow him on Twitter*

In the past, he and his team simply sent a paper newsletter to the approximately 6,000 collective members of the American Society of Hematology and the American Society of Clinical Oncology, as well as quarterly e-mails alerting them of clinical trials. "I thought that there had to be a better way to share this information."

During an episode of Larry King Live, he heard about Ashton Kutcher's attempt to become the first person on Twitter to secure one million followers. He had never heard of the tool before, but realized that by using it, he could expand his reach dramatically. "Social media is a misnomer," he says. "It is really grass roots media because I can reach future patients and referral sources directly," he adds.

Given the constraints of medical-related communication, he only permits his Facebook "fans" to comment on posts, rather than write on his wall. By having a fan page rather than friends, his followers maintain their privacy while having access to his posts. When his followers on Twitter, most of whom are patients, cancer survivors, or caregivers, have specific questions, he asks them to e-mail him directly.

Most people who contact him on social media, including those abroad, ask about their eligibility for clinical trials or the progress of a particular study. "We are among the first people to use social media for this," Younes says. "It is nice to see that people from across the world are following; it demonstrates a level of trust that they are seeking our advice," he adds.

Like Vartabedian, Younes encourages doctors to be economical with their social media usage because "it is really time consuming," he says. "It will work only for individuals, who are motivated and believe in a certain objective that they would like to reach." Younes, for example, would like to reduce the time it takes to fully enroll patients in a clinical trial from six to three months. "I am counting on it having an impact on the future of clinical trials," he notes. His efforts are working in his practice. Younes reports adding at least one new patient per week to his practice. "It is really incredible."

RECAP

- The key to innovating in a digital market is to adapt to new technologies and reengage your audience members in the way in which they are increasingly comfortable. Focus your efforts locally at the outset.
- To maximize your potential return, be transparent in your communication. Highlight your objectives in an open fashion. Doing so builds trust and creates additional opportunity for followers.
- Set goals for your social media efforts and begin to cultivate offline relationships online. Facebook and Twitter, among other medical-profession-related sites, offer physicians the opportunity to convey critical details on clinical trials and medical treatment. This usage notes what is possible in modern communication.

3

Recognize the Resiliency Revolution and Join It to Grow Your Practice

Practitioners who sense the evolution in their discipline must remain focused on their ultimate growth objectives and committed to serving their clients or patients. This chapter will illustrate how to recognize the revolution and justify adjusting to accommodate change. Whether you are a dentist or an accountant, there is a common goal of finding new opportunity. From leveraging flexible fees to aligning with a client's interests, successful practitioners veer from the traditional to provide non-traditional service.

■ ■ ■

Dr. Janet Crain is the co-director of the Center for Headaches and Facial Pain, a renowned dental practice founded by her husband, Dr. Ira Klemons, that focuses on the treatment of headaches and TMJ (temporomandibular joint disorder). The practice's high profile on the Web presents both a benefit and a burden, says Crain. While patients "Google my name before they come to me," Crain explains, the Internet also allows people to complain about services online. "Many people write very good things about you on the Web and people can write bad things about you," says Crain. "Dentistry is not cut and dried; things can go wrong even if you do everything right," she adds. The bottom line, she notes, is that every day you have to go in knowing you did your best.

"The mindset in the past was that dentists and doctors didn't have to advertise, but today hospitals are constantly advertising," Crain says. "There are billboards of a multi-cultural group of doctors in a fertility clinic throughout the public transit system," she adds. Just having a web site is increasingly common, but it depends on what is unique about them. Credentials and licenses are basic. Including forms is useful. Virtual tours of an office and patient profiles are gaining momentum.

"You have to tell people nowadays that you're unique and this is what you can offer," says Crain. "You can't just put up a sign and build your practice based on that," she adds.

Crain and Klemons send out press releases when they receive certain certifications. For example, when they took a class in cone-beam technology, they let the public know that they have advanced training in this area. They also sent it to local newspapers for their review. "We would never have done this before, but the more times your name appears in front of people for good things, the more credibility you have because people don't do things on blind trust anymore." There is also a greater sense among the public as consumers of medical care. "Wouldn't you want to go to a dentist that is current and taking advanced continuing education courses over someone that is using older technology?" Crain asks.

> You have to tell people nowadays that you're unique and this is what you can offer. You can't just put up a sign and build your practice based on that.
>
> *Dr. Janet Crain, co-director, Center for Headaches and Facial Pain,*
> *South Amboy, New Jersey*

You have to decide which innovations and products you will keep up with, she notes. "I don't know much about bleaching teeth or whitening teeth," she says. "It is very hard to know everything about dentistry because it is advancing so much," she adds. Every professional must make that choice and is faced with a rapidly advancing industry.

The changes are in every aspect of the dental practice because technology is moving so fast," she says. "We converted from a radiograph to a digital imaging x-ray machine," Crain adds. Unlike other professions, dentistry is gadget- and product-oriented, notes Crain, pointing out that some dentists use cameras instead of looking directly inside a patient's mouth. Sandblasting, tooth-whitening, and, of course, computer-assisted design for implants are among the countless courses those with a DDS after their name can take. In a competitive marketplace, it may be worthwhile to let potential patients know which skill set has been acquired.

There are also new regulations requiring education in every area all the time.

Seize Opportunity Whenever Possible

For accountants, a dramatic regulatory shift occurred in the past decade.

Gareth Davies experienced that drama firsthand, and when you meet him, there is something immediately likeable about his personality. He strikes one as confident, content, and genuinely interested in the conversation.

A partner with PricewaterhouseCoopers LLP in London, Davies has come a long way from his life as an auditor with then Coopers & Lybrand. Earlier in his career, Davies was the London partner at Coopers responsible for the 1993 and 1994 Barings Bank audits, which made him a prime public target to take responsibility for the demise of one of the United Kingdom's most significant financial institutions when it collapsed in 1995.

The Institute of Chartered Accountants in England and Wales Joint Disciplinary Scheme disciplined him with a monetary penalty in 1999 and he spent five years in litigation. "It was obvious I didn't have a future in being an audit partner," he jokes. He was not sure what he would be because, "Our business was doing audits for 50 years and we had fantastic relationships with clients, but we did not have relationships with anyone else because that was the way the world worked," he says.

So, in 2000, he set out to reinvent himself. "I was doing it on my own for three years and it was quite a lonely existence," he recalls. "Suddenly Sarbanes-Oxley comes around and there is a systematic need to find new clients; I was very lucky in that respect," he says.

The Sarbanes-Oxley Act of 2002 ushered in a new era of public company accounting reform and auditing responsibility. It set standards for the management of all U.S. public companies and their boards of directors. It also changed the nature of their relationships with their accountants.

Congress enacted this law in response to the variety of accounting scandals that cost American investors billions of dollars, including scandals at Enron, Tyco International, Adelphia, and WorldCom, among others. The law requires independent auditors, strict corporate governance, sophisticated internal controls, and broader financial disclosures.

It designates specific categories of services that an accounting firm can and cannot provide to an audit client without impairing its independence. When introduced, it limited the scope of the relationship and forced accounting firms to quickly institutionalize its client-development efforts.

In sum, it gave Davies a chance to test out the business development skills he had been honing during his years in exile from auditing. "I had learned an art form," he says, noting that accountants at large firms typically did not focus on business development. Since the same clients often remained with their advisors for life, barring some catastrophic financial event, there was little need to attract new clients on the scale that Sarbanes-Oxley suddenly required.

Every industry has generally experienced shifts like the one prompted by Sarbanes-Oxley.

Flexible Fees Make Cost Conversations More Cheerful

In the law, for example, there is increasing acceptance that it is a competitive business similar to other professional services such as finance and engineering, and that in-house attorneys are in a position of control as the buyer. Clients now realize that they have more power and influence over fees than previously realized. "Law has been viewed as a secret science, like monkhood or mysticism, shrouded by secrecy and uncertainty," says Jeffrey Carr, Senior Vice President, General Counsel, and Secretary for FMC Technologies, Inc., a global provider of technology solutions for the energy industry.

"Some even bring suspicion to the relationship," Carr adds, cautioning that a few believe their outside lawyers are charging too much and inflating their bills. They are doing so in the name of "zealous representation" while failing to understand and appreciate the notion of value commensurate with risk or the operational realities of running a business.

In medicine, insurance companies choose where patients can go for certain tests and it is harder to recoup your money, notes Dr. Gabriel Pivawer, a partner with Edison Imaging Associates, PA, in Edison, New Jersey, which operates four radiology centers in the state and services a hospital's radiologists. By way of example, a decade ago, an insurance company paid Edison Imaging $2,500 for a PET CT scan (used most frequently in oncology, surgical planning, radiation therapy, and cancer staging). "If you opened an MRI center, your patients were flocking to you and you had no issues surviving or making money," Pivawer says.

Today the insurer pays under $1,000, but the costs have probably increased ten-fold in the form of rent, malpractice insurance, and employee salaries, among other factors. "We have to be more economical, more frugal, and must go after the business," he says. "Business is not going to fall into our laps."

The same was true for Davies back in 2003. "We had to completely learn a load of new techniques to rebuild the business," he adds. In the first year of Sarbanes-Oxley, Davies reports that PricewaterhouseCoopers's tax revenues dropped significantly. Given that he had spent so much time learning to connect with prospective clients, he set out to meet 100 new corporate executives. "If you want to justify your place in the firm, you need to go out and do business development," he says.

Sales activities have always been viewed as a necessary evil in professional communities because the job of the expert is to provide advice, rather than to sell it. Moreover, redefining one's role to include this job function is an overwhelming challenge because as Davies experienced, "The level of rejection was quite crippling," he says.

Still, he began his journey with a focus on meeting people, rather than concentrating on being technically talented in conducting these meetings. From the perspective of bringing in clients, he failed frequently. "As time went on, however, I became more resilient and comfortable with people trying to reject me." He recalls. "Then I learned how to plan a meeting with the CEO."

At one point, he networked with the CEO of a large technology company who was not interested in hiring PWC. Instead, he asked Davies whether his team was interested in a joint venture. That deal ended up being worth $100 million and PWC earned $28 million on the transaction.

For a professional with a globally branded company, the initial meeting is fairly assured. "You always get a first meeting as PWC, but it is the value perceived that leads to a second meeting," he advises. "Once you've gotten yourself up that hill of dealing with early rejection, it becomes quite similar to dealing with clients in any other way."

It comes down to being a hustler who must learn how to meet people and how a business works. "My basic position on this is that if you train as a professional person without learning to hustle, you are at a disadvantage," notes Davies. More importantly, perhaps, is how you bring an edge into conversations and convince potential customers or clients to deal with you instead of your competitors. "The idea of hustling is so alien for lawyers and accountants because they are so status conscious," he adds.

When Davies and various colleagues began a coordinated effort to approach business prospects, it was somewhat unusual, but soon after the enactment of Sarbanes-Oxley and its restrictions on selling certain services to existing clients, there was a need to work with multiple competitors. "It is a very different relationship when you are competing for every piece of work versus managing a steady stream of work," he says. "You are working much harder for the sale and more creatively on how you keep the relationship fresh," he adds.

Suddenly there was a massive shift of where certain firm revenues originated. Buyers of anything, particularly professional services, still buy from people they trust and with whom they have a relationship. "The art form is to create a relationship that is not passive," says Davies. "Basically, the monkey is on your back to keep taking ideas to your client," he notes.

> The idea of hustling is so alien for lawyers and accountants because they are so status conscious. My basic position on this is that if you train as a professional person without learning to hustle, you are at a disadvantage.
>
> *Gareth Davies, partner, PricewaterhouseCoopers LLP, London*

Like Davies, professionals at all levels must establish that they are hungry and sincerely interested in their clients. "For me, taking an idea to a client is a form of respect," he says contrasting that with simply checking in with a client and asking how he or she is doing. "If you do that type of meeting in the new world, they will wonder what they got out of that," he cautions.

Consider the type of insight you can share with your client or prospect, not just so they will appreciate the first meeting, but will look forward to the second encounter. "There are loads of things that are valuable for people; you have to connect with them on a business level and a personal level," says Davies. "You become a confidant."

The key is to connect with others in a way that does not waste their time. In that effort, you need to be resilient, not only because you are certain to be ignored on occasion, but because you will always be competing against a cacophony of voices positioning before the same audience.

Your message also needs to be energized and creative. The great challenge of modern communication is adapting your message to the needs of your prospect or client. That adaptation requires thoughtfulness in an ambiguous environment where organizations recognize a need, but are not certain of the appropriate solution. They must be involved in finding it so professionals are now collaborators, rather than problem solvers. "I don't see my job as closing a sale, but actually energizing a system," says Davies. Once that level of comfort has been provided, it encourages prospects to reveal their true concerns and problems. "It is a bit like dating; people want you to court them," he adds.

They also want to see how obstacles are managed. The competition is so strong that making a connection and building trust are no longer enough to secure new business. "Executives have become very sophisticated at rejecting you and testing you," notes Davies.

Alignment Is the Answer to Better Client Relationships

It is actually not just a game of selecting the most talented individuals who demonstrate the greatest level of perseverance. It is also about finding alignment in a wired world where answers are often less important than the conveyance of those answers. The medium is as important as the message and the messenger. Professionals who can organically associate with a client's challenges will find that principles of trust, authority, collaboration, and respect will simply fall into place.

Upon graduation in 1969 from Hofstra University in Hempstead, New York, Phil Strassler began working for Peat Marwick (the predecessor to the accounting firm KPMG). Strassler worked there for a decade and learned a guiding principle that would shape his career: "It is about how you add value to clients and find a seat at the same side of the table," he says. "You don't have to be an extrovert to give great client service," he adds, noting that you must, however, convince clients that you will go the extra mile and share the same sense of urgency.

Client experience generates a buzz. It creates excitement around how the individual is treated that goes beyond how any specific problem is solved. The importance of knowing what is important to the client often ranks as highly as responding to his or her query. That simple identification sets the foundation for all communication centered on the client. "I was very aware of how things I read, for example, could apply to my client's situation," says Strassler. "Whether it was a trip they were planning or a technical article related to their business, if it was timely I sent it to them."

Describing this effort as his first foray into understanding how to differentiate himself by making his client's concerns and values an opportunity to sit on the same side of the table with them, Strassler capitalized on the power of a simple but compelling technique: courtesy with a twist. "Everyone likes being special," he says. "You cannot, however, pay attention until you learn what is important to your clients and potential clients."

That philosophy served as a central tenet of his 40-year career. He sought not only to learn about what makes his clients successful, but what bothers them, what inspires them, and a host of other characteristics to develop greater insight into their motivations. "I believe in alignment," he says. "If you can align yourself so that you win and your client wins, that is the essence of modern business." According to Strassler, sitting on the same side of the table allows you to understand how your client thinks and allows you to carefully develop a relationship based on trust.

He honed this skill working as the accountant at a family office for eight years and then left to join a large hedge fund, only to experience its liquidation 18 months later. After that incident, he decided that he would never work for anyone again. He started an accounting practice and his former employer became his first client because he owed him so much money that it was the only way he could repay the debt.

> Everyone likes being special. You cannot, however, pay attention until you learn what is important to your clients and potential clients. If you can align yourself so that you win and your client wins, that is the essence of modern business.
>
> *Phil Strassler, accountant, Marcum & Kliegman LLP (retired, 2007),*
> *New York City*

Servicing that client became his night job as he spent his days developing business for his firm. His strategy was based on "honor-by-association." Prospects assumed that if the financier who created an enormous hedge fund used his firm, then he must be talented. Clients quickly referred similar clients and he grew from one person to eight. "I was dependable, committed, practical, and technical," he recalls. "The people I hired were all exactly the same."

A few years later, his largest client, albeit still a non-paying one, advised him that he was planning to acquire a very large company. He asked Strassler to conduct the necessary due diligence and raise the necessary financing. In exchange, the client forgave the balance of his debt and retained him to execute the accounting work on the acquisition. He also permitted Strassler to invest in that company. "Being involved in that transaction made me realize how important it is to understand the motivations of this client and how I could be aligned to represent him." That client ultimately did many deals with Strassler. He became a friend and a tremendous referral source over the years.

Just as architects measure their success according to their clients' success, and as lawyers are increasingly considering the use of alternative fees, accountants are faced with similar concerns. Strassler did in the early 1990s what many professionals are struggling to do today: partner with a client. While in some industries it is not possible, there is often opportunity to share the risk and the reward. The future will be built on an era of shared possibility from both the positive and negative perspectives.

Technology allows greater monitoring, accountability, and the creation of defined metrics in real time. Most of the obstacles, other than regulatory controls, have been eliminated.

In an effort to continue growing, Strassler joined Marcum & Kliegman LLP in 1995, where he remained until his retirement in 2007. The weekend before his first partnership meeting at the firm, he bought a generic PDA and loaded the 500 or so names and addresses in his file into the tool. He grouped them by relationship and proximity and decided to stay in touch with each of them. To do so, he set out to contact five individuals every morning five days per week. Over the next 12 years, he had entered more than 10,000 names into his database.

"Every conversation was inviting," Strassler recalls. "I might ask someone to have lunch or offer to make an introduction." Most people have something that they need help with, he notes, and it is not necessarily accounting assistance. As Strassler became more involved in niche areas related to investment partnerships, hedge funds, family wealth planning, and structuring transactions, prospects increasingly associated him with those matters. "Then the intersections started occurring," he says.

People with whom he met would mention that meeting to others that he wanted to meet. That remark created an intersection, which allowed him to develop greater name recognition in various niche areas.

Occasionally, Strassler would set a lunch date and then invite someone else that his lunch partner would like to meet. "My philosophy was that if you are going to lunch with someone, you might as well invite someone who can help that person out," he says. Naturally, doing so helps you by showcasing your network and demonstrating to both of your guests that you are a thoughtful practitioner.

Instead of making a virtual introduction, the invitation guarantees that they meet. To form deep relationships, you have to show people that you care about them personally, not simply their business. By doing so you are automatically aligned with them. While this generates potential referrals, it offers guaranteed references. Those references provide the basis for intersections. That mutual respect is a key step in alignment.

Most accountants lead a very reactive life, Strassler says, because they either have too many clients or see the technical aspects of their business as more important than how to apply them to the client's needs. "It is a very low bar," he says encouraging the next generation. "When I was in private accounting, the number of times my accounting firm came to me with new ideas was limited," he recalls. He also spent a lot of time in the offices of his clients, outside of his own office. "When you are in a client's office with the client's staff, it is more likely that they will discuss a problem with you," he says. "You can't get business sitting in your office."

That very simple concept is not well understood. Rather than being motivated by increasing his practice, Strassler engaged clients or new contacts to learn about their lives and businesses. He did not do so to simply earn their work. It is the long-term relationship that creates the opportunities that result in revenue.

Rainmakers are always in motion. They are creative. Many professionals, however, are introverted and sell only technical skills. Selling expertise is different from a product. "You have to sell and then deliver at competitive rates," says Strassler. While people were satisfied with the status quo in the past, they have greater expectations today. And, that conclusion is not limited to accounting or finance.

Technology Offers Better Communication All Around

Ford Harding has been studying those expectations. He is the author of *Creating Rainmakers* (Wiley, 2006) and founder of Harding & Company, which helps professionals learn to sell. "You need to compete for business and there are legitimate and appropriate ways to go after it," Harding says, noting that the concept of selling is gaining acceptance in different professions.

That acceptance may be slower in the legal field, where there is a legitimate concern about not appearing to be ambulance chasing, and faster in architecture, but it is changing everywhere. "Actuaries have come slowly and management-consulting falls somewhere in between," he adds.

In fact, some professions have created a euphemism for selling, such as "business development" or "marketing" notes Harding. "Salespeople are called 'rainmakers'," he adds. Fundamental demographics are, however, changing this dynamic. "There has been a huge growth in the number of professionals, far outstripping the population growth, which inevitably leads to increased competition," he reports.

And, of course, technology now permits relationship tracking and more seamless communication to initiate conversations with more people, more rapidly. The techniques for doing so will continue to evolve and differ depending on the field, the market, and the individual professional. "People will continue to invest in those systems until we have a very interesting, transparent, and interactive marketplace," says Avvo's Mark Britton.

Consumers of services actually feel a certain responsibility to learn more about the person from whom they are buying those services because there is more available information about them, notes Brian D. Zeve, managing director for Microsoft Corp.'s U.S. Professional Services Group.

"There is a shift in power toward the business consumer," he says noting that the power of the crowd provides a certain level of support to help consumers and professionals to validate publicly available information in real-time. Crowd members do not want the basic contract; they want insight. They can get standard templates, but the real value is for professionals to provide their expertise.

In addition, members of the millennial generation have a much more collaborative mindset and are comfortable communicating a variety of ways, including synchronous interaction and wikis that offer a very different form of creating content. "What this generation does particularly well is that they are very good at validating content as opposed to just finding it," says Zeve. "The skill required to look at multiple data points and be able to align them is very different today from a few decades ago," he adds.

"We are seeing a disaggregation of the value chain in professional services and the reassembly of it," notes Zeve. There is more flexibility in roles and work styles, with lockstep advancement and traditional billing practices giving way to a more creative approach. The rise in prominence of the virtual law firm concept is based on this progression. "Expertise is not geographically based anymore, it is topically based," advises Zeve.

Technology is changing the way individuals and organizations leverage their intellectual capital and their collective personalities. "The consulting industry, for example, moves quickly because they understand that information and knowledge have a half-life," reports Zeve, noting that many are creating a Facebook-like experience within their own sites to establish community.

The variety of details in the public domain also allows people to pattern-match to improve leads and sales strategies. The professional services delivery tool is changing because the communication and collaboration infrastructure is allowing people to do things differently. "The traditional rule of thumb suggests that 80 percent of profits come from 20 percent of clients," says Zeve, which requires professionals to know their clients in a much more personal fashion. They are now able to gain that insight while simultaneously sharing it.

It is no longer a model of information-gathering or data-distribution. It is now a hybrid model with few restrictions other than to be authentic. And that authenticity is the hallmark of the new white-collar hustler. Social media thrives in an environment of honest interaction, flaws and all. Sincere communication builds the type of trust that has always set the foundation for longstanding relationships.

For the past two years, I have completed the Manhattan Island Foundation's Aquathlon and Swim, which is a 1.5 kilometer swim in the Hudson River and a 5 kilometer run in Hudson River Park. I was never really concerned about completing the race; I was worried (at least before my first event) about how absolutely disgusting it would be to swim in the Hudson River, an often-maligned body of water. So, when I arrived at the park for registration at 6 A.M. on July 18th, 2009, the blocks-long line of New York City Sanitation trucks and the sanitation facility on the shore of the transition area almost made me turn back. Given that I had already told friends and colleagues about the event, I stuck to my plan and literally jumped in.

That line of garbage trucks is the image that comes to mind when I think of opportunity blockers. Then I have a vivid counter visual to that pessimism.

When my daughter was almost four, to the surprise of many, she overcame her fear and started jumping off of the diving board at our town pool. Before each leap, she would pause at the edge, smile nervously, and then plunge into the cool water below.

That moment at the edge before leaping is always the biggest obstacle, but the picture of that smile always convinces me to take a calculated risk.

RECAP

- The demographic and level of sophistication of a typical client or patient has changed over the past decade. They are more familiar with the substance of the advice they are seeking and the nature of the proposed remedies.
- Modern professionals must embrace this increased access to information and respond with an equivalent level of detail. Press releases, for example, offer an opportunity to convey key points of data on a broad scale. Continuing education also offers opportunities for growth and interaction.
- With respect to fee structures, be flexible and consider tying your structure to value billing, which is an increasingly popular form of measuring professional services. It is also fueling a trend toward efficiency.
- Pay close attention to the objectives of your client or patient so that you can create alignment that harmonizes the outcome.
- Technology offers the advantage of tracking relationships and engaging in seamless communication, enabling a greater volume of richer conversations at a much faster pace.

4

Students Have Everything to Gain from the White Collar Hustle

Students are in a much more flexible position than their professional counterparts and this chapter will encourage them to hold themselves accountable to achieve certain career-oriented objectives, ranging from initiating contact with those they would like to meet, getting published, and coordinating their follow-up efforts. Perhaps most importantly, students must understand that failure is part of success.

■ ■ ■

I spent the fall semester of my junior year at Boston University studying in London. I remember being excited, but scared to leave. I was the first person in my family to receive a passport and go abroad. Students often have the opportunity to learn while facing their fears in a fairly protected environment. They have the freedom to experiment with fewer restrictions than they might have once they are employed or associated with a profession.

I took advantage of my time overseas and enthusiastically toured as many cities as I could in the few months that I had. Even so, when I returned to Boston in January just before my nineteenth birthday, I could not wait to get back on the road for my next adventure.

A few weeks later, walking from class one wintry afternoon, I saw a sign that read "Teach English in Czechoslovakia." It sounded interesting, particularly since I had experience teaching English as a second language. So I applied to an organization called "Students for Czechoslovakia." I never heard back and essentially forgot about the application. The night before one of my final exams that spring, there was a voicemail waiting for me from one of the program's directors. He offered me a job as an English teacher in a variety of summer camps throughout what is now known as the Czech Republic. I recall the job paid about $35 per week and included room and board.

Everything sounded reasonable except that the position was not actually guaranteed. I had to fly to Prague on my own and someone from the organization would meet me at the airport. As adventurous as I felt at 19, I was still a fairly risk-averse future lawyer. Students, for instance, use many more types of technology than their more senior mentors, but they struggle with the best way to engage with those beyond their immediate peers. They want proof that it will work.

I sought that verification as well so when I happened to visit Washington, D.C. after school ended that spring, I decided to stop by the Students for Czechoslovakia office. It was 1992, long before the modern concept of virtual offices became common. As I drove up to the address on my application, I found only a Mail Boxes Etc. store. I walked in nervously and confirmed that the office listing was indeed a place to receive mail.

This would not have been that shocking except that I was a junior in college with little experience. I planned to quit my summer job early, and travel to a country where I did not know a soul and could not speak the language with the hope that some unknown individual would be waiting to take me to a remote summer camp far from any major city. It actually sounds crazy now that I am recounting the decision. It should be noted that this was long before cell phones were common and the only way to reach anyone was via a pay phone and an international calling card.

With little to lose and a great story to gain, whether someone was waiting for me or not, I bought the plane ticket, which I think was about $750 dollars, and left for Prague at the beginning of July. At first when I walked off of the airplane, I didn't see anyone. Just before panic set in, however, out of the corner of my eye, I saw a sign that read: "Students for Czechoslovakia." It turned out to be a remarkable summer. The people were extraordinary and the experience was unforgettable.

There is a certain risk aversion that sets in after receiving a college or graduate degree. Maybe it is the reality of repaying student loans, or possibly the fear of wasting a tremendous investment of time and money on something that seems frivolous. Either way, students are often best positioned to take advantage of creative networking opportunities. They can chalk mistakes up to inexperience and enthusiastic follow-up is more often seen as moxie than a nuisance. There is a short window during those four years of college, and more of those enrolled in school should take advantage of it.

Still, the most popular word they use to describe networking, whenever I ask them at schools across the country, is not "relationships" or "connections" or "positive." No, the most popular word that students use to describe networking is "creepy." Most people find it annoying, distasteful, and needy, but it is the aspect of relating to someone in a way that demonstrates your interest in them that most people find awkward.

Another curious response in student polls relates to the people they would like to meet for job opportunities. Rather that identify a person or organization at which they would like to meet someone, students frequently tell me that they would like to meet 'the person who can get me a job' or 'anyone that is hiring.' The problem with these responses is that there is no way, other than by responding to job postings, to sincerely meet those who are hiring. Instead, I often advise students that it is much more effective to meet people in a field or at a company in which they would like to work.

Once you highlight a specific target, there are a variety of communication tools that you can use to reach them. Seventeen years after my trip to the Czech Republic, one of the campers saw my profile on Facebook (after no contact for almost two decades) and sent me a note. Welcome to the new era of opportunity. My former student's effort highlights that making contact with others is no longer the problem. To reach hundreds, thousands, or even tens of thousands of people in a short amount of time today is completely possible. Comment on a popular blog post, upload a catchy YouTube video, or create a group, perhaps one for long lost English teachers, on Facebook or LinkedIn and you are on your way.

Career success was once based solely on academic performance, skill, reputation, and experience. Today, commoditization means you need to add another element to the selection equation. You have all of the tools available to learn about the people you are trying to meet. You also have plenty of incentive with a tighter job market.

You simply need the hustle.

Those individuals who find success in the modern era of professional services, from students to senior practitioners, must now hustle for clients, manage their media relations, and routinely raise their profiles in an unprecedented manner. The cost of a graduate education has also raised the level of risk for new entrants into society's most honored fields and yet most of those who provide advice for a living maintain an aversion to veering from the traditional path. Ironically, by taking a few calculated risks to stand out in a genuine and positive fashion, they will position themselves as enterprising experts, rather than isolated kiosks of information.

From networking to navigating the technological landscape that has reshaped the way professionals promote their services, the formula for progress and achievement is based on overcoming fear through action. That action requires non-traditional creativity to exceed traditional expectations.

Busting Myths About Networking

In the current market, those who continue to think of ways to provide value to others will stand out in a sea of people that is only growing more crowded. They are not simply seeking to collect names; they are trying to create relationships. It is a more genuine form of interaction that is replacing traditional notions of networking in favor of a new perspective on interpersonal engagement. Start thinking about someone in your community who inspires you and why. Proactively try to meet one or all of those individuals. It is important to begin this process of finding inspiration because as those skills are honed, you will be able to nourish your appetite for interesting and unique views throughout your career.

The manner in which they can be met varies depending on style. Some people are comfortable cold-calling or e-mailing prospects. Others prefer to use technology. Still others are only comfortable with an introduction by a friend.

While all of these methods work, you may not have the luxury of pursuing only the option with which you are most comfortable. Buoyant times allow for relaxation, but in leaner periods, all possibilities for distinction must be explored. That said, personal style is critical to professional success. Many types of personalities can arrive at the same destination—they just need to do so by taking different routes.

If you are more comfortable in small groups, consider individual interviews or small discussion groups. Meal-time events, such as dinner clubs, can be productive gatherings where contacts are more inclined to discuss issues of greater importance to them, including family, sports, and hobbies. These conversations provide deeper insight into an individual than changes in the market or frustrations with billable work. The key to finding value in these meetings is to use what you learn for genuine follow-up. (See Chapter 14 for a more in-depth discussion on networking follow-up.)

The opportunity that technology offers is not just efficiency, but intergenerational interactivity. Students today are more proficient with technology and in organic self-marketing than most organizations realize. Those managers who harness talent and enable junior hires to demonstrate their potential are likely to increase their business-development initiatives. For that reason, students should lead with an offer to assist. A collaboration of this type between the generations is the ideal solution for students seeking to distinguish themselves to employers interested in raising their profiles among prospects.

Convince senior professionals to pair up with you to develop a presence in the social networking environment to create new and deeper relationships in the marketplace. For instance, offer to help optimize the text in documents they post online. Start by identifying key words that should be in boldface type because they are common search terms or those that can be linked to other resources on the individual's site. This will increase the likelihood that individuals searching for those terms on Google will find them more easily.

Be Disciplined and Accountable

Most great stories about triumph over adversity involve tenacity and persistence. While business opportunities and jobs routinely come through connections, many people are uncertain how to make the connections that yield those prospects. Discipline is the key to achieving those returns on your investment by staying committed to your goals, but remaining flexible enough to bypass the obstacles that are certain to block your path is essential. In addition, there is a dynamism associated with success that can also fuel career and business development potential.

You are unlikely to realize that potential, though, without support. As such, seek the counsel of those you trust and respect. The remarkable benefit of asking for advice is that those who provide it will want to know whether it proved useful. As a result, they are much more inclined to stay in touch and welcome your initiative in making regular contact. More importantly, you can set goals with them and hold yourself accountable to follow up.

It is very easy to avoid doing something when you only have to answer to yourself. It is often very easy to forgive things that can be rationalized as nonessential. However, by telling someone else about the goal, even if it is to contact one person, we are more likely to do it for fear of telling that person we just never got around to it. There is a certain character issue associated with making promises we don't keep.

As I point out to seasoned professionals as well, if failure occurs, don't worry. Everyone can identify with an obstacle or a setback. Each person has also learned a unique lesson from that experience and is often predisposed to sharing that insight. One's interest in benefiting from their wisdom can be the key to setting the foundation for a long-term relationship.

Distinction in the economic downturn is actually easier than most people believe because of the natural inclination of professionals to meet others in a difficult economic environment. Knowledge experts often benefit from leveraging the need for continuing education to demonstrate their style, background, and insight into a particular industry. The global nature of online outlets allows them to record something once and realize the benefit on a recurring basis.

Students are perfectly positioned to help them execute on these goals. Consider inviting to campus a professional whom you would like to meet to speak to a student group with which you are associated. Arrange for that individual to meet the dean and other key members of the faculty. Approach a student vendor such as a test-preparation company or a local restaurant to sponsor a cocktail hour. If the person is an author, buy a handful of books and auction signed copies in advance on Facebook.

In other words, do everything possible to make the person feel welcome. Prepare for the visit and plan to record the presentation (with permission, of course) so that the recording can be given to the individual as an expression of gratitude. If possible, post it on the organization's web site (again, with permission) so that he or she can share the link, rather than a large video file, with colleagues.

If the contact cannot make it to campus, consider a virtual presentation. In his "The Rise to the Top" series (Therisetothetop.com), David Siteman Garland, author of *Smarter, Faster, Cheaper: Non-Boring, Fluff-Free Strategies for Marketing and Promoting Your Business* (Wiley, 2010), conducts video interviews via Skype using software-maker Ecamm Network, LLC's $20 Call Recorder for Skype, which can be found at Ecamm.com/mac/callrecorder. Garland splits the screen and creates a professional looking program at virtually no cost. If neither the organization nor the guests have video capability (though virtually every computer sold today comes with a built-in web camera), consider registering for a FreeConferencePro.com dedicated phone number. It will allow you to host a call, invite others, and record the discussion completely free. No video, no buttons, just a phone call.

Do not be concerned with the tool or the medium. Focus instead on the relationship. The video, audio, or live engagement is the vehicle for setting the foundation for something positive. It will provide interaction before, during, and after the event. The program will need to be scheduled and its contents discussed. Then the event is produced either live or otherwise. And, finally, follow up to share the recording. Ultimately, the most powerful way to create opportunity is by doing so for others first.

From a practical perspective, the basic protocol can be as simple as:

1. Identify an individual to meet. Many students (and even professionals) struggle with this task.
2. Develop a reason for making contact other than providing a copy of a resume or trying to persuade him or her to offer a job. Convey this through action as opposed to commentary. Perhaps a student group would like to profile this person for its members.
3. E-mail the request.
4. Follow up in a day or two with a phone call.
5. Arrange the call, interview, or meeting. Record it with permission, noting the way in which it may be used. Assure the interview subject that he or she will have an opportunity

to review the content or confirm his or her quotes prior to publication.

6. Publish the piece.

Share Your Successes and Your Failures

Soon after I started practicing law in the late 1990s, I began distributing periodic updates to my friends, family, and small network of contacts. I would share a new article, a few details about my focus at work, and perhaps a personal note. It was generally short and I had no grand plan in mind; I simply wanted to stay in touch. Over the years, I migrated to a series of more formal mailing list programs, and finally introduced an unsubscribe feature (to the delight of many).

I was amazed by how many responses my e-mail often generated. In fact, many years later when I decided to leave the practice of law (after almost nine years) and pursue a full-time writing career, I let my audience know in a subsequent newsletter. Prompted by my message, the senior executive of a large public company wrote back and asked if I would be interested in serving as the CEO of a new company he was planning to form. He noted that I had been "spamming" him for seven years at that point and while he rarely, if ever, read any of my work, he had an impression that I was "someone who got things done."

I am now on the distribution lists for a number of students around the country who share their successes and failures on a periodic basis. Their updates almost always prompt me to follow up. For that reason, notes are a potent tool. MailChimp.com offers a free newsletter service for those with lists of up to 500 contacts. MadMimi.com offers one for lists of up to 100 contacts.

When I learned how to program in HTML after taking a weekend course at Baruch College in 1999, I visited NetworkSolutions.com, then the sole registrar of domain names with the goal of buying AriKaplan.com. Realizing that it was $70 for a two-year registration, I decided to wait. After all, who cares about owning AriKaplan.com? Turns out, there are no fewer than four Ari Kaplans with a presence online and soon after I made my decision, one of the smarter Aris registered the domain. *Newman!* For that reason, I actually registered the dot com names for my children when they were born. At under $10 per year now, it is worth the wait for them to have a chance to leverage that online real estate.

While I am already thinking about what my kids will do with their personal domain names years from now, I am often struck by how few students have their own web sites. Their obstacle is no longer the cost because if you register a name, for example, with 1and1 .com or GoDaddy.com, among many others, that purchase includes free space and design tools for a basic web site. It takes literally minutes to create and will immediately give you a presence online. Many people are even bypassing a traditional web site (though they are still registering a domain name) in favor of a WordPress.com blog that looks like a web site, but allows the owner to more easily update its content. It is free as well.

A web site now serves as a repository of work, both personal and professional. Most students are not opening their Facebook accounts to the public so potential employers will not get to see their full breadth of accomplishments. In addition, most of the other platforms limit the type of content that can be used.

You can leverage the power of your web site to meet prospective employers passively by simply posting your resume and other items you have created, including a video commentary, an audio interview, an article, links to guest blog posts, Facebook and LinkedIn group members, and Twitter stream, as well as many others. People tend to complicate this process by naming all of the potential tools they could use and worry about where to start. Students instead should view themselves and their accomplishments as a starting point, at a minimum. Create a central presence and then point others to that destination.

As for the domain name, register your full name if you prefer, but that element of your identity, while most obvious, is not essential. Being creative or descriptive in this regard has its advantages. In fact, I own a few domain names that are simply easier to tell people about than my company's primary web site (AriKaplanAdvisors.com). For instance, visitors to PromoteMeToday.com or PromoteMyWork.com, will be redirected to my homepage. They are just easier to share in conversation and tend to be more memorable. There are many others I could use and I'm always thinking about those ideas.

Be Prolific and Fast

Once you determine whom you want to meet and the areas in which you are interested, an article can be a powerful vehicle in modern career building. Speed is also a key consideration in a free-time-deprived culture. Profiles, conference summaries, and "how-to" tips can be written very quickly and provide maximum benefit. Consider this idea. Attend a conference in an area of interest. It could be technology or architecture or entrepreneurship—don't focus too much on the example. Your passion will determine what works best in each case. Simply visit the web site of the local convention center and review its calendar for the next few months. Find something that is free or cheap enough to enable this experiment.

Attend the event and then instead of randomly, and often awkwardly, introducing yourself to people for purposes of "networking," try this approach instead. Walk up to someone and say: "Hi, I'm Joe (assuming, of course, that is the name) and I am writing about this event for [*whatever—again, don't worry about this—it could be a blog, LinkedIn group, a school paper, a local web site. It doesn't matter very much. Now, here is the key*]. "How are you enjoying this event?" Once they respond, and almost everyone would, ask a few follow-up questions, such as: "How does this compare to last year or others that you have attended this year?"

Once he or she starts responding, learning about his or her reasons for attending, business, and goals immediately begins. But don't stop there. As the conversation is concluding, get a business card and make this offer: "I am going to be interviewing a variety of individuals today [or this week, depending on the duration of the event] and I would be happy to introduce you to the types of people with whom you would like to connect. Is there someone specific you are interested in meeting?"

That person will remember you because nobody says that. And, even if they do say it, they don't follow up. So, follow up. Set a goal to introduce every person you meet to one other person. Even if the introductions are not perfect, they demonstrate a thoughtful and creative nature. It is such a simple and straightforward exercise, yet very few people complete it. Those who do so organically stand out. They then consider sharing that experience.

Be a Resource, Focus on Others

One of the best ways for students to network and remain in touch with others is to serve as a resource. Listen for clues about the interests of those with whom interaction is occurring. After connecting with someone who, for example, wants to teach a course in a local law school or college, visit Chronicle.com, the web site of *The Chronicle of Higher Education*, and set an alert to receive e-mails when relevant positions become available. Once the alert is set, following up is no longer a worry; it will do it automatically. It provides an ideal opportunity to offer something of value to others and stay in touch. It is merely an offer of ideas for how they can improve their professional careers.

Professionals are also often seeking venues in which they can share their expertise by publishing articles. To help them, a student could study the editorial calendars of trade publications in the industry with which he or she would like to be associated after graduation. Editorial calendars are simply date-specific listings of topics a publication will focus on throughout the year. They are often posted on the publication's web site along with their advertising materials because they are typically used to draw advertisers to those issues that will attract their target market. For instance, advertisers that support lawyers bringing cases to trial (e.g., duplication services and court reporters) will likely be attracted to an issue focusing on litigation. Industry-specific newsletters, which can be found at EzineArticles.com, may also offer the potential for connection and even collaboration. Working together on an article would both showcase the talent of the practitioner and provide the student with an important writing sample.

Consider how you acknowledge your contacts. Expressing gratitude and wishing members of your audience luck are two of the most powerful forms of engagement. Yet most people overlook those opportunities for distinction. Think more proactively about people, and remind them of what they said when subsequent meetings and conversations take place. Those individuals will almost always respond to the small gesture with surprise and appreciation.

Leverage the power of social media to spotlight the work of others. Consider co-founding a group on LinkedIn, Facebook, or an industry-specific site that will provide a tangible representation of affiliation with the co-founder. The sharing of networks will generate more interest in the same field, and effectively showcase a broader base of expertise. Most people think of social media either as a frustrating hindrance to true relationship building or the holy grail of relationship management. There are a few students, however, who are successfully leveraging it to raise their profiles and those of their peers. They understand that generating content is only part of the process. The relationships built will help proliferate that content throughout the community, both online and off.

Follow your contacts on Twitter. Participation in the conversation is not necessary to derive benefit from its contents. Also, try to learn additional details about contacts using LinkedIn. It will demonstrate initiative, enthusiasm, and a sincere interest in the subject matter.

Surveys are great tools for prompting engagement. Those who ask questions that are relevant and offer to share the responses (often anonymously) will set the foundation for a deeper future connection. You can then syndicate that content online and associate yourself with a topic you want people to relate back to your message. LinkedIn, Facebook, and Twitter all serve in a syndication role, as well as offer additional tools for that purpose. As part of that sharing, for instance, ICyte.com allows web pages to be saved to highlight information of interest, drawing someone's eye right to the information that is most relevant to him or her.

Follow Up

Nothing happens without follow-up. It is the essential element of becoming a white-collar hustler. You can try as hard as you want on the initial effort, but it is often the second and third interactions that bear fruit. In fact, there is an expectation of resiliency in a modern economy.

You must incorporate so many different personality traits in order to create something memorable: telemarketer, motivational speaker, politician, deferential assistant—and all at the same time. You must fight your natural insecurity and make an attempt. Rejection is usually not a reflection of the merits of an idea or strategy. Sometimes, it is just a function of bad timing. A letter thanking you for your resume and advising that there are presently no openings could mean that there really are no openings. The collective instinct is to assign another meaning to that message and consider it a negative judgment on one's qualifications. Next time, consider following up with a thank you note and checking back in a few months.

With the help of a mentor or other individual who provided advice, draft a plan of action for how to grow your career, and then take measurable and attainable steps to get there. Be honest about the ability to accomplish what is necessary to create momentum and stay grounded. And, take a few calculated risks. Try to connect others with those people they are trying to meet. Stay committed to the goals that have been set, and do so in a fashion that helps others. It is a proven formula for success and will help turn obstacles into opportunities every time.

RECAP

- Students are in as strong a position to innovate their career activities as professionals are in their practices. Consider how few of your classmates are taking creative and dynamic steps to enhance their job prospects. Ironically, they have everything to gain and almost nothing to lose. In the same way that clients have heightened expectations that their service provider will propose unique solutions, employers are increasingly waiting for job candidates to offer the same. The generational divide that is common between employers and student employees fuels this expectation.

- To take advantage of their position in school, students must overcome their uncertainty about networking. They need to remain disciplined in their approach and accountable to someone they trust in pursuing particular goals. That accountability will allow them to easily share their successes and failures along the way.

- Students should also be prolific generators of content. They can use that material to spotlight the good work of others and share key resources with those people they are trying to reach.

- Those who develop a follow-up schedule and calendar key milestones often have an advantage over their peers.

CHAPTER

5

Know Your Clients and Patients Because They Expect You To

Clients and patients have come to expect their professional services providers to have an immediate understanding of their personal history and the detailed nature of their query. As a result, they need to more effectively tailor their approach to the particular individuals with whom they generally work. This chapter will identify how other professionals are getting to know their customer base on a personal level using interactive video, Twitter, and online groups. It will also highlight how different industries, ranging from accountants to investment advisors, are adapting to a client-centric model of service, including engaging in a cross-disciplinary approach.

■ ■ ■

Andrew Prozes is a senior adviser at Warburg Pincus and the recently retired CEO of the LexisNexis Group, a division of Reed Elsevier Plc, where he served as a member of the latter's board of directors. Prozes joined LexisNexis in 2000. During his tenure, the organization grew from a $1.7 billion company to a $4 billion-plus entity with 17,000 employees and profits in excess of $1 billion.

A member of the first graduating class in computer science from the University of Waterloo in 1969, he has had a storied career in the information-delivery market. From running the Southam Inc. newspaper chain (Canada's largest newspaper company with 13 publications) for a decade, to serving as chairman of the Information Industry Association, he has experienced firsthand the evolution of technology in the professional services community.

"Lexis moved from being a provider of information to a provider of embedded workflow solutions," Prozes says. "The application of technology has had a sea change in how legal professionals execute and interact," according to Prozes. "That is key to tremendous improvements in productivity, speed, and getting to the core of an issue." Today a legal issue can be put into a search field and a computer does all the work; despite an increased reliance on technology to execute the work, one must know his customer to get the work in the first place.

Knowing your customer, client, or patient, is critical because of the expectation that you will understand who they are, their preferences, and their history. There was a time, not so long ago, when listening was often enough. Today, you must build a complete profile to understand the individual or organization, as well as his or her place in the market. "You are much more aware of the customer you are dealing with," notes Prozes.

Social media allows you to find common connections in seconds, which helps to seamlessly open a meeting or initiate contact. You can simply pay attention to a "friend's" Facebook updates, subscribe to his or her blog, or "listen" to what the person is tweeting. One must, however, understand how that information impacts the person directly.

Even a decade ago, professionals would still call their colleagues to find common connections and read industry-specific publications to familiarize themselves with background information. Today, professionals can conduct the very same due diligence on their mobile phones in the cab on the way to the meeting.

"There have been dramatic improvements in speed, which makes us significantly better prepared for any question," Prozes points out. He is aware of this sea change in client relationships because so much of his career involved helping researchers find answers. "We want our customers to have at their fingertips the best information in every single form, which helps them instantaneously respond to almost anything their clients need."

The application of technology has had a sea change in how legal professionals execute and interact.

Andrew Prozes, senior adviser at Warburg Pincus and the recently retired CEO of the LexisNexis Group, a division of Reed Elsevier Plc, New York City

Accountants and Technology Are a Good Match

Katrina Harrell knows her customers, and is leveraging the Web to get to know them even better. The Clayton, North Carolina-based accountant is the founder of Your Simple Bookkeeper, Inc., a division of the K.M. Harrell Group LLC, which has been assisting the micro business community as a solo accountant (though not a certified public accountant) since 2008 and does business from the YourSimpleBookkeeper.com site. Her clients and prospects, however, do not typically hire a bookkeeper at their current stage, but reactively contact her when they encounter a problem. "I wanted to create a service that would allow people to be proactive," says the former corporate accountant and management consultant of her decision to develop the site in February 2010.

Her business model is based on subscription fees for micro business bookkeeping services that rise according to each client's size, as well as the operational and record-keeping matters with which it needs assistance. Basic bookkeeping subscription plans range from $35 to $100 per month for new start-up companies that have revenues up to $300,000. "My clients cannot afford the expenses of a traditional CPA, accountant, or bookkeeper in a metropolitan city," says Harrell. "Technology plays an integral role in allowing me to keep my expenses low," she adds. As a virtual bookkeeper, Harrell is able to be more proactive in reaching her target clients. In fact, one can pay for her services directly on the web.

Technology is playing an increasing role in the way accountants conduct business. Many businesses look at accountants as more than number crunchers who can provide additional services. The challenge is to get the *accountants* to recognize that they are more than that. For example, every Wednesday afternoon, Harrell leverages the power of Justin.TV, a completely free, live-streaming video service that allows her to address her audience on a specific topic that is of interest to them.

For instance, a recent program covered "27 Little Known Tax Deductions that Small Businesses Overlook." In the presentation, she shares candid advice like "making money and keeping money are not the same thing." She also allows her viewers to ask questions and chat with her during the program and continues chatting with her audience via Twitter.com/YourSimpleTweet using the hashtag #YSBLiveChat.

> My clients cannot afford the expenses of a traditional CPA, accountant, or book-keeper in a metropolitan city. Technology plays an integral role in allowing me to keep my expenses low.
>
> *Katrina Harrell, accountant and founder of Your Simple Bookkeeper, Inc.,*
> *a division of the K.M. Harrell Group LLC, North Carolina*

Harrell also has a webinar series called "Your Wealthy Business," as well as a Facebook group associated with that endeavor. She uses her Facebook.com/YourSimpleBookkeeper page to post a business or bookkeeping tip multiple times per week. "I make it personal based on the needs of my clients." Harrell's goal is to incorporate her experiences as a business owner into the information on how members of her audience can manage their businesses. She uses their feedback and creative ideas on technology to help fuel their growth.

To determine the types of programs to offer, Harrell posts direct questions via Facebook and Twitter, such as "What do you need to know from an accountant?" She also interacts via her other social networking platforms. When a prospect recently asked her for additional information related to the difference between an employee and an independent contractor, she sent her a video she had created on that issue, as well as specific pages on IRS.gov. When another prospect asked her about inventory management, she sent a proposal for ways in which she could assist the business. "I ask the questions and provide the platform for discussion," she says. "As a result, people let me know how I can help."

Lawyers, consultants, veterinarians, and a variety of professionals can utilize these same techniques to share information and engage with their audience. Despite the increasingly common nature of these efforts, fewer people are doing it than you think. You may even be the first among your peers.

Leverage a Variety of Tools to Promote Your Practice

The new media environment is forcing professionals to think more creatively to find their voices and listeners to their message beyond simply meeting in person (though that effort is still critical). "Technology is more than 50 percent of the way that I will grow my business," Harrell predicts. Her commitment to growth in that fashion stems from her experience that her efforts enable clients and potential clients to feel more attached to her based on their experiences online. Her candor and responsiveness build the type of trust that was once only possible with a live handshake and office visit. Harrell will often re-tweet information via her Twitter account, Twitter.com/YourSimpleTweet, so that her strategic partners will share her announcements and information with their respective audiences. "It creates a beneficial cycle," she says.

Charles E. McLaughlin of Andover, Massachusetts, recognizes the need for beneficial cycles. The founder and CEO of the McLaughlin Investigative Group, Inc. and EmploySecure.com, his business is about both knowing his customers and creating relationships with others who want to know more. His private investigation firm focuses on product liability, as well as international and insurance investigations. He also conducts Web-based pre-employment screening for organizations nationwide. "We use technology heavily in both sides of the business," he says.

"I do not have an IT background, but I believe in technology to leverage what I do for a living to better serve my clients," McLaughlin says, referencing his usage of a virtual work force in India to outsource his non-confidential administrative projects via Elance.com. Given the nature of his work, he actually stores many of his company's documents on the web through premier Gmail accounts and Google Docs to have universal access from anywhere. "That has probably been the biggest, most dramatic, and simplest change that we have done," he adds.

The ability to access data faster and cheaper than he could even a few years ago has resulted in a dramatic reduction in price for engaging a private investigator to conduct pre-employment screenings, a practice once reserved for the hiring of mid-level or executive managers. A basic background check used to cost an organization between $1,000 and $1,500. It is now less than $100. "It is also more thorough and compliant with the Fair Credit Reporting Act," notes McLaughlin, who conducts these investigations through EmploySecure.com (created by an India-based design firm). Nevertheless, "Technology works with you and against you." McLaughlin admits. "It streamlines communication, yet also keeps you apart." He recommends that professionals use technology to assist in creating and developing the relationship, but not in defining it.

Regardless of the industry changes associated with professional services, there must still be a counsel-client relationship that forms with credibility and conviction. "It does not need to be done face-to-face, but you need to keep everything personalized," McLaughlin says.

Answer the Question the Client Should Have Asked

Mary Ellen McCarthy is trying to personalize relationships in an industry that she feels is advancing so rapidly that the relationship is often being displaced by a vast array of information available online. Arguably, with respect to financial advisory services, there is plenty of data available for educated consumers to make basic informed decisions. Consumers no longer need to speak with licensed individuals to place most trades or to secure advanced research and planning tools. That said, however, consumers generally still need a licensed attorney to appear in court and a licensed medical professional to prescribe medication.

McCarthy, originally a biologist, moved to Wall Street in the mid-1980s after realizing that financial services firms needed scientists to evaluate biotechnology companies. She started as an analyst with Merrill Lynch Asset Management, now a division of Bank of America Corp., providing advice to money managers related to companies in the healthcare and biotechnology sectors. She moved to the sell-side as a healthcare and pharmaceuticals analyst with Shearson Lehman Brothers, where she provided industry and company research for traders, investment bankers, and money managers.

Later, with start-up Multex Systems (sold to Thompson Reuters Corp.), she helped pioneer technologies to deliver Wall Street research to individuals and independent money managers. In 2002 she retired and moved to Brookline, Massachusetts. There she began teaching individuals how to manage their money, including ways to select mutual funds and stocks, as well as techniques to manage and diversify their portfolios. "I realized as I started teaching that ordinary individuals had no idea how to use financial services to their advantage," she recalls. "They lack basic skills even in terms of reviewing their financial statements properly."

Since financial decisions and products can be confusing to many people, they engage advisors for their judgment. Those advisors traditionally bill for that judgment based on assets under management. McCarthy, however, thinks that the market has shifted.

Given the last decade's financial meltdown and mistrust of all things Wall Street-related, individual investors are increasingly committed to managing as much of their own portfolios as possible. "People want advice that they can trust to be unbiased; they want advice that's customized and provided in a way that helps them to really understand what's going on," she says.

McCarthy provides advice on asset allocation, but bills for her services on a per-hour basis only, creating personalized, prepaid financial advisory packages that include plenty of one-on-one time, much like a gym coaching package. "Most people are not terribly organized with respect to their financial papers and they are also very intimidated," she says. "I seek to empower individuals and help them sort through the maze of products and services being offered to them."

Until recently, independent financial advisors like McCarthy did not exist, but the technology in financial planning now allows an individual with an average understanding of investment products to manage his or her money. In addition, there are low-cost index funds that cover almost every sector of the market. With some inexpensive initial guidance, says McCarthy, "you can drive an individual's costs down to one-half percent from one and a half percent to two percent in fees just by switching mutual funds."

> People want advice that they can trust to be unbiased; they want advice that's customized and provided in a way that helps them to really understand what's going on.
>
> *Mary Ellen McCarthy, a Massachusetts-registered investment advisor*

As Harrell notes, there is a difference between what you earn and what you keep. "The only predictable part of a stock investment is the dividend," says McCarthy. "If most of that dividend goes to your money managers then all you are doing is speculating on prices," she adds, highlighting her efforts to help clients keep more of the wealth that the markets generate.

In fact, McCarthy says that many discount brokerage firms provide a vast array of planning tools that few clients use to their maximum value. In addition:

- Morningstar.com offers paid subscribers portfolio management tools, personalized portfolio analysis, investment ideas, and independent reports.
- Tip$ter is a free financial planner, retirement calculator, and portfolio simulator from Prospercuity, LLC (Prospercuity.com).
- ESPlanner (ESPlanner.com) provides a variety of calculators that allow individuals to create their own saving and spending plans that build in personal priorities.
- Medicare.gov offers an excellent long-term-care cost calculator that allows you to take your own or family medical history into consideration.

That is the essence of the shift not in the market, but in the way that consumers approach the market. "The tools are all out there if you know how to ask the right questions and can get educated on how best to use them," says McCarthy. They are armed with information, but need to figure out how to maximize the benefit of that information. They are increasingly calling on counselors to help sift through the details, rather than present the basic options to them. Just as patients are diagnosing basic ailments and nonlawyers are drafting standardized documents (after all, free contract-creation web sites abound), individuals are developing strategies to create and manage their own money.

"Whether they ask the right questions is often a question of luck," cautions McCarthy, because investors can misuse or misunderstand the models and calculators available online. And personal issues, such as overspending, can derail the best plans.

It can no longer be just about selling products, or demonstrating a history of returns. It is about trust and judgment. Those managers who help their clients make better decisions, rather than solely focusing on their investments, will prosper in the new dynamic. McCarthy, a Massachusetts-registered investment advisor, conducts workshops in local high school and college extension programs to grow her business. Former students make up half of her client base and the other half is referrals.

There is a certain level of emotional intelligence that is essential for financial advisors. Ironically, "The emphasis has increasingly been on minimizing the amount of contact you have with your client," reveals McCarthy. Clients are thought to pay for performance, not face time. Money managers have historically tried to grow their total pool of assets in the least amount of time, but she advises, "Out-performance is an ephemeral and generally unobtainable objective, while a caring relationship nurtured over hours and years of contact time is priceless."

Just as Matthew Shatz, head of the U.S. Equities, Sales, and Trading at MF Global Holdings, Ltd., reports in Chapter 7 on the rapidly decreasing commissions in the high-frequency trading industry, mutual funds are under similar pressure. Index funds have created a dramatic level of cost competition. In addition, "The vast majority of mutual managers under-perform the benchmarks," says McCarthy. "There is no proof that fund performance is anything other than luck," she adds. With that in mind, it is understandable that the industry would be in transition and require a more dynamic generation of professionals to face these dramatic challenges.

Enter Edward J. Finley II, a managing director at JPMorgan Chase & Co. Finley is a University of Chicago Law School graduate turned wealth consigliore. He experienced the crossover in professional services between the technical expertise and personal prowess necessary to thrive in a client-centric environment. Finley thought he wanted to be a litigator, but was less certain after completing his first rotation as a summer clerk before his second year of law school. After rethinking his choice of concentration, Finley approached his mentor, who suggested that he consider focusing on trusts and estates. The field combined substantive knowledge with constructive assistance to specific clients.

The summer following his second year of law school, he combined rotations in bankruptcy, tax, and litigation to set the foundation of his trusts and estates experience at a large law firm in New York City. He spent the next five years honing his skills there, and then moved to San Francisco, where he continued to work in a large law firm in the same practice area. "In order to do trusts and estates at the top of your game, you had to be at a big law firm," he says. In 1997, he experimented with value billing, which did not measure hourly investments. "That rubbed the bureaucrats the wrong way," he recalls. Two years later, he decided he could more innovatively serve clients as a wealth advisor and moved back to New York to work with JPMorgan. "I found that all of the work that I enjoyed as a lawyer was increased manifold when I came here."

Merge Talents Wherever Possible

Finley notes that prior to the mid-1990s, the wealth-management world consisted of separately operating accountants, lawyers, investment professionals, financial planners, and tax specialists. "Now, it isn't about siloing those skill sets," he says, reporting that in the late 1990s, accounting firms started acquiring tax law practices and operating them through subsidiaries. They no longer tracked billable hours to the client. Rather, the accounting firm simply charged a flat fee.

Multi-family offices also started emerging and offered experts in tax, investments, estate planning, and insurance, who helped coordinate the lawyers, bankers, accountants, and other professionals in exchange for a fee based on the total under management. Finley notes that JPMorgan was interested in this same model. Instead of paying by the hour, they focused on best in class. "People in the wealth-management business realized in the late 1990s that the professions needed to be integrated and that this was not a solitary business model."

According to Finley, although the lawyer was originally the primary counselor, that role diminished as wealth-management teams became more effective. "It meant for lawyers that you were kind of stuck somewhere neither here nor there," notes Finley. "Nobody can make a living being the scrivener, but law firms also do not have credit specialists, wealth managers, and accountants on their teams," he adds.

In response, lawyers tried to broaden their services. A few became adept at developing very technical and aggressive estate-planning techniques. They became the lawyer's lawyer and viewed the local lawyers as their clients rather than the client himself or herself.

Just as the lawyers have had to evolve, banks have had to shift their strategies as well. Finley highlights that individuals and families once kept all of their wealth with a single firm, which managed each class of assets. In the last decade, however, families of great wealth ($500 million and over) began to divide their wealth, including those who created their own private family offices. Smaller clients worth about $50 million tried to manage it themselves, reports Finley.

Banks have been trying to offer choices and coordinating with a variety of outside experts to provide more options to their clients. They want their team members to serve as trusted advisors for all of a customer's wealth-management needs.

Today, a client may not have to split its wealth among various firms. "As a very young lawyer, I had a senior partner tell me never to answer the question a client asks," recounts Finley. "Instead, always answer the question a client should have asked," the partner said. That effort is the key to identifying a client's objectives. Determining those objectives required his group to balance the extremes of never seeking outside guidance with the brokerage model, which has a completely open architecture. Brokers actually leverage computer models that evaluate managers in a variety of asset classes, notes Finley. "Rather than having that many choices, we wanted a narrow set of choices that reflects the firm's judgment and leaves it up to the investor to manage the mix."

The increased competition and wider selection has increased the reliance on trust in the decision-making process. In the same way that social media and technology have created more noise in the communication environment, competition and lower-cost solutions have created confusion among prospective clients. That has increased the level of influence over the selection process. "Professional advisors play a deeply meaningful role in this," Finley says.

> Always answer the question a client should have asked.
> *Edward J. Finley II, managing director, JPMorgan Chase & Co., New York City*

The essence of that trust is persuading others with information and knowledge. Lawyers are using that technique of empowerment to recommend accountants, and bankers are using it to encourage the use of various financial planners. "Their understanding of what you do differently has a big impact on the role they play," says Finley. The responsibility of a wealth advisor now expands beyond working with clients on specific wealth management, but also to maintaining the firm's relationship with the professional advisor community.

For instance, a wealth planner may ask lawyers to propose estate-planning topics that he or she can share with clients. Those kinds of programs and that interaction with an interdisciplinary group of experts make a client's experience with one bank over another fundamentally different. Financial institutions once saw lawyers as the funnel to wealth-management clients. Today, they are establishing their own diverse teams to collaborate with, rather than depend upon, their referral sources.

RECAP

- It is essential for professionals to familiarize themselves with the tools that their clients, patients, and prospects use to research information. Most of these tools are available online. For example, Justin.tv allows you to create real-time video that gives your audience a chance to interact with you in a convenient web-based environment. It also gives you the chance to demonstrate your expertise. The key is to ask the correct questions to learn as much as you can about your clients, including where they prefer to spend their time online.
- If a client prefers Facebook over Twitter, find ways to interact in a Facebook group or through a Fan page.
- Incorporate the talent of others in enriching this client interaction. That collaboration could be formal or informal, but the breadth of experience will often have a material impact on the client experience and the outcome.

CHAPTER

6

Putting Your Practice through a Wind Tunnel Will Blow You Away

I n an innovation driven market, it is critical for individuals and organizations to routinely reevaluate their efforts to determine whether they are operating at optimal efficiency and reaching their client base or pool of patients in the most effective way possible. Yet professionals often avoid this exercise because such an assessment is disruptive and tends to force change. This chapter will highlight the benefits of scrutinizing your practice to enhance the nature of how you deliver your services. It will compare changes in the legal, accounting, and consulting fields to identify a series of best practices. And, it will help identify your value in the marketplace.

■ ■ ■

In 2000, Mark Harris was an associate with a prestigious New York law firm. He was a junior lawyer thinking about billing his hours, rather than a new way of providing legal services that would revolutionize how lawyers viewed themselves and their role in the business community. He was just trying to work as hard as possible and provide exceptional legal work to the firm's clients. Like most junior professionals, he thought very little about business models and billing rates.

The day after his team completed a transaction, a partner asked him to review a bill for the client. In doing so, he noticed that at his billing rate of about $300 per hour in a month when he worked around the clock and billed between two and three hundred hours (yes, that is humanly possible), he earned the firm enough to cover a large portion of his annual salary. It was at that moment that he began studying the pyramidal model upon which most traditional professional service firms, particularly law firms, leverage their internal talent.

A typical law firm will hire permanent associates and pay them a salary based on their class year along with a merit bonus. In return, the associate will bill his or her hours to specific client matters, hopefully earning multiples of the cost for the firm. The difference between what it collects from the client and pays to the associate, with some accounting for overhead, is generally the profit of the firm. Senior lawyers are often the managers of the client relationships while junior lawyers perform the daily project management and research tasks. The goal has historically been to maximize the fees, with less attention paid to efficiency. After all, there are three cost components to the traditional professional services firm.

First, there is the apparatus and overhead that supports the attorney, such as the office, equipment, and support staff, as well as the firm's investment in training the attorney and the money it spends on the attorney's benefits and other costs of employment. Second, there is the profit-sharing pool, which is distributed to the partnership. Third, there is the leveraging of talent, which can be high in metropolitan markets.

After evaluating this model, Harris began studying the money trail, seeing at what point in the year his salary and expenses were covered. "I realized that value was a big driver of client decision-making," he recalls. In addition, many attorneys Harris knew (and didn't know) were generally unhappy. Most considered themselves neither overpaid nor under-worked, and he evaluated the sources of their dissatisfaction.

After discussing the idea with Alec Guettel, who is now his business partner, Harris concluded that in an exchange between two parties, if one party is unhappy, it is likely to be the result of a bad bargain. If, however, both parties are fundamentally unhappy, that's probably a bad exchange.

So he and Guettel decided to disrupt it. "We pulled it apart and replaced it with a system that accounts for cultural shifts and advancements in technology to leave everyone radically better off," he recalls. The two took that premise, plus the visual imagery of putting the law firm into a wind tunnel—similar to the way engineers would—to create Axiom.

It is critical to make this evaluation in the most thorough manner possible to take advantage of the mood in the market. At this moment in time, clients are, in fact, simultaneously conducting an identical analysis and often appreciate a service provider's effort to streamline operations, particularly given the hourly nature of standard billing protocols.

Even Small Elements of Inefficiency Can Have a Large Impact on the Bottom Line

Engineers strip away all of the parts that create drag or waste. That was the goal of Harris and Guettel in forming the Axiom model. "It was addition through subtraction," Harris says.

Most organizations that provide professional services, regardless of the specific discipline, operate in the same fundamental fashion as those that preceded them for decades. Their business models continue to prize those skills and personalities that fit well into the leverage model. They focus on timekeeping and hourly valuations. Clients pay both for that time and the reputations of the organizations sending the bill. The economy and technology have forced a shift in that landscape.

Axiom, for example, says it has been able to eliminate two-thirds of the law firm cost structure by targeting those areas where it could create a new tier of lawyers, who are equally talented as compared to their traditionally employed counterparts, but nimble in their ability to provide client service.

Consider that, like Harris, law firm associates can generate $1 million per year at a large law firm at an annual salary of $200,000 to $250,000. "The typical leverage ratio in a big city of four or five to one is expensive and wasteful," highlights Harris, who notes that clients are generally insensitive to this issue only in a truly exceptional event or one featuring extraordinary yet unique demand for legal services. These include large "bet-the-franchise" multi-jurisdictional matters, cross-border public mergers and acquisitions, and initial public offerings. Due to the material nature of these events to the organization's existence, "what you're buying is not the legal work and the infrastructure; it is the imprimatur and the insurance." Those buying that small slice of a law firm's capabilities often do not mind paying the tax inherent in the structure, notes Harris.

Harris and Guettel founded Axiom not to handle these large-scale matters, but to support lawyers and clients who demand legal expertise for the other 90 percent of issues that arise every day with the same quality of service at a 70 percent lower cost. "We removed about ninety percent of the physical overhead," says Harris, who notes that attorneys work out in the field or from a home office. The technological evolution that has made this possible has had a direct impact on the economics of the practice Axiom can offer. With the dramatic drop in top tier computers to under $500 and the inexpensive nature of wireless Internet access, professionals can work almost anywhere, from a coffee shop to an airport terminal.

Recently, clients have started outsourcing entire functions to Axiom, such as having the firm maintain its commercial contracts for the whole organization. In those more complex matters, attorneys work on site or in Axiom's New York City headquarters. This arrangement is consistent with a modern trend in professional services, which is outsourcing overhead or leveraging the fixed assets of the client. Similar to the idea of encouraging a contractor or even an employee to use his or her laptop or wireless Internet connection, Axiom and comparable services (including, Atlanta-based FSB Fisher Broyles, LLP; Mountain View and San Francisco, California-based GCA Law Partners LLP; Plymouth, Minnesota-based The General Counsel; and Houston, Texas-based Outsource GC) are taking advantage of the ubiquity of talent and technology.

There is no longer a need for the same type of infrastructure to support talent-driven completion of certain services. The talent can support itself. Axiom provides a leaner and flatter structure. Clients pay only for what they need and lawyers make a larger percentage of what they bill. Axiom measures that amount at about two times or more than what they retain in a law firm environment. "No attorneys at Axiom are making money off the system," Harris says. Although this arrangement caps one's earning potential, it allows skilled lawyers to perform sophisticated work for challenging clients without the pressures inherent in a traditional "up or out" law firm model.

In a dramatic shift from the way professionals engaged in the past, Axiom's lawyers can freely opt-out of engagements they cannot or prefer not to do. Self-determination without consequences is a hallmark of the modern transformation of the manner in which professionals operate. They choose to work and receive compensation.

At Axiom, one's salary stops when he or she is "on the beach" (Axiom-speak for between projects). Whether they work or not, attorneys on the beach continue to receive their baseline benefits.

Despite the logical nature of this model, it is a fairly recent phenomenon. "The big shift that we hoped was happening 10 years ago is just now beginning and was catalyzed by the financial crisis," says Harris. Even before the recession began to negatively impact the economy in 2007, organizations focused on profitability. They began reconsidering their costs and ability to influence pricing among their service providers. As they assumed more control of the relationship and began dictating the terms of that relationship, increases in competition led to price reductions. "Since cost control is a much more prominent technique for companies to drive and control profits, creative arrangements are becoming more attractive," notes Harris.

In fact, most corporate executives are requiring a drop in spending without any sacrifice in services. As a result, service providers are under enormous pressure to deliver results in an optimally efficient way. In response to that pressure, organizations should follow Axiom's lead and spend time studying what Harris calls the "rigorous segmentation of demand." "This is not complicated. It's not magical. It is profound in its simplicity," he says.

Identify the bucket of demand for your overall services in the market. At the very top of the value chain, there are risky and novel matters for which prospective clients will pay a significant premium. These matters require expertise, experience, and a unique perspective. They are not easily copied.

In contrast, at the bottom of the chain are the items that are being consumed by the free economy: quick answers to basic questions, form documents, resources, and directories. In the middle is all the run-the-company type of work. Things that require experience and expertise, but not necessarily the infrastructure and imprimatur of a major law firm.

> The big shift that we hoped was happening 10 years ago is just now beginning and was catalyzed by the financial crisis. Since cost control is a much more prominent technique for companies to drive and control profits, creative arrangements are becoming more attractive.
>
> *Mark Harris, co-founder and CEO, Axiom, New York City*

Define Your Value Proposition to Focus Your Future

Professional services firms must now determine where they reside in their eco-system to properly identify their competitive advantages. They must identify the true value they are bringing to their clients and prospects.

The commoditization of formerly value-added services is having a dramatic impact. Typically, the most expensive firms manage the most complex items in the demand chain. As you move down the spectrum of complexity, novelty, and risk, the cost to serve tends to drop accordingly.

Those who can articulate and deliver on the promises they make at the outset are more likely to find success. Like Axiom, the key is to ensure that the cost structure does not bring any excess to the table. "If you want to differentiate yourself, you have to make the business case to the client that every dollar they are spending on you is a value and will yield a return on their investment," Harris says. The relationship premium that characterized business for decades is now being impacted by the value proposition.

Companies want more specific information about what their budget is buying. They are increasingly dictating billing structures, time frames, and strategy. The markets were once so relationship driven, and fueled by inertia, that external advisers were the proverbial 'easy' button for specific departments. That is over.

The phenomenon is also much more widespread. "This is a movement that is broader than the legal industry," says Harris. Discipline is almost irrelevant. If you are a professional in any area, the idea of putting your business through a virtual wind tunnel will help you redefine your market niche, as well as your target client.

Karen Ferguson, the president of Tatum, joined Resources Global Professionals in Irvine, California, at the time of its founding, along with various colleagues as a division of a large accounting firm in 1996. Ferguson and her team focused on providing staffing support to the CPA and financial community. From a base of clients in San Francisco and Los Angeles, she moved to New York.

Resources Global completed an initial public offering in December of 2000, but Ferguson recalls that prior to the downturn in technology stocks, it was not a popular company in the public market. As a cash generating business, however, it became a successful IPO, she reports. At its peak, Ferguson notes that the company had $850 million in revenue and 85 offices worldwide. For many accounting-related entities, the passage of the Sarbanes–Oxley Act injected a lot of opportunity into the field. The new requirements were windfalls for Resources Global. "When they started in the mid-1990s, there were temp agencies, but the professional project-contract, interim-person business was not well known or understood," says Ferguson. "It was a mystery from the employment side, as well as the business and corporate side." Like Axiom, the business grew from a confluence of demand. The clients were in need of access to talent. Their choice at the time was temp agencies, which did not always offer the quality provided by talented alumni of the big accounting firms. Instead, the accounting firms would supply clients with internal talent on a temporary basis, but they were often junior with no real business experience, notes Ferguson. "If the client needed to do things internally, it wasn't the right match."

At the same time, professionals began seeking more balance in their careers. They began demanding flexibility and the revolution in technology made this increasingly possible. Those trends fueled the growth in Resources Global. It is often a combination of client needs and employee capabilities that drive change. When the marketplace offers tools to manage that change, it serves as an incubator for innovation.

The rise of the Internet and the related freedom it produced materially changed what companies could offer, and the manner in which they could do so. Remote access, secure communication, and a flatter global landscape forced professionals to reevaluate their service offerings. This shift forever altered the landscape in which experts provide advisory services.

When Ferguson arrived in New York City in 1998, prospective clients would tell her that they had no need for temporary staff of the caliber that the company offered. "It was the day of corporate culture and you were never going to leave that family," she recalls. As she probed further, however, her prospective clients were routinely "borrowing" accountants from the Big Four, which was a popular practice called "Staff Augmentation." Resources Global was offering a more cost-efficient alternative to what clients were already doing. There was a very mature business in Europe called "Interim Management." They adapted that model to the United States.

Once clients realized that they were already doing this, albeit in a different form, and that it was Resources Global's core competency, they soon began adopting this model. "Professional services firms are interesting, but it is the details of the operations that make them different," says Ferguson. "On a web site, they all look the same and it is hard to differentiate them on paper," she adds.

Finding True Worth Is Wiser Than You Realize

As individual practitioners identify their competitive landscape, they must capture the true value they are bringing to their clients and prospects. The simple fact that most professionals appreciate is that the best way to identify this value is to simply ask. Ask your clients, prospects, and the industry cognoscenti about your reputation. Consider asking others why they would call you. Listen to their reasoning. Specify the areas in which you excel and those where you falter.

If these responses are consistent, then continue to hone your message and cultivate that brand. If, however, they are contrary to or inconsistent with your mission, then be very methodical about changing your operations. Ironically, the one aspect of this transition process that most individuals and organizations miss is to continue to incorporate your critics into the resolution.

Even just a few years ago, one needed to hire a team with sophisticated data-analysis capabilities to conduct this type of market research. Today, Web-based survey tools allow instant, and often free, access to the honest thoughts of those who are best positioned to shape the development of your profile. It provides experts with additional uninterrupted thoughts from prospective and existing clients that help determine how you can assist them. It is often essential to delivering a practical message.

That insight is more important than ever because while the market shifted to produce the success stories of Axiom and Resources Global, among others, it has also moved again to make decision-making more protracted. Organizations are more thoughtful in basing decisions on a defined return on investment. Despite these challenges, they force individuals and organizations to be better at what they do. They make flexibility a value proposition that many are demanding.

Resources Global took the variable model to the client and made it acceptable internally. "It aligns with all of the phenomena in the world," says Ferguson. Ultimately, people have to be flexible and agile. "The economy has cleansed a lot of stuff out of business," says Ferguson. It's not hard to see why sending your business through a wind tunnel is essential.

The good things about professional services firms are that they are very agile businesses and have the ability to evolve in many different ways to best serve their clients. When they need more of a thoughtful consulting oriented approach, you create one. Infrastructure can help or hurt depending on why it exists. If its purpose is to perpetuate a successful model that can quickly respond to client requests, then it can help. If it is based on a system of leverage that is slowly eroding because clients are demanding a price structure that it cannot support, then it can infect the foundation of the operation.

That said, if you have positioned yourself in the marketplace as an organization that will generally capture the large-scale projects that are less sensitive to price, then using leverage to accomplish your goals and serve your clients will be successful.

Become a Chameleon to Kick Start Your Initiatives

Nimble businesses, regardless of their size, must become what a client needs in a very chameleon-like way. They need not only to be able to staff appropriately, but to consider value from a variety of perspectives. With a client-centered focus, an organization can determine how important certain outcomes will be to a client as they bill for their time and experience. "If you are smart about running a business, you are always evolving to meet the client's needs," says Ferguson. "I don't think traditional professional services firms have that kind of flexibility," she adds. For that reason, most need to be somewhat non-traditional for their market.

That doesn't necessarily mean that dentists should hire assistants capable of creating balloon animals for patients, or that lawyers should engage a singing troupe to woo prospective clients. Companies that can simply evolve toward demand and make their operations more efficient will be more successful. "Look at what your clients are asking of you and think creatively about how to be that," advises Ferguson. "It is important to hold on to your ability to innovate and create" she adds, which she cites as critical components of being successful in the future.

That innovation can be something as simple as modernizing one's client interaction. When a local hair salon approached Sajeel

Qureshi with a request to make its appointment system more efficient, the founder of Computan Innovative Solutions, a Canadian Web and mobile application developer for small- and medium-sized businesses, had a simple idea: Digitize it. "They didn't want to answer the phone to create an appointment because it is an administrative problem and removes time from the stylist," he explains. For its hair salon client, it built a booking engine to take reservations online. This permitted customers to make appointments at any time, day or night. It resulted in fewer phone calls and freed the employees to spend their time engaging their clients.

> Look at what your clients are asking of you and think creatively about how to be that. It is important to hold on to your ability to innovate and create.
>
> *Karen Ferguson, co-founder, Resources Global Professionals, New York City*

More importantly, however, it allows them to engage their clients long after the initial appointment is made. It provides them with insight into the type of person with whom they like to work, a record of how long it has been since their haircut, and the types of products they use. It offers the benefits of the survey without ever asking for a customer's time to complete it. In addition, when the salon follows up with a customer, it can sell products while gauging satisfaction. The reminder service allows the salon to offer free client service options like adjusting or trimming one's bangs at no charge within 10 days of his or her initial visit. "It creates more ways for the customer to say 'yes'," notes Qureshi. "It typically works wonders."

If you're an accountant or a lawyer providing an information product, simply creating a system for appointments may not be a fully effective strategy, given that a customer or prospect may need immediate information, as well as the ability to coordinate a time to receive it. Savvy professionals could take advantage of specific Web communities where individuals are sharing their expertise with a worldwide audience interested in their knowledge. On Avvo.com, which rates lawyers and doctors, attorneys have responded to over 175,000 different questions.

The emergence of this direct form of communication by an expert has changed the way in which prospective clients interact. It has also heightened their expectations. Clients find answers to the simple questions before reaching out to an accountant, doctor, or lawyer with the serious issues they ultimately face. Those professionals who are answering the questions are also benefiting, regardless of whether the questioner ever retains them. They are using the Web to optimize their visibility. It is a modern version of a free consultation (within the confines of all of the ethical rules associated with such communication, of course).

Similar to the hair salon example, professionals can add a button to their sites that allows a visitor to instantly chat with him or her (or a virtual staff member). Consider the most popular questions that people will ask an accountant: How do I file for an extension? Is there a cap on the mortgage interest deduction? How much of my home office can I deduct? "You are making it easier for a potential customer to become a current customer," Qureshi says. "The scale should be increasing if the amount of leads are increasing," he advises. You must deliver the service, but you can leverage a variety of the tools to generate the leads and connect with potential clients. He suggests that reminder programs, chat systems, and surveys help generate opportunities much more quickly.

"Competition is so high now," says Qureshi. One does not need a premium expert for basic matters. "We beat companies that are much larger than us and lose to four guys in a basement in India," he adds. Often an established expert can overcome the challenge of a few kids in a garage. Today, however, it is hard to make that distinction and a sensitive economy encourages people to take calculated risks with commodity-type projects that require little sophistication. "If they can get the job done, you will have to adapt," says Qureshi.

Liann Eden and Dena McCallum adapted. They were in some ways the proverbial kids in the garage competing against the major forces in an industry that was always fairly insulated from competition other than its peers. The founders of independent consulting powerhouse Eden McCallum started the company near the end of the Internet boom in 2000. The London-based firm did not even have a web site for about a year.

Like Harris in the legal field and Ferguson in accounting, Eden and McCallum, both former McKinsey & Co. consultants, believed that clients were interested in retaining top-quality consulting resources in a different way than they could access it from the top-tier consultancies. In addition, as with their peers in the United States, the rise of the Internet changed the way professionals in the United Kingdom thought about the balance in their lives. "People were management consultants because they loved the work and did not want to be part of big corporate organizations," says McCallum. "They wanted to be independent and be part of something that was innovative rather than blue chip," she adds.

They studied the marketplace and realized that the number of alumni from large consulting firms across the globe began to outpace the current number of employees at those firms. This shifted the supply of talent. Technology then allowed those talented individuals to work remotely and access information that was once too expensive for freelancers to access. The dot com boom and bust changed the way professionals thought about their careers. "People who had blue chip educations and experience defined success differently," notes McCallum. They began to characterize success as broader than financial rewards and sought freedom over wealth.

Since they were not initially expecting to compete for the sophisticated work for which a global corporation might seek the assistance of a traditional consulting firm, Eden and McCallum networked with their former colleagues and other contacts. Their goal was to secure consulting projects and place highly experienced and well-educated professionals in those organizations.

> People were management consultants because they loved the work and did not want to be part of big corporate organizations. We are part of disaggregating the full bells and whistles.
>
> *Liann Eden and Dena McCallum, co-founders, London-based Eden McCallum*

One of their first clients was referred to them by a colleague at a large firm that helped to create the company's global strategy. When the company, an Internet service provider targeting small businesses, needed a UK approach and a web site to link all of its offerings throughout Europe, it determined that a smaller organization like Eden McCallum would be better suited to provide support. "As we have evolved over the years, we are now doing the global corporate strategies ourselves, but back then there was a view that we were synergistically a very good option for follow-on work," says McCallum.

The firm and its flexible model have proven to be very resilient over the past 10 years. "During the last two recessions the firm performed well. Many companies let their internal strategy and group corporate resources go during the downturns, but they still had important issues to resolve and turned to us for support," reports McCallum.

Leveraging the talents of Eden McCallum allows an organization to perform the project quasi-internally since the consultant is often resident on site, but the outside expert offers more objective answers. "Clients that want to be involved in crafting solutions and developing their strategies want to work with Eden McCallum," says Eden. The company has taken two important steps to ensure success.

First, it has generally identified the population of people to whom its services are most valuable and in what situation. While it might compete for large-scale global consulting work, it is more frequently considered the alternative to the mainstream consulting organizations. It is perceived to be more nimble and cost-effective, yet equally as talented because its employees are alumni of those larger organizations.

Second, the company has cultivated a vast network of referral sources within its client and consultant pool. Most of its new consultants and clients come via referral. "We are usually quite good at maintaining contact with people and following them through their careers," says Eden. "It is an old-fashioned relationship business, but it is fundamentally about genuine interest in others, rather than a marketing tool or system," adds McCallum.

There has to be a conviction to start, Eden points out. She was four months pregnant when she and McCallum (who was one month pregnant) started the company. "There is no ideal time, but in retrospect it was great to start in a downturn because clients were thinking creatively about how to bring in external support and the traditional firms were not recruiting as much," she advises. "If you think about things too much, you will never do it."

Traditionally, large consulting organizations attracted large clients because they appeared to have a tremendous infrastructure with a proprietary team of experts and unparalleled research capabilities. Today, there are vast networks of independent forensic accounting experts, medical professionals, legal authorities, and, of course, talented consultants. Even LinkedIn and alumni networks allow one to access a host of web-enabled information. Access to that information was once a unique feature of large consulting firms, notes McCallum. "We are part of disaggregating the full bells and whistles business model," adds Eden.

There are also freely available answers to millions of common research questions available online that a fairly basic user can find in minutes. Market research and competitive intelligence could be free, but is certainly available for a fraction of the cost that it was when Eden and McCallum founded the company.

Travel and document production are similarly commoditized functions. There is no longer a need for internal travel agents or an entire document management center. Professionals can arrange worldwide travel on a variety of simple web sites and technology has made paper copies almost unnecessary. "When the tricks of the trade became accessible to everyone, it became about the consultant purely as an intellectual body," says Eden. "The fact that you can work remotely and share documents releases the industry's view that you need to be based at a desk in an office every day," she adds.

That realization made a freelancing career acceptable to a mainstream workforce of highly educated and experienced professionals. "Early on there was a sense that only people who weren't very good consultants would leave the traditional firms" says McCallum. "There has been a big shift and it is not a dubious career choice anymore."

As individuals become chameleons to changing industries, they are fueling improvements centered on client concerns and streamlined operations. Professionals have an opportunity to seize this moment to reshape their practices to grow more steadily and efficiently.

RECAP

- With professional services firms facing shrinking margins and rising costs, it is essential that they find their optimal operating equilibrium. By measuring their efficiency and finding ways to streamline, they will be better positioned to respond to client and patient concerns at a reduced cost, but at a high level of responsiveness.
- To that end, professionals may want to consider adding features to their web sites to help automate certain functions like scheduling appointments or responding to general questions.
- Consider responding to questions posted on trusted web sites. Leverage web-based survey tools to poll your clients, patients, and prospects to help determine your value proposition. This exercise will help you alter your brand to meet the needs and expectations of your audience.

It's a Small Street, So Befriend Your Neighbors

Professional communities are small, whether your business is on Wall Street or on Main Street. To grow a practice and a reputation, one needs to befriend and interact with colleagues in the area. This chapter will highlight how to promote your identity in the market while also recognizing the complementary nature of your competitors. It will also provide guidance on redefining your business in the face of external challenges. Creative profit arrangements where profits are tied to success are also emerging as a leading tool for encouraging progress.

■ ■ ■

Six months into his college career, Matthew Shatz decided he was much more likely to be a success at picking stocks than classes. So he began his career in a self-described "boiler room" to prepare himself for the industry's General Securities Representative Examination, known as the Series 7, to become a licensed broker. Passing on his third attempt, he borrowed the $30,000 his parents had saved for college and lost every penny. That was the inauspicious beginning of his career in the mid 1990s.

Then Shatz learned about successful trading during his six-year tenure working for Steven Schonfeld, CEO of The Schonfeld Group. In the last 15 years, the 33-year-old head of the U.S. Equities, Sales, and Trading team at MF Global Holdings, Ltd. has become well known for his familiarity with "black box" trading techniques and his ability to serve clients utilizing such efforts in large-volume transactions on a high frequency across the globe.

From Schonfeld, Shatz moved briefly to E* Trade Professional, a division of E*Trade Securities LLC and then, with a colleague, helped start CyberTrader Institutional, a division of CyberHoldings, Inc., a subsidiary of Charles Schwab & Co., Inc. "We approached [CyberTrader creator] Butch Jones and told him we wanted to start a mini-prime broker," recalls Shatz. At 26, Shatz received funding to create this business unit at the company, alongside industry luminaries like Jones and Schwab himself, as well as senior executives at many major Wall Street banks, that would compete directly with more well-established entities.

They called themselves a "Hedge Fund Hotel" because, like a number of prime brokers at the time, they permitted their biggest traders to use their office space on the 47th floor of the U.S. Trust building in midtown Manhattan. "Every time I have moved, it might not have been the right place, but I was always moving up," Shatz says, which identifies a generational shift in workplace culture. "You have to be active in this business; you are only as good as your last deal."

According to a U.S. Bureau of Labor Statistics survey in 2010, the median number of years that male wage and salary workers aged 25 to 34 had been with their current employer was 3.2.[1] In fact, professional and business services employees had the second-lowest tenure out of eight different categories. As such, it is not surprising that Shatz continued to move in search of opportunity. After CyberTrader, he moved to FIMAT, which was acquired in a joint venture by Société Générale and Crédit Agricole and now operates as the Newedge Group. Newedge is among the three largest futures-clearing merchants in the world.

In his four-year tenure, his strategy was to attract high-frequency traders who could sell upward of 100 million shares per day. Yet like many professionals, Shatz felt constrained. "Moving is often the only way in this industry to get yourself to that next level," he says. This phenomenon is not unique to Wall Street traders. Lawyers routinely leave large firms as senior associates. They are well respected and talented, but leave because another firm offers them a partnership, even if it is non-equity in its character.

---

[1]See www.bls.gov/opub/ted/2010/ted_20100927_data.htm#ted_20100927a.

In fact, changing jobs is not new, yet the frequency with which people move represents a cultural shift and a different mindset in the way individuals view their roles in a profession. In addition, the portability of a client is a paramount concern. If a client will not leave, a professional will not either. If, however, a client chooses the lawyer, doctor, or accountant, rather than the practice with which he or she is associated, then movement no longer poses any barrier. "If you're good, someone always wants you," says Shatz. After all, he points out, "It is a small street."

While professionals commonly call Wall Street a small street because of its interconnected quality, you could insert the name of any street in its place. Main Street is now a small street. From Broadway in New York to Wilshire Boulevard in Los Angeles, the size of every street is shrinking because the ease with which one can cross has increased.

Technology has transformed the way individuals interact. The rise of social media has made everyone a neighbor and linked every industry to another. If you want to be a magazine publisher, you can create an online e-zine or a blog. If you want to have your own radio show, you establish a free program on BlogTalkRadio. And, of course, visit Justin.TV for a completely turnkey video show. Despite the advancements in how interaction occurs, it is still often about direct communication in professional services.

Know Yourself to Better Understand Others

In 1987, Nancy Ruddy and John Cetra established a small architectural firm in New York City. The company thrived based upon its reputation of high-quality design and creative thinking. Both principals were experienced in large-scale new construction, which is the bedrock of the city's real estate, but soon after they formed CetraRuddy Inc., the stock market crashed.

While the duo focused on architecture and interior design, the weak economy limited the availability of high-rise construction projects. To account for this deficiency, they decided to market the small part of their practice concentrating on the renovation and adaptive reuse of existing properties. They became recognized experts at analyzing structures and determining how to maximize the asset. In a down market, the firm grew because of its dynamic focus on the type of work that was available.

During the challenging economic climate of the early 1990s, CetraRuddy was suddenly competing against large well-known firms even for the smallest projects. "We had to build on our expertise and communicate what differentiated CetraRuddy from the pack," Ruddy recalls.

Markets ebb and flow in every industry. Some are positively impacted by the recession, while others are forever changed. Industries themselves, however, rarely fade away. They reconfigure and adjust to their newly appropriate size, but they are generally not eliminated. As such, professionals in those industries who adjust their businesses tend to thrive regardless of the market. CetraRuddy was flexible and nimble enough to focus its efforts to actually grow in difficult economic times.

As CetraRuddy was building its presence in adaptive reuse, it began studying the employment trends. After a client approached the team asking for guidance on moving a 50,000 square foot facility into a smaller 30,000 square foot office, it realized that downsizing corporate office space was another niche market. "We assisted firms in the banking, publication, and nonprofit sectors to downsize in existing office space while maintaining their identity and productivity," Ruddy says.

The company's executives contacted attorneys, real estate brokers, and business professionals with knowledge of firms seeking to downsize. They also studied workstation sharing and multi-purpose conference usage, as well as other planning methods that enhanced their expertise. Again, they not only survived but thrived by ingeniously repositioning themselves according to the needs of their clients and prospects.

Each time the economy shifts, Ruddy notes that the company analyzes its market sector distribution and refocuses on a proper equilibrium. Although CetraRuddy has always had a business-development strategy, it never prepared a formal strategic plan. To continue its growth trajectory, the firm hired a director of strategic development, who was responsible for conducting, along with the executive team, an analysis of the company's strengths, weaknesses, opportunities, and threats (SWOT).

Every professional services firm can benefit from a similar analysis to determine what contributes to its success and how it can maximize those opportunities. CetraRuddy evaluated the competitive field and made some difficult decisions to narrow the firm's focus. "It was a way to redefine our mission and it really helped us determine which markets were important and profitable," Ruddy recalls. "It also helped define where to spend our marketing budget," she adds.

To consider your strengths, weaknesses, opportunities, and threats, create an increased dialogue with your clients, patients, colleagues, and friends. Start by formally assigning a trusted individual to lead the analysis, either internally or externally. Consider the strengths of your practice, including ideas related to service, efficiency, innovation, responsiveness, and reputation, among others. Repeat the process for each element of the evaluation.

Following the SWOT analysis, "We realized that instead of looking at new markets where we did not have expertise, we looked at the markets that build on our strengths," says Ruddy. While the company of 55 employees recently completed construction of a 1.3 million square-foot building, she notes that those projects will be rare in the next few years given the difficulty in obtaining financing and the current economic climate.

Known for its highly crafted luxury residences and lifestyle communities, the company evaluated how it could broaden its focus on housing. With its unique signature capturing the attention of top-tier hotel and industry leaders, "We felt it was a very easy shift going from housing to hospitality," Ruddy says.

The firm also broadened its geographic markets, which previously had focused on the New York metro area. Close to home, it expanded into the northeast corridor's gateway cities with projects from Boston to Baltimore. In addition, it increased its global presence with projects overseas.

CetraRuddy's evolution from a talented architectural duo concentrating on regional metropolitan projects to an internationally recognized creative force in construction and design is the direct result of its thoughtful approach to innovation, among other efforts. Professional services firms seeking to emulate its success must adapt to changing markets with a client-centered focus and a self-reflective process.

From SWOT to Sales Is a Path to Prosperity

Like finance, the architectural community operates on a series of small streets. There are a variety of market sectors and leaders in those areas. CetraRuddy had already achieved the hard part, which is general brand awareness, which, like the experiences financier Shatz related here, was associated with client service and long-term success. Through a coordinated campaign of public relations and external publishing on matters of design, the CetraRuddy team has become adept at taking advantage of its high-profile work, as well as the public's fascination with big city real estate.

The firm has also been pursuing more recognition for its work, which is increasingly common for those who once focused more on doing their work than getting new work. Web sites like AwardSync .com, which enable individuals to identify potential accolades both for themselves and their clients, have the potential to create previously unforeseen value.

Other industry praise may be valuable even if it does not directly relate to one's core function. For instance, an investment banker who writes an article may achieve recognition through an Apex Award for his or her written work on an industry topic instead of the industry work itself. Or, the banker could recommend that a client apply for the award and solidify his or her relationship if the client is ultimately recognized.

The publishing and pursuit of industry recognition leads to panel presentations and wide-ranging lectures to developers and institutional clients. "Ten years ago, we just wanted to sit and do our work, but we realized in a much more competitive world, we had to be out there and really help the public learn about our brand," says Ruddy.

CetraRuddy is also marketing to existing clients. "We do an awful lot of repeat business, but were not very proactive about it," admits Ruddy. Many professionals struggle with this strategy. They are either unsure about what else is possible with existing clients or concerned about selling too hard. "It makes sense in any time, but to go to your existing clients and see if they have other departments that are doing something has been very successful for us," she says.

That marketing effort is prompting the company to think more broadly about its role and the potential for collaboration. As work becomes scarce, the idea of organizations partnering to weather an economic downturn is not new. The idea of licensed professionals leveraging their talents to strengthen a bid in a more competitive environment is, however, becoming increasingly effective.

> Ten years ago, we just wanted to sit and do our work, but we realized in a much more competitive world, we had to be out there and really help the public learn about our brand.
>
> *Nancy Ruddy, co-founder, New York-based CetraRuddy Incorporated*

Many industries are struggling with whether that collaboration dilutes the potency of an industry's value. In the legal community, for instance, lawyers in the United Kingdom and Australia are permitted to create formal alliances and partnerships with non-legal counterparts like accountants and consultants. They are prohibited from doing so in the United States. And, when they want to reach into other markets or different practice areas, they tend to merge their firms.

In the same way that professionals combine expertise by co-authoring industry articles or join their networks to conduct formal research, there is a common purpose in redefining their roles in a client-centered era. The technology revolution, for example, has fostered a remarkable level of teamwork from open source software to guest blogging.

In a recent bid for a large contract on a college campus, CetraRuddy submitted its proposal in partnership with a well-known university specialist. "It is better to get a piece of the pie rather than no pie at all," she says. After all, the company is looking toward the future and recognizes that if it can gain additional experience, it will be better positioned.

Change But Don't Change Who You Are

Despite being smaller than it was five years ago, Ruddy highlights that it has not changed very much. It has modified its approach and evaluated its marketing, but "what we have done is kept our DNA of who we are as a firm," she says. The field is shifting to require firms to include modeling technology as part of its process. Building information modeling and integrated design is currently changing the manner in which architects create and complete their projects. CetraRuddy, which embraced this option in 2007, is applying that integration on selected projects, including a 300-key hotel and a synagogue. The firm uses advanced design systems that allow an architect to reflect the mechanical and structural systems into a drawing in a more organic fashion because the construction manager, structural engineer, mechanical engineer, and others must use it as well.

Oscia Timschell is an associate and a construction contract administrator at KMD Architects in San Francisco, where she is responsible for executing the vision of the design architects. She notes that the building-information modeling trend is revolutionary because it requires collaboration and fosters innovation. Timschell says that traditional projects expect an architect to design a building, an engineer to create a supplemental design, and a contractor along with subcontractors to bid on the project.

For decades, however, she says that this has been an increasingly inefficient system because of the complexity in building codes. At one time, architects were considered the master builders and assumed responsibility for the completion of an entire project, serving as the designer and general contractor. Given the separate licensing requirements, their duties are now split. "There is a clear dichotomy between the design of the structure and the execution of the design," Timschell says. "As a result, constructing a building today is very inefficient, both in time and in cost."

In other manufacturing processes, builders and designers collaborate more efficiently to ensure consistency in their approaches, determine appropriate materials or technology, and synchronize timing. The new software allows teams to design a building in three dimensions, which combines the specifications of the contractor and the engineer in one cohesive format. It can also incorporate cost information throughout the building process. Teams can even export the electronic model to a manufacturing facility that can prefabricate parts of the building.

Despite the emergence of revolutionary technology, in certain professional services, one cannot exploit the full potential of the technology unless you change the business, notes Timschell. "You need to tie the designer's and builder's profits and losses to each other, as well as to the ultimate success of the project in order to achieve full collaboration," she says. "This Integrated Project Delivery method could change the whole industry."

You need to tie the designer's and builder's profits and losses to each other as well as to the ultimate success of the project in order to achieve full collaboration. This Integrated Project Delivery method could change the whole industry.

Oscia Timschell, associate and construction contract administrator, KMD Architects, San Francisco

Tie Profits to Success to Build Trust and Motivate

Lawyers, though they work in a very different profession, struggle with the idea of tying profits to success in order to motivate and build trust. Of course, personal injury lawyers have been operating on this contingency-style basis for decades. To thrive in a transformed market, however, there is among many lawyers a renewed focus on value and alignment of interests. "In some ways, we have a business that is masquerading as a profession," says FMC Technologies, Inc. General Counsel Jeff Carr.

Carr uses a well-regarded performance-based system that provides outside law firms with an incentive to resolve a matter efficiently using targets and multipliers. The company and the firm agree at the outset on a billing system, which could be hourly, fixed fee, project-based, or retainer-driven. The company pays 80 cents on the dollar and holds back 20. At the end of the engagement—or matter—the company provides the firm with a "report card," which details its performance in six areas. If it earns a 3.0, it receives 100 percent of the holdback and if it gets a 1.0, it can expect none of the holdback. Firms that perform at an exceptional level, rating a 5.0, receive their 20 percent, plus an additional 20 percent. One year, Carr paid on average 107 percent of most law firm invoices.

In this same fashion, if the architectural, construction, and engineering teams complete a project under budget, Timschell suggests they should profit from the savings. A profit model partially based on cost savings would address one of the biggest issues in the U.S. building industry, Timschell says. There are now industry group contracts that seek to incorporate profit and loss directly into the compensation scheme. Architects have historically viewed themselves as protectors of building owners against contractors, notes Timschell. "That does not apply in today's world," she says, because owners are quite comfortable dealing with contractors, who are able to sell the value they provide as guardians of the budget.

Architects are instead occasionally viewed as creative, but less concerned with the budget, which makes it more difficult to secure higher fees or to do more of the work, according to Timschell. For instance, they may not be retained to administer the work during construction if the property owner gives that responsibility to the general contractor. "New architects or those growing their businesses need to find better ways to communicate their value to owners," Timschell says.

This includes providing owners with hard data in real numbers about what an architectural team adds to the project, such as how much money one design might save over another while achieving the same objectives and aesthetics. They will also need to emphasize collaboration with builders because the alternative is an ineffective way to market. This approach is not taught in architecture school, according to Timschell.

Professionals in various disciplines repeatedly echo these themes. There are constant calls for law school reform and suggestions that institutions accredited by the American Bar Association offer comprehensive instruction not just on the ability to practice law, but on the art of building a practice. Similarly, for every accountant like David Bukzin, (see Chapter 10) there are scores that focus on the numbers, rather than making the numbers work. It is an issue that plagues professional schools in a multi-disciplinary way and will need to be resolved as the next cohort rises to reshape the landscape.

While Timschell notes that architects are generally not focused on marketing, there is a new generation emerging with a flair for marketing as much as design. As an example, she offers Modative in Los Angeles. The firm's web site, Modative.com, offers free downloads of its 13-page Architecture Process Guide covering the various design phases, how to set expectations with an architect, billing options, and the role of other consultants involved in the process.

The site also provides guidance on building codes in Los Angeles with its Small Lot Subdivision Guide and Small Lot Subdivision Information Report. It also features a Site Evaluation and Planning Services sample report to demonstrate its capability in providing feasibility studies for developers interested in evaluating certain properties. "Most people don't even know that architects can do this," says Timschell.

Trust and Respect Now Matter More Than Ever

Marketing in professional services is about content and character. "Personally, it is about treating everyone with respect," says Shatz, of MF Global. His team caters to small- to mid-sized hedge funds and proprietary trading organizations that use their own capital. These clients are individuals who used to work at large institutions, and his goal is to help them grow from funds managing $10 million in assets to those with $100 million. His division at MF Global offers them lower commission rates to encourage them to trade in higher volumes, and they also provide more leverage, enabling them to take more calculated risks.

There has, however, been a dramatic shift. In the same way that Intel Corporation co-founder Gordon Moore predicted that the number of transistors on a chip will double about every two years and drive down the cost of each function, the speed of trading has reached a new peak. As a result, the fee that high volume traders are willing to pay per transaction has dropped significantly, requiring even higher volumes and riskier trades. "We are at a breaking point in the industry," says Shatz, who reports that MF Global only charges its clients a fraction of a cent per share in commissions for its premium active traders.

> It is about treating everyone with respect.
>
> *Matthew Shatz, head of the U.S. Equities, Sales, and Trading team at MF Global Holdings, Ltd., New York City*

While MF Global would earn a six-figure commission on a company that trades one billion shares, that amount was substantially higher on the same transaction two years ago. "Just as the speed can't get any faster [because MF Global already executes trades in micro seconds], the cost can't get any lower," notes Shatz. That said, his group's hedge fund clients can occasionally dictate what they want to pay. "We are at the mercy of the client," he adds.

Every industry is now at the mercy of the client. It is one of the great shifts in global business. Clients are empowered with information and options. They have greater choice and less pressure to choose. If Shatz focused only on the speed of the trade and the cost of the transaction, his team's success would be in jeopardy. Instead, he focuses on the growth of the client. "I am here to help you build so you will want to be with me forever," he says. Due to that philosophy, despite evolving and changing employers over the years, his clients remain with him as they have prospered.

To fuel the success of his team's clients, Shatz must know them as well as he knows his own practice. He must identify the best ways to communicate and cultivate trust. His clients generally share two common traits: They play professional poker and have an extraordinary aptitude for math. "You wouldn't know who they are if you Googled them, but when you read the news about the 2008 market collapse, they were making millions per day." The technology that some clients use is so secretive and secure that they do not permit Shatz or anyone on his team to enter their offices.

That relationship requires trust—a lot of trust. Sometimes it takes a year or two, but Shatz eventually gets to access a client's office. After all, they have a lot to discuss. The U.S. Securities and Exchange Commission (SEC) is considering the viability of high-frequency trading following the highly-publicized flash crash on May 6, 2010 that forced a drop in the Dow Jones Industrial Average of 700 points in minutes. Shatz admits that if the SEC eliminates high-frequency trading, it could destroy his business. Then again, his clients will still need to trade and they are not quick to trust anyone to help, so he is probably secure. He is an optimist. After all, it is a small street.

RECAP

- As individuals and practices become more specialized, the community in which they find themselves shrinks. As a result, it is essential to properly convey your value proposition and reputation in the most effective manner possible.
- To do so, you might host a regular show on BlogTalkRadio.com and profile members of the business community.
- Firms that are considering where to focus their efforts in a challenging market should conduct a SWOT analysis to tailor their strengths to opportunities in the marketplace.
- Create payment schedules that appeal to your clients and patients. Consider tying compensation to success or more efficient forms of collaboration.

CHAPTER

8

Networking Is Dead;
Long Live Networking

Networking is a tremendous challenge for many providers of professional services. Despite the transformation of the operations and need to exceed even higher expectations in various practice types, they remain reluctant to take advantage of networking opportunities. With the rise of social media platforms, that endeavor has become even more confusing. This chapter will clarify how to execute effective networking efforts, which tools to explore, and the benefits of doing so.

■ ■ ■

During my second summer of law school (and into my third year), I had the opportunity to work for the U.S. Department of State. It was my dream-come-true. I was a law clerk to the Chief Legal Counsel in the Office of Foreign Missions. At the time, the office was responsible for relationships with the diplomatic community.

I acquired two pieces of identity swag upon commencement of my position. The first was essential for anyone living in Washington, D.C.: A government ID hanging proudly from a metal lanyard chain around my neck. I was so pleased with the necklace that I wore it everywhere, even on the Metro back to class and on campus during the school year. In addition to my ID, I was also allowed to print business cards (at my own expense) with the seal of the U.S. State Department, indicating that I was a legal assistant. You would have thought that I was the Secretary of State given the pride I took in those cards.

I am not sure where I got the idea I held back then about the art of traditional networking, but I misinterpreted the lesson. My impression of networking was collecting business cards. In fact, I associated skill in meeting people with counting those cards. The more I had, the better I was, I figured. Today, people think that networking has changed because of technology. But just as my impression was wrong about networking and collecting business cards, today's conclusion about the role of technology is flawed as well. Technology has enhanced one's ability to network, but the fundamental principles of networking have not changed.

Those principles never were centered on collecting cards; that is a great misimpression. And today, the total number of friends or fans on Facebook, the number of followers on Twitter, or the number of connections on LinkedIn don't affect them. The cards, like their modern counterpart—contacts on the Web—enabled (and still enable) one to follow up on a meeting to create a rich relationship. In essence, networking as professionals thought they knew it is dead, but the art itself remains very much a core element of personal interaction.

Go Where Your Audience Goes

Today, the essence of connecting and relating to people initially, or after you've have a chance to meet, is often by going to the place where they congregate online. "In any industry, step one is to embrace and use the tools that your customers are using," says Rich Barton, the founder of online travel service Expedia, Inc. and online real estate marketplace information provider Zillow, Inc. For instance, he points out that Zillow had 13 million unique visitors in November of 2010, and of those, over two million were professionals, including realtors, mortgage brokers, or loan officers. "It is a really good sign that a subset of the professionals in the category are embracing the tools that their customers are using," he says. While change is uncomfortable, you must be progressively minded, advises Barton, given the industry transformations that are occurring across disciplines.

Start by asking your existing clients, patients, and customers where they congregate and what tools they use. Consider including that request on an intake form when meeting with a new prospect. In addition to an individual's telephone number and home address, ask about their usage of social media and other technology. Determine whether they use mobile phone applications to coordinate their schedules or get information. Ask whether they participate in webinars or tele-seminars. Find out about their professional interests and personal hobbies. There needn't be a requirement to respond and one can share as much or as little as he or she prefers. If the questions are not asked, however, they are unlikely to supply the answers.

Consider the reason a prospect has sought you out for counsel. Clients generally come with a problem. A doctor might see a patient who is ill or worried about becoming ill. A lawyer might be connecting with a nervous individual who has just been wronged or may have committed a wrong. Accountants, veterinarians, dentists, and others all occasionally face a similar group. You learn a lot about their motivations and concerns. The key is to consider all of that information throughout the interaction.

"You now have a super-empowered consumer who can spend more time researching information than the professional," says Barton. That said, "A smart, informed consumer is a much better customer," he adds noting, for example, that when he goes to the doctor, he already knows the basics and can tap the full wisdom of his physician.

Use Tools that Your Audience Uses

Once you know where your target audience gathers, consider using the devices and tools that are best suited to reach them. "Most of my healthcare from my doctor is delivered by e-mail," notes Barton. Instead of a series of random visits, he describes their relationship as "an ongoing conversation."

Talented professionals are recognizing that they need to be radically more efficient, which will help them increase their productivity. Many, for example, participate in answering questions either on LinkedIn or other industry specific tools, which permit them to share their expertise with a broad group of those interested in their work. "While painful and time consuming, the professionals that are engaging in these new information marketplaces are the winners," says Barton because they are driving business and building their reputations. And if they don't, people will know about it.

The rise of review sites like Yelp.com, and other, more targeted sites like Barton's Glassdoor.com, which allows job applicants to share information about companies where they have interviewed, is making information about performance, both substantive and interpersonal, much more public. "If it can be known, it will be known by the consumer," says Barton. "If it can be rated, it will be rated."

Find sites in your industry that allow interactivity. Real estate professionals can use Zillow as a way to showcase their expertise by answering questions posed by prospects. Lawyers and doctors can use Avvo. Consumers can use Yelp or Glassdoor.com. Architects are developing OpeningDesign.com.

Before engaging on these sites, however, you must think about what you want your personal brand to be. It's important to recognize that your reputation is much more accessible in what Barton describes as a "super transparent world," which the Web and smart phones are enabling. "You must understand that every day you are building your brand and marketing yourself whether or not you know it," he says, because word-of-mouth is no longer reserved for interesting chats at the coffee shop. The risk of not using these tools is ultimately the risk of being used by them. Barton recommends that professionals encourage every client or patient to review their work. In fact, he says, send him or her a link to the exact place online where the user can enter a review. It takes a minute or two and could be a great excuse to have a conversation with a client about prior work and possibly future interaction.

> You must understand that every day you are building your brand and marketing yourself whether or not you know it.
>
> *Rich Barton, founder of online travel service, Expedia, Inc., and online real estate marketplace information provider, Zillow, Inc., Seattle*

Find a Geek to Help You Get LinkedIn

Professionals who are unfamiliar with social media and even the proper use of technology should enlist support. "It is critical for you to find the 'passionate geek'," Barton says. That could be a friend or acquaintance, a teenage child, or a person at the company who is "fully swimming in this social media world," he adds.

Students are perfect for this role.

To recruit a student, contact the career placement office of a local college or professional institution, and indicate the possibility of an opportunity for a student in this effort. It is likely that this will result in a flood of responses. It is also possible that an ad on craigslist may provide similar results.

Pair up with your "geek" and ask him or her to either create or further build out a LinkedIn profile. Plan to spend a few hours building an initial presence on the site, but then no more than 15 to 30 minutes per week. Start by comparing e-mail contact lists to the LinkedIn database. Experimenting with LinkedIn will help most professionals develop a presence in the social networking environment.

To build out the profile, have the assistant research to use LinkedIn's Answers tool to participate in conversations on topics of interest, and to explore its business pages feature to provide a virtual umbrella for all of the company's employees on the network. "You need a guide," says Barton. "You are taking an adventure to a new land; it is a little scary and threatening," he cautions.

To determine whether Barton is correct, simply ask if it is comfortable to discuss Twitter, Facebook, or LinkedIn during a casual conversation. There are so many services that might benefit the practice (see the Resources section), but to make this effort accessible, consider experimenting with the most popular tools and then following up with those that are more closely tailored to the industry of interest.

"I don't think it pays too much for a professional to be on the bleeding edge," notes Barton. That said, recognizing when a tool or activity appeals to a mass audience and has become one that your customers and fellow professionals use is important. If your clients are on Twitter, try it. There is no mandate to master anything, but there is no progress without the attempt. "You might think about Twitter as a much more accessible way to blog," advises Barton. "Ninety-five percent of all blog posts I read could have been 140 characters and probably should have," he jokes.

Integrate Your Efforts to Save Time and Sanity

You probably already have a web site, though it is not updated with any regularity. It is often little more than a static place online that contains contact details and some background information. By simply adding a feed to your web site from anything you post on Twitter, even if they are simply interesting links from other respected people, it will result in a much more dynamic web site.

Twitter will automatically create the code you need to associate it to your page.

Consider leveraging a mobile phone for something more than a quick game of Angry Birds or Fruit Ninja, two of the iPhone's most popular games. Zillow.com, JDSupra.com (a site that offers and distributes law-related content, among other information), LinkedIn, Facebook, Twitter, and others all have an iPhone application. Once the foundation is set, the tool can be used from anywhere.

On one occasion, I saw Barton post a recommendation for Join.me, a free Web-based meetings tool, on Twitter. I immediately tried it and was excited about the prospect of an item of this type. "Before, the number of people I would have been able to share that suggestion with was limited to the people in my immediate network," Barton says. "The social media sphere is the world's most powerful recommendation engine ever created."

According to Barton, the accessibility of information has transformed the real estate industry over the past 15 years. Once Zillow and others put the database of industry-driven information on the Web for free, consumers took control and forced professionals to be more creative. That doesn't mean there's less important or less complex work for realtors to do. "People are going to realtors just as often as they did before, but their interactions are now much richer and more efficient," says Barton. "Just because you can research your knee surgery before seeing your doctor doesn't mean you don't need one."

> The social media sphere is the world's most powerful recommendation engine ever created.
>
> *Rich Barton, founder, Expedia, Inc. and Zillow, Inc.*

Ultimately, consumers don't want to bypass the professional, they just want a better result.

Given how important it is for people to find you when they search for specific topics in which they are interested, you must optimize the content that you create online. Professionals who have a LinkedIn profile, for instance, increase their cyber-visibility, but it should not stop with that effort since they generate content in different forms. Those who publish articles that appear in digital format or post presentations online, for example, should optimize the text in those documents.

They can do so by identifying key words that serve as common search terms or are terms that can be linked to other resources on the firm's site. Taking these steps will increase the likelihood of individuals finding you when they searching not for *you*, but for what you *do*. This technical task is perfect for your assistant. The investment in setting this up can be as little as 20 to 30 minutes per piece of content.

Explore Facebook for Fun and Professional Potential

Have your "geek" give you a tour of Facebook. Learn the possibilities of connecting and associating with your network on a more personal level. Senior professionals may be surprised to learn that they are just as likely to have colleagues on the popular social networking platform because, although Generation Y popularized the site, a large number of seasoned experts have accounts to interact. Contact in this environment will allow you to connect your business profile and your personal profile.

Consider creating a fan page for a business or interest. This is as easy to create as a LinkedIn group and will permit migration from Facebook's traditional private network to a more public and open architecture. The privacy settings can still be controlled by the page owner, but this environment can be designed based on interests in expanding reach beyond an existing network. Simply visit www .facebook.com/pages/create.php and enter the name of the group. Press "Create Official Page" and *voila*! You now will have a Facebook fan page. Use this just as an ordinary Facebook page is used, except that there are no personal features to share with the general public. Then add a variety of applications available here: www.facebook.com/ apps/directory.php. Whenever you get confused, there is an answer online to virtually any question. Type your question into Google and you will find tutorials, quick answers, and step-by-step instructions.

How to Decide Whether You Should Blog

Whether you want to shape opinions or share them, blogging has a number of benefits ranging from increased name recognition to better search engine optimization. In the end, one of the best reasons to blog is that it gives you something to share everywhere else. You can use the blog as your central point of contact and then post the content in all of the different areas where your audience congregates. You don't even need to have your own blog. Instead, consider using Google or a blog directory to find other sites in your area and outline guest posting opportunities. It is only a few paragraphs, but could have a tremendous impact.

Name five topics on which you could write a single paragraph. If you run short, ask a colleague or even a client for suggestions, if necessary. Call that client and mention your interest in writing about the kinds of issues that are affecting his or her business right now. Not only will this demonstrate your sincerity in the work that you do, but it will also yield some great responses. Then brainstorm for a few minutes to develop one or more of those ideas. Consider starting with answers to basic questions that plague your audience. A guest post will help you expand your audience reach, further solidify your expertise, and, of course, enhance your Google-ability.

Start with WordPress.org to create a blog. It is robust and free. You can select background colors and designs. It also provides lots of options in terms of formatting and content. I have also used Typepad.com, which also worked well, but requires a monthly subscription fee.

Consider pre-writing posts to enhance efficiency. Executing comes down to sharing ideas on a topic of interest so that you are not bored in a few months. "You have to be driven by passion," says David Siteman Garland, author of *Smarter, Faster, Cheaper: Non-Boring, Fluff-free Strategies for Marketing and Promoting Your Business* (Wiley, 2010). "Quantify your passion on something that other people can relate to," he adds. The mere creation of the content gives your audience the impression of expertise.

Also, Garland recommends thinking about the medium in which content is created. It is not just about text. You can create audio, video, and even animation to promote your ideas. XtraNormal. com, for instance, now allows individuals to create animated video out of simple scripts.

Find the area in which you are most comfortable and act like a publisher. "Publishers do not think product first, they think audience first," notes Garland. "No one cares about products; they care about being entertained or inspired," he adds. In professional services, they also care about being well informed. Simple answers are not as valuable as simple ways of offering complex details. But the act of becoming a trusted resource is at the core of any effort to expand your brand.

In terms of frequency, Garland recommends worrying less about quantity and focusing more on consistency. Pick a day to show up and simply produce something. To blog or guest blog, try to build it into a routine. If Tuesday is the day, get your audience used to a message on Tuesday. In addition, pick a time as well. "The community must understand when to show up," says Garland, who prefers to reach business people in the morning. That said, "Different rules apply for different people."

Garland cites famed social media expert Chris Brogan, co-author with Julien Smith of *Trust Agents: Using the Web to Build Influence, Improve Reputation, and Earn Trust* (Wiley, 2010), who blogs seven days a week at ChrisBrogan.com, and contrasts him with Chris Guillebeau, author of *The Art of Non-Conformity: Set Your Own Rules, Live the Life You Want, and Change the World* (Perigee Trade, 2010), who generally posts to his blog on Tuesdays, Thursdays, and Saturdays at ChrisGuillebeau.com.

Garland cautions that the lack of consistency is what most often results in failure. "It is a combination of creating content and showing up on the sites," he says. "I wish it was a complicated formula, but it is just offering quality content, getting in there and talking to people," he says, noting that you must go where you are comfortable. Garland uses Facebook as opposed to LinkedIn, as a matter of personal preference. He also notes that, "The best digital schmoozers selectively attend parties so you don't need to get to every party online." Consider your personality. If you like quick interaction, Twitter may be most appropriate. Are you more comfortable sharing personal details or professional expertise? Choose accordingly.

> It is a combination of creating content and showing up on the sites. I wish it was a complicated formula, but it is just offering quality content, getting in there and talking to people. The fear of technology is an illusion.
>
> David Siteman Garland, host of TheRisetotheTop.com, St. Louis, and author of Smarter, Faster, Cheaper: Non-Boring, Fluff-free Strategies for Marketing and Promoting Your Business *(Wiley, 2010)*

Spend Time with Your Audience and the Members Will Spend Time with You

Ultimately, building community takes some effort. Garland recommends an hour per day, but depending on the platforms you choose, more or less time may be necessary. Start with one and increase the duration as you become comfortable. Avoid the mistake that many people make, which is focusing so much on the content that they fail to make time for the promotion. The difference the technology is making in professional services is not in the facts one can share or the medium in which to share them. The difference comes in the ability to distribute that information on a much broader scale to an incredibly wide audience.

Garland suggests that most people spend 20 percent of their time creating content. They should spend the other 80 percent in meeting, interacting, and becoming part of communities. Do this by answering questions, commenting on blog posts, and making introductions, among other techniques.

Pick one or two sites and begin sharing your content and that of others whom you trust. Focus on the conversations. Worrying about getting it right will only distract you from your goal. Be authentic and you will create honest interaction. "The fear of technology is an illusion," says Garland.

RECAP

- The primary key to networking is to participate in the areas where those you are trying to reach are interacting. Start by asking your existing clients, patients, and customers where they congregate and what tools they use, then begin experimenting with them to gauge their level of interest. Webinar tools like GoToWebinar.com or tele-seminar tools like FreeConferencePro.com are excellent places to start.
- To explore social media sites such as LinkedIn and Facebook enlist the support of a junior member of your team, who is an enthusiastic proponent of these platforms.
- As you begin participating, combine your efforts so that your message on one network also appears on another.
- They key to building an audience is to share content in which people are interested and to do so on a regular basis.

9

Proactive Professionals Pay
Attention to Progress

While clients and patients once simply walked through the door or called for appointments almost effortlessly in the past, they no longer make it that easy. One must understand a client's goals and then work tirelessly to help achieve them. There is an increasing value placed on trusted advisors as opposed to merely licensed professionals. This is forcing even the most conservative individuals to market in an unprecedented way. This chapter will highlight how proactive professionals can create opportunity in a shifting market. It provides examples in various industries, from veterinarians to radiologists, to illustrate this point.

■ ■ ■

Leisa Mohler-Erickson is a partner with the Advantage Performance Group in St. Petersburg, Florida, which helps organizations develop their business. She spent 12 years working with mid-sized accounting firms, among various other professional services organizations, and highlights that the most pressing issue for a licensed expert is to find ways to distinguish himself or herself in a world of commoditization.

Consider the example of one of the world's largest paper manufacturers, which was seeking to distinguish its products and create a competitive edge in the modern marketplace. The image of duplicate rolls of paper enveloping a factory floor serves to visualize the current concern.

The paper manufacturer routinely acquires different companies that make paper products like cardboard boxes, coatings for juice boxes, point of purchase displays, or multi-wall bags for pet food. Once it does so, it must integrate them into its seamless culture. Ultimately, creating value is a mixture of art and science. "You have to be your own differentiator and not rely on the output of services you provide as the glue to seal a new client," says Mohler-Erickson. The most successful professionals view each interaction with a client as akin to executing a sales call, she says. Turn the discussion to a client's ambition and how you can partner to achieve it. Identify the connection point first and then develop a strategy.

As shown in earlier chapters, the Internet now provides basic answers to many consumer questions. "The self-diagnosis problem is rampant," agrees Mohler-Erickson. The antidote is providing something unique and irreplaceable, which includes the experience a client associates with your interaction. "It is not just about the deliverable; it is more about what I as a professional can bring to the table that you cannot get from a web site," she adds.

> It is not just about the deliverable; it is more about what I as a professional can bring to the table that you cannot get from a web site.
>
> *Leisa Mohler-Erickson, partner, Advantage Performance Group,*
> *St. Petersburg, Florida*

In addition, it is not about solving a single problem anymore. In a previous era, licensed professionals solved problems—period. Today, "I just don't want to close the deal; I want to open the pipeline for a continuum of deals," remarks Mohler-Erickson. Continuity is often the most effective way to combat a changing market.

While many businesses appreciate when the phone rings and the revenue that ringing generates, they cannot focus solely on the reactive nature of those calls. To build longevity, they must foster relationships beyond the immediate. Instead of merely answering the question the prospect asks, anticipate the issues that could raise further inquiries. Building a relationship becomes a secondary issue for many when the primary concern is survival. Mohler-Erickson notes, for example, that while accounting firms provide compliance services to business owners that need to perform financial reporting, those who excel think beyond compliance toward growth. They are looking to create value by being a true trusted advisor rather than a provider of information that a savvy researcher could find on the Internet.

The professions are changing and their evolution of interaction with clients and prospects is evident in many ways.

Veterinarians in the United Kingdom, for example, generally were once partnerships based in homes, reports Tim Puddle, the founder of U.K.-based marketing firm, Smart Kits. Among many other clients he has represented over the years, the Hills Pet Nutrition, Inc. division of Colgate Palmolive Company provides insight on the dramatic transformation of the veterinary profession. Puddle notes that veterinarians often focused their practices on large animals and used to travel to different towns to treat them. "They were a pillar of society 50 years ago," he says.

In the early 1990s, the profession started to become increasingly commercial and smaller practices began combining with one another to create branches. "Business-minded vets saw the opportunity to become more powerful and increase their ability to consult with suppliers," Puddle recalls. He compares veterinarians to lawyers in that they were typically male and worked as junior vets until their peers promoted them to partnership, when they bought equity stakes in the business.

Since 1995, the profession has consolidated even more, Puddle observes. The consolidation is being led by a handful of large firms comprised of practices throughout the country, for example CVS (UK) Limited, which has more than 210 practices, is listed on the London Stock Exchange. Another group, The Medivet Partnership, some of whose partners originally came from South Africa, has more than 70 practices throughout London and southeastern England. Companion Care (Services) Ltd. of Wantage, England, operates more than 70 veterinary clinics within Pets at Home stores in the United Kingdom, taking a joint venture partnership approach of ownership with vets.

Vets4Pets Group is a company with more than 50 clinics that essentially associates smaller veterinary practices into a larger group, similar to a law firm network such as LexMundi, the MSI Global Alliance, or TerraLex, Inc., among others. Interestingly, a business professional with success franchising optometry practices throughout the United Kingdom founded Vets4Pets.

In an industry once comprised of mostly local veterinarians dotting the British countryside, the top practices and corporate parents of those practices now dominate the field. Non-veterinarians serve as directors of veterinary businesses and individual investors own shares of publicly-traded CVS (UK). In fact, according to Puddle's research, there are approximately 20,000 actively licensed veterinarians in the United Kingdom, with about half of these operating in approximately 3,000 practices; however, the top 800 practices account for a significant amount of the revenue.

The faltering economy has also had an impact. As an industry analyst for two decades, Puddle reports that a variety of factors are resulting in an oversupply of veterinarians to meet a drop in demand. They include: An increasing number of individuals reducing their expenditures on their pets; fewer people using pet insurance or veterinary services; and a wider selection of inexpensive pet foods. This shift has hit the profession in a dramatic way since historically there had been year-on-year real growth until 2008. "It was nearly automatic before then that people would come in and spend more on their pets," recalls Puddle. "The cost of fees had been going up in terms of salaries and equipment as well." Groups like Scotland-based XL Vet UK, Ltd., with more than 45 independently owned practices focusing on livestock have been routinely recruiting practices to join the group around the United Kingdom. This helps them gain a competitive advantage by sharing their collective skills, knowledge, and experience as well as achieving buying efficiencies or marketing to both large and small animal owners in the marketplace.

Practices have also been experimenting with alternative staffing models. Many are, for example, increasing their use of veterinary nurses. The role of the vet nurse has become an essential part of the efficiency equation at optimizing these practices. These para-professionals receive training and can provide basic services, engage with the pet owners, and spend additional time explaining the issues that arise. This allows the customer to ask questions and develop a stronger connection to the practice.

Puddle also notes that veterinarians from outside the United Kingdom are entering the market, which is reshaping the model, because professionals from outside, "haven't bought into the old paradigms," he says. "By crossing boundaries and markets, you will see opportunities for doing things differently."

Instead of veterinarians, one can insert lawyers, architects, or dentists into these examples. Large law firms were historically growing at a routine pace for years prior to the end of the last decade. The recession completely changed their longstanding business model, which they are still redefining. Architects once survived as small partnerships, but as the industry changed, they too were evolving to meet a very different real estate market than their predecessors.

As for dentists, Puddle highlights that they experienced a dramatic shift in the United Kingdom in the late 1990s when the structure of payment for dental treatments led to increasing numbers of private patients. Whitecross Dental Care Ltd., which operates a number of practices throughout London, created procedures for relating to clients and even published a guidebook for its professionals. "They deliberately recruited dentists who excelled at communicating because they realized that it was the key to dentists and their office," he says. "There is a huge parallel with veterinarians because it is a blending together of technical know-how with customer service skills." Puddle points out that the key is to balance financial viability and quality care. "You need to have an overall philosophy; determine whether you are an inexpensive volume practice or a smaller boutique at the top of the range."

> By crossing boundaries and markets, you will see opportunities for doing things differently. There is a huge parallel with veterinarians because it is a blending together of technical know-how with customer service skills.
>
> *Tim Puddle, founder, U.K.-based marketing firm Smart Kits*

He cautions that some professionals may focus too heavily on technology, without spending enough time training the staff or considering their budget for such equipment. Others may concentrate too much of their practice on developing patient relationships that they give away their time without properly charging for their expertise. Individuals who enter a particular profession often enjoy the technical side of the work or find satisfaction in caring for others. They are not necessarily comfortable with the commercial or customer service aspects of the business. Some are now leveraging the expertise of others more experienced in client development. Banfield, The Pet Hospital, for example, is a chain of veterinarians located in hundreds of PetSmart stores throughout the United States.

Whether they reside in a larger store or on their own, veterinary practices once simply offered prescription drugs and medical treatment for animals. Today, they sell healthy premium pet food, lifestyle diet regimens, and specialty accessories, among other products.

Veterinarians provide clinics on pet behavior, bereavement counseling, nutrition, obesity, and other topics. "Lots of things happening to humans are mirrored in the pet community," says Puddle. "Geriatric concerns, arthritis, and diabetes are all very real issues," he adds noting that there is a large population of pets that are prone to more diseases, as well as problems with their joints and hearing, as they get older. Veterinarians actually call it the "Seniors Club" to highlight issues pets face, he says, and much of the practice is focused on preventive care. As a result, vets have had to modify their marketing to appeal to those interested in sustaining the health of their pets, rather than simply treating them.

Sales and Marketing Have Evolved So You Should Too

While vets and caregivers both want healthy pets, traditional sales and marketing are often inapplicable because of the nature of the relationship. The medical professional provides the diagnosis and a recommendation, but instead of selling the options, he or she offers the customer time to consider the next step. The emphasis is on the intention at the beginning and the follow up at the end.

Although the standard selling process starts with an objective and ends with a close, professionals need to start with the benefit and identify a mutually beneficial outcome. "That is a more holistic way of selling and speaking with people," says Puddle. "We have found the more complex you make it, the less likely things are to be done," he adds. For that reason the entire environment has changed. Each member of the contact team is an essential part of the relationship because clients now have connections with all of the staff members. They want understanding from their counselors, as well as a proactive demonstration of that understanding.

Tony Williams conveys that idea to his clients in periodic research studies, which he shares with them personally. The United Kingdom-licensed attorney, former managing partner of Clifford Chance LLP, one of the largest law firms in the world, and Andersen Legal, a top legal team—prior to the downfall of Arthur Andersen—provides strategic consulting. Given that Williams's firm, Jomati Consultants LLP, focuses on the legal industry, it is a very targeted market. He connects personally with 130 to 150 firms per year and many of his clients come to his office through a referral.

In an effort to cultivate those referrals and to maintain current contact with the law firm chairpersons or managing partners, Jomati issues research reports to about 1,000 professionals across the globe. In an information-driven society, original research is an ideal tool for finding distinction. Jomati issued three 30- to 40-page reports in 2010. The March release covered the globalization of legal services, the June release focused on the evolving client relationship, and the September release highlighted challenges associated with the U.K. bar. In Jomati's business of strategic consulting, his team helps executives identify the growth trajectory of their firms, where to focus, how to staff, and ways to implement new initiatives.

Like most professionals, it is relatively rare for Williams to meet a prospect that hires him immediately. "It is a dripping tap approach because these tend not to be impulse buys," he says. "They get to know you over a period of time or get a recommendation from someone they know and respect," he adds. A new contact once hired him after a month and another waited six years.

The market, however, has changed dramatically in the past few years. An industry with a traditional undersupply of top talent has become oversaturated. Those who hire consultants like Williams are savvier and more demanding, using client teams to maintain more control of their legal matters. In fact, "To a greater or lesser extent, it has happened in most professions," says Williams, citing the accounting and medical fields. "Doctors have to answer all of a patient's questions today, rather than offer a pat on the head and a prescription as they used to."

The greater availability of information has reduced the collective level of patience. There once was a certain deference to the experience and knowledge of experts, but "We are more wired up so we don't expect to have to wait," notes Williams. As a result, he uses that information and processes it in a way that demonstrates his expertise.

His research compiles responses from surveys of members of his industry, but adds commentary interpreting the trends they reveal. "I don't think there is one knock-out proposition." His reports put Jomati's name on the desk of his prospects multiple times per year.

"I can point to specific pieces of work that came directly from the research reports," he says noting that on a recent occasion, a new client brought the report to an introductory meeting.

Ultimately, successful professionals are certainly aware of what interests their clients, but speed and relevance are key. There is a benefit to immediacy, which is why Williams will call before e-mailing and e-mail before snail mailing. Following up on relevant concerns that are important to your target market conveys thoughtfulness. The important thing is to continually adapt, he says.

Frédéric Brunner, CEO of a-connect, is very familiar with the reinvigorating aspects of adaptation. The Swiss orthopedic surgeon spent six years at McKinsey & Company both in Europe and the United States, as well as time at Novartis prior to joining a-connect, a global consultancy and project execution partner.

Transformations in the marketplace, the shift in focus to emerging markets, and a dramatically regulated business environment, have caused disruption or change in the way that companies conduct their work. a-connect was created in 2002 to give clients the ability to complete work with more flexible and experienced experts who can react to the increased importance and speed of change caused by these factors. The company's 1,200 independent professionals (IPs) combine industry expertise and top-tier consulting experience that helps them cleanly integrate within organizations that need help reaching a very specific goal. A company might use a-connect's IPs when it wants to understand how a finite financial or pharmaceutical regulation will impact its business model. It might also use IPs to understand how a change in consumer habits requires a complete reorganization. While the idea of change is not new, "in the context of change, companies want to move faster and more effectively," says Brunner.

The traditional consulting model would apply a full team of bright professionals with varying levels of experience to a broad matter, notes Brunner. a-connect selects IPs whose unique skill set helps clients navigate from strategy to execution quickly.

Financial services firms, for example, endeavoring to shift to online services such as e-banking can experience a disruption in daily operations caused by the additional work in the transition, while at the same time they are still required to keep the organization running efficiently. Similarly, just as patients search for medical diagnostic information on the Web before speaking to a physician, doctors themselves search for clinical data prior to meeting with pharmaceutical sales and marketing teams.

> The corporation of the future will be made out of strong brands, top managers, and very good contractors that can enable a large organization to adjust to small variations in its business.
>
> *Frédéric Brunner, CEO of a-connect, a global consultancy and project execution partner, Zurich*

Brunner compares transforming one's business model to keeping the water running while simultaneously changing the sink. Since the operations of the business don't stop even when management is modifying its business, there need to be components of the organization that can temporarily fill critical gaps. As a result, "the corporation of the future will be made out of strong brands, top managers, and very good contractors that can enable a large organization to adjust to small variations in its business," predicts Brunner. Major restructuring is expensive and there is a market premium on flexibility given that the hiring and firing cycles tend to be slower, particularly in non-U.S. markets.

He suggests that the independence trend coupled with a variable project workforce model will only grow because employers value the continuity associated with maintaining a relationship with those familiar with their corporate character. It prevents knowledge leakage and maintains consistency. The more efficient and flexible a company is with its staffing of key initiatives, the more it can do to invest for the future. And, an external team familiar with the field and specific project can serve as a virtual backup when changes occur.

Medical Records Are Right on the Money

The medical profession is not immune from the need for backup. Gabriel Pivawer, the New Jersey radiologist whom we introduced in Chapter 1 in a discussion of flexible fees, co-founded Valor Network, Inc. with Jolienne Rutter, Ph.D and retired U.S. Army Lieutenant Colonel Scott E. Rutter, to take advantage of the need for additional teleradiology support. Lieutenant Colonel Rutter is a retired service-disabled veteran of the first and second Gulf wars, who commanded the brigade that stormed into the Baghdad Airport in 2002. They are growing Valor Network to provide medical care to U.S. veterans, service members, and their families.

Teleradiology, which is the art of transmitting and reviewing medical images remotely, has been an available resource for years. While it was once typically used to allow on-call physicians to rapidly interpret off-hour emergency room, intensive care, and other life-impacting situations, occasionally across time zones or as a means of consulting with a specialist, technology has made this practice much more accessible in the past few years.

In February of 2008, the Valor Network began bidding on tele-radiology contracts with the Department of Defense. By September of 2008, the group acquired its first contract with a 10-bed U.S. Air Force treatment facility in Idaho. Unfortunately, Valor quickly realized that the Air Force base's IT and security requirements were much greater than what it had in place, causing a lengthy delay.

Over the next two and a half years, Valor developed a series of protocols and procedures to transfer the images from a military treatment facility in another state to a server room in New Jersey. It finally received its certification attesting to the security and accuracy of the data processes in November of 2010, and began working with the base in Idaho soon after.

Between September of 2008 and November of 2010, Valor Network started connecting with Veterans Administrations (VA) hospitals, which required lower levels of security than military bases. On one occasion, Pivawer contacted the imaging administrator at the Brooklyn Campus of the VA New York Harbor Healthcare System, which serendipitously had been searching for teleradiology assistance, as well as on-site mammography support. By February of 2009, Valor Network had secured those contracts. "I was in the right place at the right time," Pivawer says. "I happened to call the right people asking questions about services with which they actually needed help." Valor Network also provides teleradiology services to additional military treatment facilities, including Pensacola Naval base and Nellis Air Force base in Las Vegas.

Part of Valor Network's success in working with one of the most closely guarded computer systems in the world is its willingness to find solutions to novel problems. Pivawer advises that Valor Network is the only teleradiology company with an "Authority to Connect" certification allowing it to interact with any U.S. Department of Defense network and transfer information. He notes that the data is encrypted and protected at every point on the exchange. In addition, their systems have been extensively tested and evaluated.

Valor Network representatives conduct monthly quality control conference calls and meet with military contract representatives on a quarterly basis. "This is the beginning of teleradiology as we know it using a secure network," says Pivawer, given the dramatic increase of veterans and active service members. As active duty radiologists are typically stationed at a military facility and transferred to a combat zone, Valor Network provides the military treatment facilities with continuity, as well as efficient alternatives that include specialists or sub-specialists.

It is not surprising that this revolution would feature this field at the vanguard. After all, "radiology is symbiotic with technology," advises Pivawer. "It is no different to sit 40 feet from the workstation scanner or 400 miles away," he adds, noting that even when his team reviews patient films, they enter their network remotely.

Pivawer highlights that the future of radiology is remote because it is cheaper, faster, and offers universal access by the most skilled experts. He cites telehealth in general as a rising trend, including psychiatrists discussing personal issues with patients through secure Internet-enabled television or Web-chat.

The mobile medicine phenomenon is forcing a broad reconsideration of traditional practices. Sleep medicine, for example, typically requires advanced equipment, overnight polysomnographic evaluation of patients in a sleep testing center, and ongoing follow-up evaluation. David Liss is board certified in sleep medicine, pulmonary medicine, critical care medicine, and internal medicine. He is a physician with Gaylord Sleep Medicine in North Haven, Connecticut, which operates five comprehensive sleep centers throughout the state and conducts more than 5,000 sleep studies annually.

To streamline these studies, the practice has incorporated computerized digital data collection and an electronic medical record, but the greatest challenge is rapidly becoming reimbursement. The Center for Medicare and Medicaid Services (CMMS), which is the federal agency that administers Medicare, Medicaid, and the Children's Health Insurance Program, sets rates for these diagnostic tools and continues to announce steep cuts in sleep medicine reimbursement. "It has changed the practice in that the people who do the studies now must complete three instead of two to generate the same revenue," says Liss, highlighting that while CMMS sets separate reimbursement standards, the insurance industry generally adopts their recommendations.

These expense issues have prompted many patients to consider home sleep study testing, particularly in individuals with private high-deductible insurance plans, where a patient may be responsible for paying the full cost of office visits, testing, and equipment. Labs perform studies that require overnight evaluation in a hotel-like setting equipped with medical machinery that monitors brain activity, body position, eye movement, sleep stages, leg movements, respiratory rate, airflow at the nose and mouth, heart rate, and oxygenation, among other parameters. Home tests generally only monitor oxygen levels, heart rate, airflow, and respiratory effort. "It is a wild west frontier," says Liss, who notes that most home tests are used to diagnose sleep apnea, which he notes is the most common sleep disorder among patients referred to his practice for evaluation.

> [Steep cuts in sleep medicine reimbursements have] changed the practice in that the people who do the studies now must complete three instead of two to generate the same revenue.
>
> *Dr. David Liss, Gaylord Sleep Medicine in North Haven, Connecticut*

The typical treatment for sleep apnea uses a continuous positive airway pressure (CPAP) machine, which blows air in the back of the throat to pneumatically prevent it from narrowing or closing, advises Liss. Patients once came into the lab to determine the required pressure setting, but many machines now make automatic adjustments at home. "I think home testing and treatment with auto titrating CPAP machines are great, but testing and implementing treatment at home may miss important findings, such as seizure activity, cardiac abnormalities, sleepwalking, and evidence of people acting out in their dreams," says Liss.

Seeing the shift in the nature of their relationships with patients, Liss and his colleagues offer certain value-added services that include sleep hygiene guidance to help patients optimize their sleep habits, cognitive-behavioral treatments for insomnia, and mask-fitting services. They also provide instruction on the usage of home-based equipment, conduct clinical research studies in sleep, and follow up on new technologies or treatment options.

The customary issues that once brought patients into the clinic may not be those that keep them associated with it. The entire medical team needs to expand the nature of its guidance in a way that most professionals are doing across the interdisciplinary spectrum.

RECAP

- To create opportunity, professionals need to start the process with a goal in mind and identify a mutually beneficial outcome. The key is to keep it simple and to collaborate with as many team members as possible.
- Be a resource in achievement of your client's goals and objectives.
- Cross boundaries and markets to identify new opportunities. Blend your technical know-how with your customer service skills.
- Shift focus away from expensive tests and dramatic overhead, to portable equipment and remote access.

CHAPTER 10

When You're Allergic to Wool, Wear Cotton or Suffer for Your Entire Career

Modern professional services offer a greater range of options given the borderless nature of commerce. As such, individuals should determine where they will be most successful and focus their efforts on their top choice. This chapter will reveal successful strategies for identifying a target market and cultivating referrals in that sector.

■ ■ ■

When John Korff, the founder of Korff Enterprises, Inc., which owns and operates sporting and other events, graduated from Harvard Business School in the late 1970s, he interviewed for a traditional job in marketing and realized something about himself: He is allergic to wool. During that first meeting, he developed a painful rash from his standard blue suit and immediately began fearing for his lifelong welfare in the white-collar work force.

There are countless stories like this one. Some involve the starched collar. Others lament the strain of the necktie. And some even have issues with dress shoes that are too tight. Most people complain. Change, however, only occurs through action. In the same sense, people don't network to impress their friends with the size of their contact list. They do so to exponentially increase their chances of being in the right place at the right time.

Korff had that moment when he met tennis legend Billie Jean King, who was starting a women's tennis tour. She offered him a job that did not require any wool apparel so he seized the opportunity. The A&P Tennis Classic, which he owned and operated for 25 years, beginning in 1976, turned out to be one of the most profitable events in the sport thanks to the timing of the A&P Classic the week before the U.S. Open. "I didn't have to put anything up other than a lot of fear of waking up," he says, smiling. "I never asked whether I knew what I was doing because I didn't know what I didn't know."

In the late 1970s, not knowing everything about your business or its leaders was forgivable because there was little public information about most people that was instantly accessible. There were industry guides like Martindale-Hubbell for lawyers, which began publishing *The Martindale Directory* in 1968, or even the Yellow Pages, with minimal contact information. Extensive details about an individual's background and history, however, were generally inaccessible.

Today, the contrary is true. You can almost instantaneously develop a general overview of a person's career in seconds. You can generally find commentary about his or her work within minutes. And, with just a little bit of effort, you can learn about his or her interests and abilities. The Internet punishes ignorance and creates an expectation of understanding. It allows professionals to at least talk the talk, as well as customize that discussion to include detail about the other party to the conversation.

That understanding of individuals has been a hallmark of Korff's career, even in the face of setbacks. Despite its success, after the events of September 11, 2001, A&P discontinued its sponsorship of the Tennis Classic and the tournament ended. Luckily for him, the summer prior to the competition's closure, he was the architect of the Nautica New York City Triathlon created in connection with New York City's bid for the 2012 Olympic Games.

It has become so popular that the 2011 event used a lottery system like the New York City Marathon to ensure fairness to the thousands of prospective applicants. There were almost 5,000 registrants in 2010 and the race closed out in minutes.

"My philosophy is that the requirements to promote all sporting events are the same: 10 percent sport-specific knowledge and 90 percent marketing and management." In addition to triathlon, Korff also helped raise the profile of other Olympic events like Greco-Roman wrestling and archery (for which he famously hired an archer to shoot an arrow from the top of a moving New York City taxi through the hole of a bagel on another moving vehicle nearby).

Most professionals today, regardless of industry, will highlight some form of equation for success that measures substantive knowledge against a variety of intangible qualities related to marketing, relationship management, and client service. The need for dynamic creativity in how one approaches his or her business is an essential component of commerce in the modern marketplace. The fundamental traits are the same, but the manner in which we display them has changed dramatically.

Passion, Time, and Luck—Plus Relationships

We are in a transformational time, but what it takes to be successful today in the professional services area is no different fundamentally from what it took to be successful in the last generation and the generation before it, says Brad Kaufman, co-chair of the National Securities Litigation group at Greenberg Traurig LLP, a law firm with 1,800 lawyers in more than 30 offices around the world.

"You must have a passion for what you do, you have to be willing to work harder than anybody else and put in your 10,000 hours to develop your expertise, and you have to be a little bit lucky," he says. Essentially, you have to be in the right marketplace working passionately at the right time in history in order to be successful.

"I thought that if the Olympic bid fails, archery will never make money; neither will fencing, table tennis, or wrestling," Korff says. "But triathlon had potential," he recalls. Although there were 623 registrants in 2000 and the event lost money, Korff's team developed a growth plan. Ten years later it is one of the largest triathlons in America and sells more merchandise that any other race of its kind in the country, other than the Ironman series, because "athletes believe that this is the best experience in America, the regulators feel that it is great for the city, and it offers a unique sponsorship opportunity." As a result, Korff's team has created a variety of recurring revenue streams from that single race.

For example, the Jamaica Underwear Run holds a place in the Guinness Book of World Records for having 446 people gathered in their underwear, including Times Square's own Naked Cowboy, a popular Times Square entertainer. The initial event had four sponsors, including the Jamaica Tourist Board. In addition, Korff created a dog race as part of the triathlon and enlisted IAMS, a Proter & Gamble Company pet food label, as the sponsor. The Janus Financial Executive Challenge, the Skechers Shape-ups Go Mommy Go race for new mothers, and even the Huggies Little Movers Diaper Race, in which 40 babies crawled 10 feet, are others. "If your head is in it, there are opportunities for this," he says. "As long as we keep being creative, we'll be successful."

Korff's creative philosophy is not necessarily about artistic imagery or graphic design; it is about the power of relevant relationships. Those who create opportunity for others perpetuate their business. Those who seek only opportunity for themselves perpetuate their struggle for business.

> If your head is in it, there are opportunities. As long as we keep being creative, we'll be successful.
>
> *John Korff, founder of Korff Enterprises, Inc., owner of*
> *the New York City Triathlon*

After considering the types of organizations with which his team should align, they sought to create chances for visibility and brand management that exceeded the value of whatever he was charging. Become familiar with each company in your industry and its leaders.

The easiest way to develop that knowledge is to attend an industry conference and study the vendors, exhibitors, and sponsors who are trying to reach your audience. Also, engage the attendees and consider their purpose for attending. If you can connect the attendees with those trying to reach them, you will not only create good will, you will develop ways to generate business; it is the manner in which you arrange that collaboration that will define your effort. It is also the thoughtfulness with which you approach the process that will enhance your profile.

Make a list of the organizations with which you are familiar and those you are not. Create ways to deepen your relationships with the groups on both lists. If there is already a chance to collaborate, pursue it. For instance, Korff and his team created a variety of events around their principal function, the New York City Triathlon. When they conceived of an event with infants, they had a short list of sponsors and reached out to Huggies, among others. They repeated that same process with pets in their pursuit of IAMS, and Janus in their effort to engage corporate executives.

In addition to attending events, one can easily identify key industry leaders and organizations seeking to meet them by reading general and niche industry publications. They will regularly feature the industry's experts and also showcase the advertisers trying to meet them. You can learn their engagement style, their branding, and what they offer simply by evaluating their advertisements. "My philosophy is that an event is as much fun as an organizer is capable of having," says Korff. "You have to be in the 'yes' business, not the 'no' business."

The "Yes" Business

On his first day of practice in 1986, a partner advised Kaufman that he would be working on securities matters and "I'll never forget that within a very short period of time, I realized that the pulse of the business world made it the place to be and I fell in love with it," he says. "The beginning of what launched my career, however, was that I was willing to do anything to work with these clients," he adds. If they had an employment matter, a garnishment, or even a personal issue, Kaufman was there to assist.

Three years into his legal career, Kaufman received a call that proved his point and "turned out to be the most significant opportunity of my life." It was a hot and sunny fall Monday in West Palm Beach and the phone rang at about 11:45 A.M. The caller was the head of litigation for a division at a large financial institution asking him if he could make it to Fort Lauderdale by 1:30 P.M. for a hearing. There was a dispute involving the agreement of a newly hired executive that the company said contained a provision barring him from competing with his prior employer. The in-house lawyer provided Kaufman with some background and he left the office to make the 50-mile drive in a little over an hour.

While driving, he realized that he had never handled a breach of a non-compete agreement in his few years of practice and had nothing more than a generic background on the case. There were no fax machines, so he could not review any of the documents and there were no cell phones, so he and his client could not discuss strategy in the car.

Sweating, he rushed into court after the proceedings had commenced. Before he had even introduced himself to his client, the judge paused, looked at him and asked, "What happened?" Kaufman simply explained that he was hired an hour before and apologized for his tardiness. To his surprise, the judge reprimanded his adversary for failing to provide enough notice and denied their motion. In an instant, Kaufman had won.

After his promotion to partner at the law firm, Kaufman traveled to New York City with a few colleagues to visit his contact at the same bank, whom the company had promoted to manage litigation for the entire organization. In the midst of pitching the firm's breadth of capabilities and noting its interest in handling a greater volume of work, the in-house litigation chief stopped him.

He then revealed what he had learned about Kaufman following his drive to Ft. Lauderdale a few years before. "Here's the reason why I always decided I would work with you," he began. "I knew that you had no background on the matter and that you might not make it to court on time given the notice, but anyone who is crazy enough to be willing to make that effort is someone I wanted on my team." That revelation has shaped Kaufman's philosophy for his entire career.

"Early on, I thought it was better to be visible among my clients, and as the world became more specialized, I was already there," he recalls. As the work increased, "I had the good sense to make sure that I hired smart people and we take a team approach to our matters." Over the last 25 years, nothing has fundamentally changed about Kaufman's philosophy, although now his team has incorporated technology and enlisted the support of lawyers who are skilled in its usage.

There is a lot of focus on the professional side of professional services; there has not always been enough focus on the service side. Being good at what you do is a given and there are lots of people who are good at what they do. With technology leveling the playing field and with clients so aware of value in the delivery of services, the manner in which you provide your service makes all the difference.

Beyond the problem that you are seeking to address, never lose sight of the human beings involved. Consider their personal pressures, stresses, and goals. Act in a way that furthers those interests and care about the people with whom you are dealing. "Do so and you will go much further than your much brighter colleague who does not take that into consideration," Kaufman advises. "This isn't science and I am not trying to split an atom; the human element always matters." Keep your clients informed. "Never let them have to find out about something through the mail or from someone else," he cautions. His ultimate advice: Accept the blame and share your victory. If something doesn't go right, take responsibility for it. If things go great, make sure the victory is shared.

Since Kaufman's arrival in Greenberg Traurig's West Palm Beach office from another law firm in 2000, the securities litigation group has grown to 75 lawyers across the globe and the value of the practice has risen to $25 million. He attributes that success to the talent of his team. For both Kaufman and Korff, the philosophy of accepting responsibility applies to both their clients and employees. "Team building is all about me relying on, empowering, teaching, and motivating," says Korff. "Go make a mistake, I'll back you up," he adds.

Make Every Client a Secret Shopper

In practice, Korff routinely holds himself personally accountable for his team's actions, and his team takes responsibility for any issues associated with the Triathlon. "We constantly seek athlete feedback," he says. In fact, Korff originally hired secret shoppers to experience the process from registration to race. Then his team realized that every single racer is, in a sense, a secret shopper, so they started emailing everyone in the race after they entered to obtain feedback. That effort took three months. After the race, they changed the Triathlon according to their suggestions and let them know by e-mail. "People would be stunned that we remembered," Korff recalls.

While there are certainly professionals who ask their clients about their service, most do not do so to the extent that builds loyalty and trust. How often do you receive feedback forms from your doctor, lawyer, or accountant? If he or she did, what would you tell them? How would sharing that information make you feel?

Despite the fact that the traditional notions of business and relationship management have remained constant, "What has changed is the ability to deliver information about the fact that you are passionate, have worked hard, and that you are in the right marketplace," says Kaufman. The value expectation from the client base has shifted dramatically and will continue to do so.

Global Roots in Virtual Spaces

Although he is based in Florida, and attended Florida State University and Stetson University College of Law, technology and trust have allowed Kaufman to build a national practice assisting mostly New York-based financial institutions. Unlike the model two decades ago, companies can now find lawyers at law firms they like, who are passionate about those clients, that can deliver services at the greatest value, and ship them across the country. "You no longer have to be rooted to a desk because lawyers do not necessarily meet clients in a physical space," says Kaufman. Location no longer has relevance because advisors increasingly hold virtual meetings with clients. "On the whole, technology has freed professionals to take on larger markets and compete in ways they couldn't have imagined a generation ago," he adds.

The securities litigation group at Greenberg Traurig, for example, uses a proprietary electronic data room that contains all of the information, transcripts, memoranda, and relevant resources to every matter it handles. They can also grant access to their clients. "You can be in an airport waiting room and have access to the entire file," he says. If a client has a question, his or her attorney can immediately answer it by downloading the relevant information. Matters can also be staffed in lower-cost jurisdictions because the same information is available to everyone, which is a tremendous advantage.

> On the whole, technology has freed professionals to take on larger markets and compete in ways they couldn't have imagined a generation ago. If you have a good reputation, are passionate about what you do, are willing to work hard, and you can deliver your services at greater value than your competition, you have more opportunity today than you ever did.
>
> *Brad Kaufman, partner, Greenberg Traurig, LLP,*
> *West Palm Beach, Florida*

To a certain degree, credentialing matters. Education and scholastic pedigree is less important than the institution with which you are associated because there may be a given quality across the board. That said, because of the demand to deliver your services at greater value today, you can even overcome institutional profile or pedigree deficiencies. "If you have a good reputation, are passionate about what you do, are willing to work hard, and you can deliver your services at greater value than your competition, you have more opportunity today than you ever did," says Kaufman. That is what is transforming most professions.

There was a time when those who didn't live in a certain city, go to a certain law school, and belong to certain clubs and organizations would not be considered by certain blue-chip clients. Today, such a client may evaluate someone anywhere in the world without regard to preconceived notions about location. Instead, those clients want to know whether the lawyers can deliver greater quality results, with higher efficiency, at a better price.

From the general counsel's perspective, Michael Callahan, Executive Vice President, General Counsel, and Secretary for Yahoo! Inc., says "law firms have to adjust their practices to the reality that clients are no longer definitely tied to a firm, but rather to the lawyers they have come to trust and rely on."

Set Expectations

There is an expectation that modern professionals will not only know more, but that they will share more with prospective clients before a relationship exists. Dr. Ira Klemons, the dentist we first met in Chapter 2, is an example of this shift. A New Jersey pain expert, Klemons holds a rare doctoral degree related to the diagnosis and treatment of headaches, facial pain, and TMJ dysfunctions .

In 1971, he was treating a patient for a breakdown of bone in the jaw. The patient called a few days later to say that the migraine headaches from which he suffered for 20 years were completely gone. After researching the problem, he found an article published in 1934 relating the jaw joint to headaches, ringing in the ear, dizziness, and other common problems.

At that moment, he had an epiphany: "I want to treat pain." He set out to find a Ph.D. program and learned that there were none which offered training using an orthopedic approach to the treatment of chronic headaches and facial pain. He convinced Pennsylvania State University to allow him to design the program and after nine years (the first four of which he spent studying as well as teaching part-time and practicing part-time in central Pennsylvania), he was awarded the first Ph.D. in this field. As part of his training, Klemons performed surgery in villages throughout Nepal and treated patients in the open with no electricity.

To date, he has had almost 20,000 patients come to his office in New Jersey. His patients include people from six continents around the world and from almost every U.S. state. One patient claimed to have seen 300 doctors over a period of 65 years before Klemons was able to relieve her pain. Over the years, his practice garnered a reputation among patients seeking head pain relief. Realizing that that renown may not be enough, Dr. Klemons had the foresight to register the domain name Headaches.com back in 1996. His team did not use the site for a number of years, but more recently has found that prospective patients still want to study his success before they call. They also want to learn more about him personally before making an appointment.

Most want to read what others have said, learn more about his philosophy in treating patients, and see the types of challenges he has helped individuals overcome. As his practice evolved, he realized the breadth of his capability and continued to leverage the Web. Since facial joint issues can also impact sleep apnea and Tourette's Syndrome, Klemons registered SleepApneaUSA.com and MovementDisordersUSA.com He shares information with his worldwide audience on those topics.

He uses audio and video on both sites to explain the substantive medical issues, but also to give visitors a sense of his philosophy. Often a short audio clip revealing the sound of one's voice and the passion in one's tone will be more powerful than a resume (which Klemons includes on the site as well). "These days, people like to look at the Internet before they make an appointment," he says. "When they come in, they are a lot more comfortable," he adds noting that the "Testimonials" section shares images to which people can relate. "Some people on the site just grab them and they relate to that particular person." Professionals posting content to their sites should ensure that it is clear, truthful, and not deceptive in any way.

Klemons writes a comprehensive report for each patient describing the condition at the time of the examination and the recommended methods of treatment. When the patient reports a complete recovery, he writes a shorter report detailing, in the patient's own words, his or her experiences with the problem and the solution. Thousands of these signed statements appear on his various web sites and in his files. "Anybody can say that they can do something," he notes. "Until the patient signs off and certifies that it worked out, there's no way to know."

Klemons advises that physicians, dentists, other professionals, and satisfied patients often refer people to him.

The Art of the Referral

In the mid-1990s, David Bukzin, a certified public accountant and member of the executive committee at Marcum LLP, recognized that industries were changing. It was not just technology and the Internet, but variety. Organizations had more choices of people with whom they could work. Travel was becoming easier and, like Kaufman, Bukzin recognized that clients would choose a person they trusted, rather than simply an organization they knew, and adjust his location to service their needs. So he decided to go to them first. "I realized that banks would have beauty contests and that sourcing capital was critical to enhancing the value of a potential relationship with a prospect," he says. "Representing the money and having access to the money was a way to multiply the referral base by ten," he adds.

Along with his multi-million dollar practice, Bukzin built a referral network of securities lawyers, investment bankers, private equity fund managers, and others who could help facilitate the closing of corporate deals.

The importance to clients of good performance by an accountant is a given, but Bukzin routinely engages in additional activities that bring value to his relationships. He recently served as an advisor to a company interested in raising capital. Leveraging the power of his referral network, he spent two-days in 16 meetings with investment banking firms, private funds, and other financiers interested in new opportunities.

They trusted his judgment and after the 48 hours, the meetings resulted in substantial accounting issues that Bukzin and his team will manage. "They saw that I added value by navigating through the nefarious capital people on Wall Street," he says. "I proved my credibility to them on Day One because they met 16 legitimate firms who vouched for me saying 'David at Marcum is the best' and they wound up walking away with a term sheet." In addition, the advisor who recommended that the company meet Bukzin also looks influential.

In a sensitive market, through no fault of any professional, companies are going out of business, going to low cost providers, or are being acquired, notes Bukzin. Professionals must offer their clients and prospects something other than good advice. This is a sea change from what was common practice even a decade ago. Licensed experts would perform the tasks for which they were paid and repeat that practice for the life of their relationship, which, if they did not commit malpractice, generally lasted for an entire career. "Now, if you don't add value, you're seen as a commodity," cautions Bukzin. "If you boil yourself down to a commodity, you will be out of business, won't make money, or you will see your client drift to the lowest-cost provider," he adds.

The son of a magazine deliveryman from the Bronx working three jobs, Bukzin knows about hard work and commitment. The new era of marketing and client development is more than simply about constant effort. It is about connecting to people in an organic way that values who they are as much as what they do. "I don't mind helping people assemble transactions because they remember when I introduce them," remarks Bukzin.

> If you don't add value, you're seen as a commodity. If you boil yourself down to a commodity, you will be out of business, won't make money, or see your client drift to the lowest-cost provider.
>
> *David Bukzin, CPA and member of the management committee, Marcum LLP, New York City*

Whether that introduction produces business is almost less important to him than the certainty that it will produce a relationship. It is that relationship, rather than the outcome of the introduction, that will yield fruit over the long term. "It shows the importance of being a hustler," he adds.

There is a special way to market to referral sources as opposed to direct buyers and those providing a service will benefit from understanding that distinction. Instead of solving the problem of the ultimate client, one must identify ways to positively influence the businesses of his or her referral sources, notes Bukzin. Being an enthusiastic influencer has been the hallmark of Bukzin's career.

In 1986, following his graduation from Baruch College in Manhattan at 21, he joined a small accounting firm with four professionals. "I always thought of myself as an entrepreneur even though I was in public accounting," he recalls. That drive is founded on his philosophy that to control your destiny, you must be self-sufficient.

In order to be self-sufficient, you must be able to relate to your audience.

"There are three kinds of professionals—good ones, bad ones, and ones with clients," says Bukzin. "When 'it' hits the fan, it is the professional with clients that stays in business, that keeps his job, and keeps the firm afloat," he adds. As a result of that mindset, from the outset of his career he wanted to think of creative ways to connect with others who could become or introduce him to partners with whom he could collaborate. "I wanted to build my practice around methodologies to generate clients."

In 1990, Bukzin was making $25,000 to $30,000 per year and his boss, who later became his partner, allowed him to hire a cold caller at his own expense of $200 to $300 per week. At the time, accountants were not cold-calling prospects, but he saw his stock-broker colleagues having success with the technique so he tried it. He retained seven clients and began developing a practice. Within two years, he generated 40 percent of the firm's revenues and the office had grown to 17 professionals.

As his practice expanded and the size of his clients grew, he needed a greater infrastructure. In 1995, he joined his current firm, then known as Marcum & Kliegman, LLP. It was looking to open a full-service office in New York City. At the time, Bukzin reports that Marcum was a firm with $6 million dollars in revenue. Bukzin's practice generated about $800,000 of that amount. Recently, he notes that the firm had over $200 million in revenue and Bukzin generated more than $8 million, supervising a team of 50 professionals.

The transformation in the industry is allowing more accounting firms to assist in managing transactions associated with raising money, mergers and acquisitions, turnarounds, public offerings, and, depending on the market, liquidations. Not long ago, clients would use the accounting firm required by their investment bank, which was often one of the Big Four. Today, there is an array of options, which fills the market with opportunity, depending on the nature of your practice and personality.

In his continuing quest to bring added value to his referral sources, Bukzin is routinely offering insight into the marketplace. Although he rarely spoke at conferences or produced Marcum-branded seminars in the past, he recently offered a program on reverse mergers and alternative public offerings, during which he shared ideas on how attendees could access the capital markets in unique ways. "I expected 40 people in my conference room, and 150 showed up," he says.

In addition to providing paid guidance, most organizations need to share information on a regular basis with their audiences. There is an expectation from the general public that basic data and strategies will be essentially free. They hire experts for the more complex questions and are willing to pay a premium to those who can answer them. While there are often many who can provide those answers, they reach out to the people that have taken the time to nurture a relationship with them or to someone they trust.

Bukzin leverages the power of his mailing list to reach his contacts, who may decide to share his insights with their contacts, as we are in a perpetual referral economy where almost every piece of digital correspondence contains a way to forward and recommend information.

Every item of news offers multiple ways to reach a broader audience. The entire social media landscape is founded on the premise that success comes not from creating a network of resources, but by reaching out to the networks created by the members of your network to exponentially increase your audience. The issue is, of course, making those connections in fine enough detail that each is well placed and focused.

"When I was young I realized that my mental capacity had room to maintain relationships with a finite number of clients and referral sources, so I had to make a choice if I wanted to be a standard tax accountant with relationships paying an average of $5,000 or play in the M&A and transactional space where relationships paid $200,000 or more," notes Bukzin. "I always went for entrepreneurial corporate projects where fees were the biggest, but as a professional you should decide early on where you want to focus your efforts because it takes years to build up a network."

RECAP

- You can generate opportunity by focusing on solutions for clients and maintaining creativity.
- Technology has given professionals the option to expand their global reach and increased their competitiveness.
- The key is a strong reputation, passion, and the ability to deliver services at greater value than your competition.
- That said, if you do not add value, you will be viewed as a commodity.

CHAPTER

11

Meet Your Clients and Patients Directly

One of the most powerful elements of technology in professional services is that it enables experts to directly target potential contacts. It allows one to create a connection that might not exist without the digital marketplace. This chapter will reveal strategies for creating and cultivating relationships with members of the local community and throughout the globe. It also highlights innovative tools for strengthening client and patient relationships.

■ ■ ■

I have often found that individuals are more likely to meet with you when you are going to be in their city or their neighborhood. There is a human instinct associated with convenience that prompts them to accept an invitation if you are able to make it as easy as possible for them. Salespeople are effective at securing a second meeting with a different contact at the same location once they confirm the first, because the second person appreciates the logistical ease of the encounter. For this reason, I often recommend that professionals reach out to potential referral sources, members of the media, colleagues, and even unknown alumni from their colleges or graduate schools in an effort to meet them when they are on the road.

On a trip to Chicago for a keynote address, I wanted to e-mail the producer of a local television station. To find the contact's name, I used the "advanced search" feature on LinkedIn (available in the top right-hand corner next to the search box) and queried the terms "producer" in the "Title" box and "WGN-TV" in the "Company" box.

On the second page of the results, I saw one that looked correct and sent an e-mail (guessing that the address was first name-dot-last name at Wgntv.com, which was correct for its related radio station, WGN Radio). I was wrong and the server returned the e-mail.

Most people would give up at this point. After all, if you make an effort and it results in immediate failure, as this did, then it must be fate. This is especially true for professionals, who are particularly resistant to cold contact. Well-educated and generally well-respected authorities in one area or another typically avoid rejection. Like most of my peers, I did not follow up.

A few days later, on the night before I left, I thought that I would give the producer one more try. The e-mail address was wrong, but I had a name. So I called the television station's switchboard and left him a voicemail message. An hour later, I received a call from his colleague, who invited me to appear on the evening news two days later.

My secret was not in the follow-up call, though that is essential, or even in my pitch. The essential component of creating this opportunity was identifying the correct name of the producer of the show. Thanks to LinkedIn and a simple query for "producer" and the name of the station, I was able to focus my efforts.

The same strategy has worked for Levan Iordanishvili, a video game music composer and founder of Vel9 Studios in Los Angeles. His is a slightly less common vocation than, say, an accountant or a financial planner. There is no traditional route to take or profession of trailblazers to emulate for his career path.

The 2010 New York University graduate started writing music for a video game during his freshman year. It paid almost nothing, but he loved the process and decided that he would pursue that path as a career. "I wanted to make sure that I was able to do what I loved to do when I graduated," he recalls. "I worked really hard when I was in school to make it happen." In 2007, he completed four projects that generated less than $600 in revenue. In 2008, he completed 18 projects and made $3,400. In 2009, he earned $7,440 from 20 projects, and also began licensing his music. In 2010, he earned about $30,000 from an array of different projects.

After completing his first video game project, he immediately read Aaron Marks' *The Complete Guide to Game Audio: For Composers, Musicians, Sound Designers, Game Developers (2d edition)* (Focal Press, 2001), to learn how composers get their work. One of the key lessons the book taught him was to carefully target potential clients. "Since then I have been e-mailing people non-stop," Iordanishvili says.

Years after sending those e-mails in college, Vel9 Studios has composed music for Ubisoft Entertainment's Settlers VII debut trailer, EA Sport's Web series opener, and various casual games published by Big Fish Games Inc. It has also licensed more than 400 tracks to various media projects through premiumbeat.com, for clients that include Lufthansa and Burton Snowboards.

As part of his outreach, Iordanishvili regularly updates his web site and contemplates ways to more effectively reach video game developers and software architects. Early in his career, he found a video game engine called unity-3D, which featured a community section that permitted composers to post their work.

Like my effort to find the evening news producer, Iordanishvili is a consistent user of LinkedIn. I am a basic member, but he finds the service so valuable that he invests in a paid Business Plus account. "It has been an awesome resource for me," he says. He regularly conducts advanced searches using the terms "creative director," "online media," "media production," "video production," and others. He spends time every day e-mailing contacts. "There are so many places on the planet that need music, so if I don't get the work it is because I am not trying hard enough."

When I am concerned about my workflow, or hear similar trepidation from other professionals and students that are job searching, I echo Iordanishvili's maxim. I encourage them to think more creatively about how to provide value. I often approach the clients that I trust the most and ask them about additional areas in which they struggle, to determine whether I can assist, or if I can refer the organization to someone who can. "LinkedIn has been a revelation," he says of his ability to create opportunity.

Iordanishvili makes a list of the specific people and organizations with which he would like to work. From a recent series of 40 e-mails, he received a reply that the company was accepting bids on a new project. Although the contact did not end up selecting his submission, the producer liked his work and has become a good connection. "Maybe a year or two down the road something will happen," he notes.

With his success on LinkedIn, Iordanishvili is building his following on Twitter, particularly since a Swedish animation company that follows him recently contacted him about a potential project. "Twitter is a place where you hope someone finds you, but on LinkedIn, you can find him or her directly," he advises. "If people understood that you could talk to people you want to meet directly, it would make their lives so much better."

Mike Dwyer, a Chicago-based Senior Consultant for New Media and Creative Strategies at human resource consulting and outsourcing company Aon Hewitt, recognizes how it can offer advantages. "I got into the *Wall Street Journal* because of Twitter and in the *Chicago Sun-Times* and *Los Angeles Times* because of LinkedIn," he reports. By tweeting a link to his Workforce.com article—"A Social Networking Solution for Retail Recruiting's Challenges"—and citing it in a LinkedIn update, he attracted reporters working on various story leads.

He helps businesses use technology to similarly engage their employees on a variety of objectives ranging from recruitment and wellness to benefits and changes in management. In areas that require dialogue between the institution and its employees or clients, there is a direct connection between the method of communication and the message. "There are opportunities for the human resources department to become similar to a marketing group," he says, because it has a target audience and can effectively showcase its unique insight.

As business continues to rapidly evolve, social media tools provide yet another distribution channel. "The way that we are getting and sharing information is changing radically," he says. Dwyer encourages organizations and individuals to strengthen those connections by both creating and repurposing a signature type of content that their target audience would find valuable.

Just as Iordanishvili is sharing links to build his credibility and following, all professionals should consider what separates them from others in the market, who occupies their target audience, and the most effective techniques for creating community.

The way that we are getting and sharing information is changing radically.

Mike Dwyer, Senior Consultant for New Media and Creative Strategies,
Aon Hewitt in Chicago

Most people are not doing the things they should do on a weekly basis to use these types of tools to shorten the sales and relationship cycle. Like diet and exercise, habitual participation is the key to deriving value from many of the tools available.

After identifying relevant content, which could consist of a simple paragraph about an area of interest, share those details as an update on a LinkedIn profile. Dwyer recommends contributing to the knowledge base on LinkedIn's Answers feature to help individuals who need their expertise. Also, connect postings to Twitter to a LinkedIn account for maximum exposure. For PowerPoint users, SlideShare allows a few slides from a recent presentation to be posted in order to further engage your audience, depending on their preferences.

Those preferences are at the core of the revolution in how professional services firms provide guidance to their clients in a way that fundamentally differs from how they did it even a decade ago. There is a self-service trend afoot and professionals are trying to determine their new roles in the process.

An Accelerant of Change

Kevin Spreng is a partner with Robins, Kaplan, Miller & Ciresi LLP who splits his time between Minneapolis and Menlo Park, California. He counsels early-stage and growing technology companies as well as investors in those businesses. He also helps entities monetize their intellectual property through licensing or syndicating royalty revenues.

His team's challenge has always been that companies need time to develop before they reach the stage when they actually are able to pay for advice to help them with corporate financing and intellectual property monetization. In order to be selected for that lucrative work, ideally a lawyer would want to establish the relationship much earlier in the company's history. In a cost-conscious environment, it is an issue that increasingly plagues business-development-minded professionals.

With that conundrum in mind, Spreng and his partner, Ryan Miest, launched Accelerant, an online, subscription-based legal resources tool, which they saw as a way to provide legal services to companies during their earliest stages, setting the foundation for a stronger relationship once the business is more developed.

The 2010 launch was designed to accommodate the needs of their prospects, as well as to continue to fuel the firm's interest in supporting innovators and entrepreneurs that can become its future Fortune 1000 clients. Robins Kaplan's corporate team developed the suite of legal resources for the start-up companies in the pre-venture capital stage that are featured in Accelerant (available at Rkmc.com/Accelerant.htm). Spreng and his team realized that while many entrepreneurs appreciate the value of capable legal counsel and the ability to scale up with a lawyer from a simple contract to a multi-million dollar round of funding, they rarely have the budget for a significant retainer agreement.

The firm limits participation in Accelerant to highly skilled entrepreneurs with high-growth business models for a maximum of 12 months. In addition, "They need to be folks that we trust and are reasonable." To make that determination, the firm conducts a conflicts check and meets individually with each potential client.

The firm charges a modest annual subscription fee for the basic Accelerant program and a slightly higher fee for Accelerant Preferred. All subscribers receive complete entity creation services from the law firm, as well as access to frequently asked questions and a variety of documents including confidentiality agreements, stock subscriptions, and records.

Clients that use Accelerant Preferred have access to the firm's document vault where they can archive, access, and manage their company's documentation online. This allows early stage companies to organize their materials in a manner that will permit them to more seamlessly prepare for a future financing or sale. The document vault is organized into the same categories as a typical due diligence checklist and gives the company online storage for all of its final executed documents in PDF, similar to an electronic data room.

Most importantly, preferred participants are able to use the firm's answer center, which enables them to ask certain questions that are not time-sensitive, to which lawyers in the firm's corporate department will provide direct and tailored responses.

In the first three months of its subscription, one company's questions cost the firm $2,700 in billable time, but its partners are confident in the model since it states in the engagement letter the types of questions that it will address in this structure. For instance, it will not answer any questions that implicate adverse parties or broad questions relating to the mechanics of a merger or acquisition. That said, if a user has a question about a consulting agreement or its web site, for example, it can submit the question and expect to receive an answer within seven days.

"If you are willing to do some of the work yourself and wait a few days for a response, then we will provide this service at a lower fixed cost," says Spreng. Naturally, Accelerant members are welcome to call members of the legal team directly, but when they do so, the firm will charge its typical hourly rates. The subscription arrangement allows entrepreneurs to pay a flat annual fee to access a catalogue of approved documents that include instructions on their use.

Robins Kaplan created Accelerant to address two issues. First, an unusual number of young companies were coming in for legal advice related to financing of entities that were incorrectly formed in an effort to save money. Second, "We want to work with companies as they grow and create a relationship with them early on," says Spreng. "For an early stage unfunded company, our assistance can be prohibitive," he adds.

In order to create the relationship in advance of when they can afford its services, the firm decided to offer this nontraditional model. In the current market, there is a divide between traditional hourly legal services and "DIY" online document-assembly services assisted by searching the Web for answers to corporate functionality questions, notes Spreng. The 10 to 30 clients that enrolled during the program's first year are divided between the first tier and the second tier. "It is just another step in the slow progression to integrate technology into the practice of law to provide more cost-effective and time-efficient service," Spreng says.

Other firms are offering similar resources, and some are completely free (though they may not meet personally with their users). The Technology Companies Group at Boston-based Goodwin Procter LLP, for example, created Founder's Workbench, which provides free access to forms, instructional memoranda, best practices, and other resources to help new companies develop. The team's 160 lawyers represent 500 technology and life sciences companies, as well as 200 venture capital and private equity firms. Visitors to Goodwinfoundersworkbench.com can use the law firm's automatic document generator to create a professional certificate of incorporation, consent of sole incorporator, consent in lieu of first meeting of board of directors, subscription letter, founders agreement, founder stock restriction agreement, and contribution and assignment agreement, as well as by-laws.

There are even resources available for companies that are fully formed and interested in obtaining financing. Silicon Valley's Wilson Sonsini Goodrich & Rosati offers a free tool (via Dealbuilder .wsgr.com) that will generate a venture financing term sheet based on a user's responses to an online questionnaire. It also contains basic tutorials and remarks about certain terms. "These are all good signposts that technology is going to play a much more integral part in how we do what we do," predicts Spreng. "It is going to reduce the amount of time that lawyers spend on commodity-type work."

This revolution is not just impacting lawyers.

Minneapolis-based Zipnosis, Inc., a Web-based medical services company, is trying to dramatically change the way doctors deliver basic medical services. For a flat fee of $25, an individual in Minnesota can buy a 'Zip' with a basic or health savings account credit card to be used at Zipnosis.com. (Another Web-based service, Kooldocs.com, offers callers the opportunity to speak with an actual doctor for $100.)

> These are all good signposts that technology is going to play a much more integral part in how we do what we do. It is going to reduce the amount of time that lawyers spend on commodity-type work.
>
> *Kevin Spreng, partner, Minneapolis-based Robins, Kaplan, Miller & Ciresi LLP, and co-creator of Accelerant, an online, subscription-based legal resources tool*

A Zip starts with a Web-based interview guided by a software-driven questionnaire. The number of questions may vary, but the company notes that a typical Zip takes about five minutes to complete. The site highlights that all information sent through Zipnosis. com is secure and encrypted to protect a user's privacy.

Within an hour, a board-certified and licensed clinician from Park Nicollet Health Services in Minneapolis reviews the symptoms you entered, but the site identifies the most common diagnoses on its web site to be colds, sinus infections, strep throat, acne, seasonal allergies, cold/canker sores, or recommendations to quit tobacco, as well as bladder and yeast infections for women. The clinician responds with a treatment plan by e-mail or text message.

The answer will generally recommend an over-the-counter remedy, suggest that you visit your local physician, or offer a prescription. If a basic (non-narcotic) prescription is necessary, the clinician will send it to the pharmacy closest to the address you enter for immediate processing.

As simple as that sounds, traveling to fill prescriptions can even be a burden for some patients. In response, Eden Prairie, Minnesota-based InstyMeds.com offers pharmaceutical dispensers at outpatient medical facilities in a variety of locations. It allows patients to obtain medicine from a vending machine-style tool in minutes, rather than traveling to a pharmacy and waiting for a pharmacist to fill a prescription. These models embrace both the interest in generating more revenue by being more efficient, but also engaging clients by making basic interaction more productive. In fact, InstyMeds shares revenue with the facilities that house its kiosks.

Professionals are more likely to profit from services that demonstrate their unique expertise, rather than their full range of capabilities. Savvy individuals will identify the products and services that they can offer at little or no cost, which will generate more lucrative future work. In addition, when they earn that compensation, they will already have a level of trust with a patient or a client that will be difficult for a competitor to match.

Displacement Anxiety

There is a classic movie starring Spencer Tracy and Katharine Hepburn about an investor who introduces a giant computer into the research department of a newspaper and disrupts the entire office with concern over the possible displacement of the staff. The film, *Desk Set*, came out in 1957, but its theme still resonates today.

I have a voice-activated Google app on my iPhone that will do what people once contacted a live operator at the *New York Times* research department to do: Find answers to general questions immediately. The pool of common work is shrinking and, therefore, the competition for the more complex matters is growing. There is also a generational shift occurring. Senior professionals are reconfiguring their entire model while more junior counterparts only know the current environment.

Real estate brokers, for instance, once invested heavily in prime office space, desks, and phones to answer calls from potential buyers and sellers. "Today, the location of a real estate office is superfluous," says R. Randy Lee, an attorney and real estate developer in Staten Island, New York. The broker and the customer meet at the property and will communicate by phone or e-mail, he notes. As such, clients are increasingly attracted to low overhead professionals, who can charge less and yet provide the same level of service in terms of their industry knowledge. "People don't equate age, a nice office, or hard assets with the value of services," Lee adds.

He attributes part of this trend to the increasing self-reliance of the current generation of clients. A young smart builder today can guide his lawyer on the nuances of a particular property redevelopment. Consequently, that ability expands the pool of potential advisors. It also eliminates much of the unnecessary trappings of professional life. For example, Lee recalls spending thousands of dollars on photocopies of architectural plans until very recently. Now, architects no longer need to make as many hard copies of their designs. Lee reports that most municipal building departments accept plans by e-mail or via portable disk. They generate comments and reply electronically to the designers and developers. It is also much easier for Lee to solicit and receive bids from non-local subcontractors. "You can send out a digital notice to 20 plumbers and increase the competitive landscape tremendously," he says.

He cautions, however, that there is a downside to virtualization. "I think it is taking us to a world where social engagement among people and personal relationships are less important." In addition, there is less balance between personal and professional activities. The remedy to this dilemma is direct engagement. Determine the five people with whom you want to speak today, rather than waiting for just any five people to call.

Before social networking became popular, Chris Winfield founded 10e20, a new media marketing agency based in New York. As the success of the field grew, 10e20 became a regular acquisition target. Each time a potential suitor contacted Winfield, he reactively tried to determine whether the two were a match. After a few failed attempts, he realized that a proactive approach might be more effective.

He and his team, therefore, made a list of the industry veterans they respected and the brands with which they could align. Quickly, he found strong partners and ended up merging five organizations together to form BlueGlass Interactive, Inc., which offers social media marketing, search engine optimization, and pay-per-click advertising campaigns, among other services.

That direct approach is the hallmark of modern marketing. Connect directly with your referral sources and your potential clients. "One of the big problems is that a lot of professionals get caught up in the shiny new object syndrome," says Winfield, referring to the need to use popular tools, whether they are most appropriate for their style and business. "Social media is such a broad term," he adds, noting that focusing on your local market is often very effective. "It is like a giant conversation online that is very different for a global company than for a neighborhood dentist."

Winfield recommends that everyone with a web site incorporate Google analytics (Google.com/analytics) there so that they can see the sources of their traffic. "That is one of the easiest ways to start," he says. Also, set Google alerts (Google.com/alerts) on your name, your company's name, and the names of key competitors.

> One of the big problems is that a lot of professionals get caught up in the shiny new object syndrome. Social media is such a broad term. It is like a giant conversation online that is very different for a global company than for a neighborhood dentist.
>
> *Chris Winfield, managing director, social media marketing firm,*
> *BlueGlass Interactive, Inc., Tampa, Florida*

Instead of looking at the time involved in communicating online in any forum that appeals to you, consider the opportunity costs of not engaging in the conversation with the target audience. "Once you need to address the audience, it will not be as authentic," cautions Winfield. It is almost like calling someone you never speak to and asking him or her for a favor.

Winfield suggests archiving conversations on your own web site, rather than relying on external sites to help you build an audience. "It is so important to have content and a community on your own site, where you are making it relevant," he says. Despite the current popularity of Twitter or Facebook, he cites Friendster and MySpace as examples of sites where users may have contributed a lot of content and then needed to migrate it to another platform. "Right now the social side and search side are so connected because many of the search engines are ranking in part based on social signals," he adds.

That means that creating rich content is only half of the hurdle. One must also find ways to share it and encourage others to do the same.

RECAP

- The manner in which individuals obtain and share information has changed dramatically because they are essentially always connected.
- Technology is going to permit professionals to reduce the amount of time they spend on commodity-type work.
- The term "social media" has a variety of meanings, but generally it is similar to a giant conversation online. That conversation, however, can be very different for organizations of different sizes.
- Consider using LinkedIn to specifically target individuals with whom you would like to connect.

12

Mailing Lists, the Media, and Making Mistakes

Sincere engagement is the key to creating opportunity. Professionals who combat doubts about their outreach strategies and experiment are often rewarded with goodwill, reputation enhancement, and client feedback. This chapter will guide readers through the steps necessary to target a market segment, create appropriate content for prospective recipients, and overcome the fear of making mistakes.

■ ■ ■

Unlike entrepreneurs, who recognize the need for failure on the road to success, most professionals are meticulous about their craft to the point of near perfection. Their ability to complete a certain task with talent has always been the hallmark of professional services. If one needs to file for personal bankruptcy, see Lawyer A. Need a checkup for the poodle? See Vet B. A physical? See Doctor C. Until recently, many of these practitioners, among others, and the students hoping to someday emulate their work, believed that the document, pet, or injury itself was the situation. They focused on the task, rather than the person behind that assignment.

Today, being able to do the work is presumed. The ability to complete the task is expected. The issues are more often about aptitude, value, and responsiveness. To ensure consistency, professionals need to determine what their story is, how they will convey it, and whom they will enlist to promote their messages.

Become an Umbrella Salesman

Dale Carnegie is reported to have valued his client list over money and appreciable assets because he could lose the latter, but earn them back with the former. In modern marketing, regular interaction with the members of a mailing list provides consistent opportunity to generate new business and other leads, as well as reconnect with friends and mentors.

With the proliferation of free professional newsletter tools such as MailChimp.com, managing contacts and business cards is easier than ever. The tools allow one to time a message and motivate one to accomplish a relevant task for each monthly, semi-monthly, even weekly communication. They can also provide a forum in which to recognize clients, colleagues, and prospects, or engage in cross marketing to a shared audience.

Instead of blindly sending information out into cyberspace, a newsletter tool can provide metrics that detail who reads which part of the update and how many people follow that pattern. Sophisticated systems will even indicate whether a recipient forwarded the newsletter to a colleague. This allows the producer to better gauge the issues that are of the greatest concern and the topics in which the audience is most interested, including any personal stories that could be shared to demonstrate a constructive point.

Yet professionals struggle to use this tool most effectively. I recently received an e-mail alert from a colleague of mine at 7:00 P.M. on the Friday evening before a three-day weekend. I would guess that regardless of the quality of that message, very few people opened it or took any amount of time to fully review it. He expended the effort to craft an appealing message and then sent it at an inconvenient moment for his audience, which is contrary to best practices for effective e-mail.

I could, however, relate to his logic. He was probably trying to complete a variety of client and business development matters before the long weekend. Imagine a doctor reviewing a series of lingering charts or a lawyer getting through the last box of due diligence materials. Professionals commonly leave something like an e-mail blast that could generate new business to the end of the day or the to-do list.

So, he was probably just about to leave a on a Friday night and hit send. Check. Time to go home.

The problem is that when it comes to e-mail marketing, it is better to be just like an umbrella salesman, notes Stephanie Miller, vice president of digital messaging for Aprimo, Inc. Just as an enterprising umbrella salesperson appears at an urban metro station or bus stop the minute rain begins pouring down, professionals marketing with e-mail newsletters need to offer information that their recipients will find relevant and timely. Focusing on them will keep a positive level of interest and ensure readership.

If one fails to do so, he or she is basically wasting energy. It might be better to wait until the following week than send a message when no one is checking e-mail. And, if something they don't like is sent at a time when they don't want it, someone on the list may mark it as spam, which the e-mail system records. That complaint could negatively impact the delivery of subsequent messages.

Also, most programs allow an unlimited number of e-mails to be sent to those on a list for a relatively small monthly fee, depending on the number of recipients. Some even allow small numbers to be sent for free. "The best thing about e-mail marketing is that it is inexpensive, and the worst thing about e-mail marketing is that it is inexpensive," says Miller.

There is intense competition for one's attention in an already crowded inbox. Miller noted that for *The Global Email Deliverability Benchmark Report, 2H 2009*, which Return Path, Inc. released in 2010, the organization reviewed data from 131 Internet service providers in the United States, Canada, Europe, and the Asia Pacific territories from July through December of 2009.[1] It found that those ISPs do not deliver about 20 percent of permission-based e-mail messages to the recipient's inbox because of a variety of tools guarding against spam.

> The best thing about e-mail marketing is that it is inexpensive, and the worst thing about e-mail marketing is that it is inexpensive.
>
> *Stephanie Miller, vice president of digital messaging, Aprimo, Inc.,*
> *New York City*

---

[1] Available at www.returnpath.net/landing/globaldeliverability/.

Despite its challenges, leveraging the benefits of an e-mail newsletter can be very effective for busy professionals. It applies the principle of regularity as one can decide to send a message with any frequency. Monthly should be the minimum, but quarterly updates could certainly be sent, depending on the purpose. If there is enough valuable information to share, a weekly newsletter may be appropriate.

The key is *valuable*. Determine what one can provide to the audience that each member would find of value. Just as one decides whether a 140-character tweet or a two-paragraph blog post is consistent with the overall message, do the same with a newsletter.

If a veterinarian wants to promote the wellness of personal pets, for example, he or she could provide a newsletter sharing tips to care for different types of pets each month or week, depending on his or her ability to produce the content. If, however, that veterinarian's audience were comprised mostly of farmers who rely on his or her advice for their cows, sheep, and horses, that newsletter would likely be irrelevant over time.

For those just getting started, consider a monthly newsletter because it is frequent, but not too much of a burden. Try to design a simple template, many of which are freely included with most e-mail newsletter services. And, each of those services offers a free trial period.

As for what should be included, be brief, at least at the outset. Share some type of story, perhaps a recent professional experience (without any identifiable names, of course), or a meaningful personal event, depending on how typical communication with the audience occurs.

Once they are engaged with the message, provide some resource information that is consistent with that theme, such as a link to an article, a video produced or found, a webinar, a whitepaper, and so on.

Consistent with my theme of creating opportunity for others, I routinely share with my audience a recorded interview with an industry leader so that my recipients can learn from the insight of other professionals with interesting ideas.

One of those individuals was Dan Nye, the former CEO of LinkedIn and President & CEO at San Francisco-based Rocket Lawyer, Inc., who discussed the transformative effect that technology is having on a variety of fields. "Technology can simplify complexity; it can reduce time to make things more efficient; and, it can drive down cost," he said. "As you think about what one experiences today, the work is done in a more efficient way, as well as a higher integrity way," he added because of the very specific digital trail.

With the goal of specificity in mind, try tailoring the subject line and the content you share to particular groups within the mailing list by job title, location, or the nature of the interaction, among others. Doing so will help ensure that they will both open the note and actually read its contents.

> Technology can simplify complexity; it can reduce time to make things more efficient and it can drive down cost. As you think about what one experiences today, the work is done in a more efficient way, as well as a higher integrity way.
>
> *Dan Nye, former CEO of LinkedIn and President & CEO at San Francisco-based Rocket Lawyer, Inc.*

Review your mailing list every three to six months to delete incorrect or inactive addresses. This will help keep the list current, but also prompt follow-up with those who have fallen out of touch.

Take note of the information that appeals to the audience and try to craft messages to appeal to those preferences, because continuously sending irrelevant e-mail will just result in lots of requests to unsubscribe.

If blogging, consider using FeedBlitz.com, which allows one to create, brand, and install custom e-mail services that will reach out to an audience on a set schedule. It will automatically aggregate blog posts into a newsletter format at whatever frequency is designated. Pricing is based on the total number of subscribers and the fees are low for those who are just beginning the process. E-mail newsletters have no barrier to entry and are simple to use, but they require relevance and a consistent commitment. "If you send me something interesting today, I am more likely to look at your e-mail next week," says Miller.

Benefits, Business Development, and Beyond

I routinely feel like I have had a conversation with a contact after reading his or her newsletter, particularly if it is done well. I also have gained a bit of value, perhaps some insight, and hopefully a new resource. Regular e-mail interaction of this type helps to remind clients, prospective clients, referral sources, colleagues, and friends what one does, how well one does it, and why. It gives an opportunity to regain prominence in their minds every month or at whatever interval is decided to be appropriate, assuming that you time the correspondence properly.

I have sent e-mail newsletters on Tuesdays, Wednesdays, and Thursdays at different times of the day. Messages sent to my list on Tuesday mornings before 8:00 A.M. seem to yield the highest open and response rates. While this is important information for planning future campaigns, professionals just starting out should not focus too heavily on any particular numbers. Instead, they should simply monitor whether the e-mail is generating some type of inbound traffic or inquiry. A call or note may not relate to the substance of the correspondence, but it likely helped to prompt the person to make contact.

Sometimes people are not motivated by the work, but by the story. E-mail newsletters provide the sender with the opportunity to convey a message beyond his or her practice. It could be the impact of a patient, the excitement of a client, or a personal story about a family pet that provides the impetus. It is a customized way of communicating, and if even one person is reached via the hoped-for manner, it is likely to have an impact on one's day, and often on one's business or practice.

It does so by reconnecting the sender. At any given interval, the message might reach different people for different reasons. One will generally not reach everyone for reasons that have nothing to do with the note. They may be away, busy, or distracted at that moment. The act of sending the note, however, does provide an opportunity to associate with the colleague. That association has the potential to yield benefits for both.

If a contact of mine is offering a webinar, for example, and I think my readers will benefit, I share it with them in my newsletter. Doing so allows one to cross-promote the work of others and introduce additional resources that recipients would find useful. The newsletter becomes a distribution tool for the practice, as well as for others. It also demonstrates to audience members that they are being thought about from a much broader perspective than just the sender's contributions.

Finally, by interacting on a periodic basis, one effectively archives his or her work, including the calendar of activities, media mentions, and scheduled events. It helps keep track of accomplishments and initiatives. It serves as a guidepost for what has been shared in the past and what can be shared in the future.

Meeting the Media

Just as the core audience is searching for interesting content in a very noisy marketplace, the media, both trade and mainstream, is always looking for the same. Those who can effectively relate what they do with that search will find personal public relations success. Savvy hustlers routinely connect with local journalists directly.

Each professional should become familiar with the media landscape in his or her locality. Get to know the editors and producers of each publication. Keep the effort simple, but coordinate contacts. Consider reaching out to one individual per week. MondoTimes.com, for example, is a resource that provides listings of every media outlet in a given city (its site claims to contain "30,185 media outlets in 212 countries.") It organizes those outlets by medium (e.g., print, Web, radio, or TV) and offers links to each outlet indicating the most popular.

Print publications tend to offer details on the proper contacts more easily than other forms of broadcast media. For instance, visitors to the web site of a mainstream print publication, a legal trade newspaper, or an accounting magazine, among others, will find a link for "Contact Us" across either the top of the home page or buried in a series of links at the bottom. That link will likely provide various contact options for subscribers and advertisers. One of them should lead to a directory of employees in the newsroom.

After those contacts are found, select an editor who suits the idea. If pitching a story related to mainstream business, then find the business editor or a senior writer that covers business issues. If there are only a few contacts that may be appropriate, conduct a search within the site for each of their names to review a list of articles they have written. Compare that list to the idea to determine whether the two are consistent.

Alternatively, start with a search of key terms that relate to the idea, particularly when a niche industry expert is pitching a mainstream publication. Pick out a few terms from the industry like "law firm" or "computer-aided architectural design" to highlight stories on those topics. Eliminate the errant responses and focus on the few writers who cover the industry. This brief exercise will help narrow down the pool of potential contacts in minutes and tremendously enhance prospects for success.

Most professionals with little media relations experience are genuinely afraid or, at a minimum, confused by the art of engaging with journalists. They don't realize that writers and producers are often looking not only for good ideas, but for great sources, who could help make those ideas even better. On a deadline, they frequently look to those individuals with whom they have a relationship. Establishing that relationship will add one to the small pool of resources, and will also position one for an opportunity when an attractive idea is presented in the future.

Make Mini Muffins with the Media

My wife is both a remarkable lawyer and a talented chef. Her meals, desserts, and snacks are fantastic, and almost always healthy. When our kids were small she decided to make them a certain type of healthy muffin that did not really appeal to them. They weren't chocolate or sweet and they didn't have creamy frosting or powdered sugar. Undeterred, she went to a bakeware shop to buy mini muffin trays and create attractive shapes for the same snack. When the fresh batch was done and resembled their favorite characters, they were eager to try one (or five).

Professionals need to give the media mini muffins: good ideas coming from credible individuals that appeal to their sense of timing. In many ways, one's goals for an e-mail newsletter and his or her idea for reaching the media are the same: relevance and timeliness. If there is a large medical convention in town, contact the appropriate beat reporter or editor, identify oneself as a physician who will be speaking (or even attending) the event. Tell him or her (by phone or e-mail) why the event matters and the key issues the audience will discuss.

At a minimum, the idea could be interesting for the industry trade publications. Tailored to a larger issue like local health care, it could just as easily appeal to a reporter who covers the topic for a regional or metropolitan newspaper. The same is true for an architect and a new skyscraper that is opening, or a veterinarian and a new mascot for a local team or a presidential pet. It is even possible to generate the idea when traveling to a particular city, not a hometown, and request a meeting based on the visit.

Here is a sample e-mail for a professional with some trade publication experience (taken from one of my first queries as a writer):

> Dear [Editor – address the person by first or last name depending on your preference]:
>
> I am interested in writing an article for NEWSPAPER / MAGAZINE / WEB SITE on emerging issues in international e-commerce. I spoke with [Chris] earlier today and [she]- thought that it was an interesting idea that I should pursue with you.
>
> I am a [corporate attorney practicing in New York City]. I currently [co-author a column in *The Journal of Commerce* on international matters]. I have also written for [the *New York Law Journal* and will have a book review published in the *Federal Lawyer* next month].
>
> In the past few months, [new legislative proposals have been fueling an interest in international e-commerce]. A column on this topic would combine my experience in international transactions with the general public's excitement for the Internet's potential.
>
> I have included links to samples of my recently published work for your reference. I hope that we have an opportunity to work together and I look forward to hearing from you.
> Sincerely,
>
> [Your Name]

Consider how one will pitch the idea as the expert and what makes him or her the ideal voice on the subject. If a marketing team or public relations support exists, consult with them for additional guidance.

Depending on the schedule or the issue, one may want to wait a few hours or days to follow up, but absolutely follow up if there is no response. Simply contact the main switchboard number or use the individual's direct line, which is often listed on the publication's web site.

The conversation or voicemail should be simple:

> **Caller:** Hi, this is Janet Smith and I am a financial planner following up on my e-mail about sharing ideas on market pitfalls your readers should avoid given the upcoming investment conference in the city next week.

Technology and the 24-hour news cycle have made members of the media more accessible. Print and Web journalists still seem to be more approachable than radio and television producers, but the Internet has impacted that barrier as well. When I need to contact a radio or print journalist, I turn to LinkedIn. The initial benefits of its search tool are available for anyone, even unregistered users to find individuals on the network. Yet, consider becoming a member for free to experiment with the advanced search capabilities that helped me reach the television news producer in Chicago.

Once I have the name of a producer, I try to find his or her e-mail address to send an initial note like the one cited above for print journalists. If a Google search for the producer's first and last name, as well as the station's URL, such as "John Smith WKRP. com," does not yield the necessary contact information, I will simply call and ask the receptionist. If he or she cannot provide it, I just ask to speak with the person directly. Once connected, I will leave a brief message noting the reason for my call, who I am, and why what I'm saying is relevant.

Those who are thinking that this will be unsuccessful are correct. Missteps will occur. It will be frustrating. Someone will, however, appreciate the idea. If it is a good one presented by a credible expert, one will find opportunities to share his or her expertise with a broad audience. The pitch about this year's annual conference may falter, but throughout the year when an issue arises in the area of expertise, one will be a contact on the reporter's mind.

In addition, I occasionally introduce the reporters who reject me to more prominent experts in my industry or community, with whom they would like to connect. For instance, if I travel to a major city and try to coordinate a meeting with a reporter in my field and get rejected, I still think of that reporter. During my meetings that visit, I may speak with the founder of a business or a prominent expert in the area. If appropriate, I might offer to introduce him or her to the journalist who rejected me. My new contact appreciates the gesture for obvious reasons, but the journalist also welcomes the effort because he or she is always looking for local authorities to add to a file of resources.

Two great examples of free services that offer direct access to reporters seeking experts to quote are ReporterConnection.com and HelpAReporter.com. HelpAReporter.com, started by Peter Shankman, author of *Customer Service: New Rules for a Social Media World* (Que Publishing, 2010), is the larger of the two services. It sends queries from journalists directly to your inbox for free three times per day, five days per week. Urgent queries can also be found on Twitter by following Twitter.com/HelpAReporter. The service essentially provides up to 500 opportunities to be quoted per week.

"The concept of being quoted as an expert is the cheapest and most effective form of advertising," says Shankman. While many of the queries may be irrelevant since they range in focus from finance and law to travel and technology, some may be directly on point. In addition, by reviewing the listings with the personal network in mind, the chances are exponentially increased that one of them will be related to a contact. "Helping someone else get quoted is the easiest way in the world to make yourself look like a hero," adds Shankman, a social media strategist who works with brands and companies globally to help them improve their communication with customers and clients.

Simply reviewing the leads will provide an education on what kinds of issues reporters are covering and help tailor a potential pitch someday down the road to their specific interests. MuckRack. com provides the ability to track the Twitter messages of journalists from major media outlets to study real-time reporting. All of this will help professionals feel more comfortable offering what the media is looking for.

> The concept of being quoted as an expert is the cheapest and most effective form of advertising. Helping someone else get quoted is the easiest way in the world to make yourself look like a hero.
>
> *Peter Shankman, founder, New York City-based HelpAReporter.com, and author of* Customer Service: New Rules for a Social Media World *(Que Publishing, 2010)*

Being the Media

Web TV show founder and producer, David Siteman Garland, who was discussed in chapters 4 and 8, often accompanied his grandfather to work and, like John Korff, the sports event marketer, decided at an early age that he did not want to work in a traditional office. After graduating from Washington University in St. Louis in 2006, the creator of TheRisetotheTop.com began managing a professional in-line hockey league in the city. The job offered no pay or benefits and yet Garland decided it would be a great opportunity if he could attract sponsors. Quickly, he enlisted the support of Anheuser-Busch Companies, Inc., PepsiCo Inc., and United Parcel Service of America, Inc. (UPS), among others.

Two years later, at 23, he decided to convey his passion for business on television. "I came up with this idea to create a TV show," he recalls. "I wanted it to be a resource that would also let me hang out with really cool people and share their stories." He initially self-funded the production of the show (with his bar mitzvah money), which aired on the local ABC affiliate station in St. Louis. He spent $15,000 to shoot a pilot and smaller amounts for the subsequent episodes, never exceeding his $50,000 budget or his sponsorship revenues. Facing mounting production expenses, he sought out creative professionals with equipment to help him shoot the show in his home for the second season. Without any marketing budget at all, he averaged 100,000 viewers per month online.

That first season he featured guests he knew, including a small-restaurant owner and a business coach. For the first two seasons, his guests were predominantly from St. Louis or the region. In the second season, however, he began interviewing guests when he visited different cities. As technology shifted to make video increasingly accessible either through Skype or handheld Flip cameras, Garland began asking prospective guests to tape themselves. He could then broadcast those discussions on the show. He spent the first three seasons on the ABC affiliate and then decided to move completely online beginning January 1, 2010.

There were almost no production costs since he filmed in his apartment and he used the camera built into his Apple computer. Also, he could reach a much broader audience of viewers and guests when he moved online. He evolved from offering insights from a local panel of successful but relatively unknown experts to a "who's who" of insightful thought leaders, ranging from famed authors Seth Godin (*The Purple Cow* (Portfolio, 2003)) and Timothy Ferriss [*The 4-Hour Workweek* (Crown, 2007)], to visionary industry leaders, including Zappos Development, Inc. chief executive officer Tony Hsieh, founder of web site shoe retailer Zappos.com, and Scottevest, Inc. travel clothes company creator, Scott Jordan. "Online was where I built my business," says Garland. It enabled him to create a diverse community, which is the essence of thriving in a socially driven business climate.

There are many ways to become the media. Garland found success with video using Skype, which is a completely free tool that one can download for Mac or PC at Skype.com. In addition to Ecamm's $20 Call Recorder (Mac only), available for purchase at Ecamm .com, he uses Ecamm's iGlasses (for another $10) to enhance the quality of the camera on his computer, Screenflow (for $99) to convert static pictures into video, and iMovie (which is included with the purchase of an Apple computer) to edit the footage.

For professionals interested in modeling themselves after Garland, there is mostly good news. It is generally as easy as he says, particularly for someone with an assistant to help with some of the logistics of coordinating the interviews. For those doing it themselves, I use Tungle.me to schedule interviews for my various projects. Simply designate the intervals available and invite recipients to select a few different time slots that are mutually convenient. It streamlines the process tremendously.

Whatever the field, one doesn't need to do five shows a week like Garland. Start with one per month. Select 12 people one would like to meet and begin with them. His advice: "It takes a consistent effort to do this." According to Garland, "You can start small and in a specific niche." His focus is entrepreneurs. Chief financial officers, commercial real estate developers, or pediatricians, are among the many possibilities.

You, Too, Can YouTube

One doesn't need to appear on screen at all, or even use a camera. I created a YouTube.com channel to serve as a repository of various interviews I take when I am on the road at conferences. They are raw and unedited short segments that I generally shoot with my iPhone. The people I am interviewing appreciate the additional visibility and I enjoy sharing their insight on the market. On one occasion, I actually edited one of the videos using the iPhone's cropping software.

There are also software programs that will allow one to narrate a series of moves on a computer screen. For example, SnapzProX (for the Mac, available at Ambrosiasw.com for $69) and CamStudio (open source for the PC, available at Camstudio.org) permit one to record both static screen shots of a computer and video so that one can give a visual tutorial on anything at all.

For example, to walk someone through completing an application for a building permit, filing his or her tax returns, or downloading a piece of legislation, one can record himself or herself clicking through the various sites on the Internet. Simultaneously, describe the efforts and merge the audio with the video. Windows Video Player and iMovie both permit this effort. I use Audacity, which is a free open source program for the Mac and PC, to edit the audio files. It is self-explanatory and available at Audacity .sourceforge.net.

All of these tools require a single mindset to be successful. It is not the skill to manipulate them to create good content or a desire to reach out to a core audience in a creative way. It is simply being open to failing. Garland admits that he was not as capable in his first attempt as he was on episode 100. He also learned something from each mistake he made.

In approaching the media or members of a mailing list with a sincere interest in sharing information that is timely and relevant, one immediately overcomes the initial hurdle of taking a chance. If the journalist does not call back or rejects the idea outright, there is always another time. For every person that unsubscribes from the newsletter, there will be many others who remain interested in the content. The entire effort is a balancing act, which will eventually lead to the correct result. Embrace the small mistakes and occasional rejection. They often create opportunity in the future.

RECAP

- E-mail marketing offers tremendous brand recognition and outreach potential if executed properly. It is, however, inexpensive, which is both an advantage and a disadvantage.
- Engaging the media has the potential to secure significant visibility for your practice and there are free services that allow you to take advantage of these opportunities.
- Online video and audio are more accessible than ever before. There are free tools for hosting and editing, which feature user-friendly interfaces and require little, if any, training time.

13

Forget Technology, Remember Others to Build True Relationships

Despite the zeal associated with technology and its ubiquitous place in our professional lives, the most meaningful efforts are still occasionally those that relate us to one another on a direct level—a handwritten note, a call, or a gift. While technology offers advantages in terms of setting the foundation for sincere relationships, personal interaction is what helps it develop. This chapter will focus on the down side of the digital domain and provide guidance on actions to avoid.

■ ■ ■

A few years ago, just prior to submitting my first book to my publisher, my daughter, then two years old, was particularly excited to see me after a nap on a Friday afternoon. Running around my office, the power cord to my laptop was obstructing her path. She tugged at it more than once, but for some reason I still left the laptop computer where it was, on the far corner of the table.

In a flash at around 4:30 P.M., my daughter won the tug of war and my PowerBook G4 literally crashed onto the hard tile floor. I watched it fall in the surreal slow motion haze that accompanies an eyewitness experience, but I could not imagine the potential damage. To my surprise, it worked for a minute and I thought nothing of the accident. I picked it up and breathed a sigh of relief.

When the colored pinwheel (rotating hourglass for PC users) locked up my computer, I tried to reboot. Alas, there was nothing but a gray screen. Game over. The support technician I called warned me that the drive was probably cracked and that I could have lost absolutely all of my data. Since I hadn't backed up in four months, I was noticeably bothered, but thought he had to be wrong. After all, it was 2007.

Two weeks and a refundable $700 fee later, it was still all gone. Not a single item was recovered. Much of my work was backed up in some decentralized fashion through various e-mail accounts, but I was sad to have lost other items, like my family photos (many of Little Miss Sunshine herself), that had no quantifiable value. With no luck at retail stores, a corporate e-discovery colleague of mine suggested that I reach out to a team in New England and ship the drive to them. After another week or two of effort, they were unable to recover anything.

A few days later, we were in the mall shopping and my BlackBerry was sleeping safely in my coat pocket. My kids, however, were running around the store with that coat and the phone fell out. I did not realize it was missing until we got home and I tried to check my e-mail. I was almost at the point of a meltdown between my computer and now, my phone. I didn't have my name on the phone and assumed it was lost.

Finally, later that month, my daughter was playing with my iPod shuffle (the first clip-on version) and hid it in one of her toys. So within a small window of time, I had lost my laptop, my BlackBerry, and my iPod. It struck me as something of a conspiracy. My daughter was somehow sending me a message that I was too reliant on technology and she was right.

During my brief tech-deficiency, I felt liberated. With fewer reminder tools, I seemed to have a much sharper memory. I was also more efficient with my time and made additional personal calls. I was less technologically reliant and more self-reliant. Given that a few weeks later the amazing data recovery team at Kroll Ontrack, Inc. in Eden Prairie, Minnesota, was able to recover all of my files, I located my phone in the lost and found area of the department store, and that my shuffle showed up in the basement, it was a fairly painless long-term lesson.

Mastering the balance between technology and the relationships that it impacts, however, often contributes to professional success. "As digital as the world is, I still believe that there is a very big difference and degree in feeling between doing something electronic, which is impersonal, relative to writing a letter or calling someone," says Robert L. Goldstein, Managing Director and head of BlackRock Solutions in New York City. The first analyst hired straight out of college to become a managing director at the company, he was named one of *Institutional Investor* magazine's 2010 "Technology 40" Wall Street financial technology innovators. He is also in many ways a key witness to the remarkable transformation in financial services over the past decade.

Soon after arriving at BlackRock as a 20-year-old analyst in 1994, Goldstein was part of the team hired by General Electric to provide risk reporting and analysis for investment bank Kidder, Peabody & Co.'s mortgage securities portfolio. The firm used its proprietary analytics and software to manage the information.

> As digital as the world is, I still believe that there is a very big difference and degree in feeling between doing something electronic, which is impersonal, relative to writing a letter or calling someone.
>
> *Robert L. Goldstein, Managing Director and head of*
> *BlackRock Solutions, BlackRock, Inc., New York*

At the time, few of the firm's clients used e-mail, as Goldstein recalls, and since the nature of the company's business has always been to exchange information, he often sent diskettes and documents via overnight mail to his contacts. In fact, his team called its portfolio of risk reports the "Green Package" because they were printed on green paper so they could always be found, no matter how messy someone's desk was. By 1998, the notion of exchanging hard copies became obsolete, he says.

Today at BlackRock, thousands of computers overseen by a team of engineers, mathematicians, analysts, and programmers operate 24 hours per day. They monitor millions of daily analytical calculations and scrutinize all of the securities in a particular client's investment portfolio to gauge the risk from any change in the economy. The system, known as Aladdin, completes 200 million calculations each week considering different shifts in interest rates and the overall financial markets, among others.

Part of the team that created BlackRock Solutions in 2000, Goldstein has served as its chief since 2009. His group provides risk reporting on more than $9.5 trillion dollars of assets and over the past three years has provided analysis on more than $7 trillion of structured credit and mortgage products that were under great stress during the credit crisis. In fact, BlackRock Solutions manages a variety of bailed-out portfolios on behalf of the U.S. government. The technological prowess in this sector has grown to rival even Silicon Valley. "Financial services is in many ways an information-processing industry, which employs as many computer scientists and engineers as those industries themselves," notes Goldstein. "Wall Street has become a game of leveraging technology to create more financial products; BlackRock Solutions' role is to help its clients understand and have transparency into how these instruments behave."

Despite all of the technology available, Goldstein still highlights that the value of having a personal meal with someone is among the best ways to engage in conversation to which he or she will pay attention. Such a meeting is much more likely to influence and convey understanding. "Video conferencing may take off 10 to 20 percent of frequent flyer miles, but by no means replaces the act of meeting," says Goldstein, who notes that he travels more than 100,000 miles per year to physically engage with clients, prospective clients, and team members.

In addition, while e-mail has been very effective for staying in touch, Goldstein prefers to connect on a more personal level when appropriate. "I still believe strongly that email is a flawed mechanism for communications and certain things are not well served through e-mail," he admits. He cites the example of an important firm client, who experienced a death in his family. Goldstein made a trip to visit the client's team, but due to the emergency, his primary contact was unable to attend. A number of people sent this individual an e-mail expressing their concern. Goldstein sent a handwritten note on his personal stationary. He also offered to make the trip back to deliver a live briefing at the client's convenience.

Goldstein relates this struggle for simplification in part to the overwhelming volume of information that he receives on a regular basis. "I have a lot of people sending stuff that is almost counterintuitive to their cause," he says. For example, he notes that after a week of vacation, he will often have 1,000 e-mails but only 15 pieces of postal mail. "As ironic as this sounds, if they mailed it to me, I'm more likely to read it because the chances are better than one in a thousand." In fact, he applies a varied approach when marketing BlackRock Solutions to potential clients, using e-mail, phone calls, and letters as opposed to just one of those options.

Still, he admits that a device is available nearly every 10 feet in his home that allows him to be connected to his office by e-mail or other means. He was also recently in a meeting with 50 colleagues, each responding to status requests for information on various projects. Most were reciting details from memory while one was effortlessly swiping his finger across an iPad providing exact facts, figures, dates, and details. "You could put 100 years of paper directly on your iPad and be ready for any conversation in an instant," he says highlighting that the device will transform the client setting in the future. "It is a truly transformational difference in technology," he adds.

If a client expresses concern about liquidity risk, and shows interest in learning more about the company's analysis on this topic, there is an instinct to illustrate the points seamlessly and immediately. Technology used to break the rhythm of a meeting, but Goldstein predicts that it will be a central component and that the changes will cross industries.

He recognizes that advancements have enabled globalization and effectively given his company access to various emerging economies. Communicating and managing information, including the flow of wealth between the United States and countries in Asia, South America, and the Middle East, is seamless. "Sending an e-mail to Abu Dhabi is no different from sending one two blocks away," he says. The same is true for a phone call or a videoconference. "There are large portfolios across the world and the ability to communicate with them is now location independent," he adds noting that 85 percent of BlackRock Solutions clients are based in the United States while 15 percent are overseas. "We view a world that is more fifty-fifty and mimic's the global profile of money owners."

Goldstein notes, however, that such representation will not likely result from e-mails and conference calls alone. "We are providing a very high-end institutional service that requires having great transparency into very sensitive information," he advises. "This degree of sensitivity needs trust in terms of our fee and the services provided so there will always be a significant face to face component."

Use Technology to Say Thanks and More

Sensitivity to client concerns and information, as well as trust related to pricing and responsiveness are all key issues for professional services providers across disciplines. Delivering superior work product and honoring the concerns of clients is an ever-present balance. The key today is to achieve that equilibrium by leveraging technology to enhance the client experience.

It is possible to create complete virtual practices, but those relationships are built on a personal and professional composite. Those interested in thriving must learn more about their clients and incorporate that knowledge into their interaction. The reason that you remember your client or patient, for example, is more important, even in a digital world, than the means through which you demonstrate that thoughtfulness.

If your client is more comfortable with a text message than a call, then send it. A handwritten note, however, is often more memorable. It is more interesting. And, as simple as it may be, it is more unique in the current hierarchy of communication habits.

Start by calendaring dates that arise in conversation. List milestones that demonstrate your interest in your contacts as individuals. For instance, if a colleague mentions a wedding anniversary or an important business event, note that on the calendar, even if it will not occur for months. Birthdays are a good opportunity to follow up, though online remembrances of birthdays have become more common since Facebook has made that easier. (See the discussion of birthdays and networking in Chapter 14.) Messages of luck are also always welcome. They are often more appropriate and better received than one would imagine.

Instead of worrying about memory, these follow-ups can be entered in a calendar. They are often tremendously valuable. To make acknowledgement of a special occasion more noteworthy, try to recall details that are unique to that person. Just as Goldstein prefers handwritten notes to quick e-mail messages in certain instances, efforts to wish a colleague luck, express gratitude, and offer congratulations are often underutilized.

Ask questions about milestones during the intake phase of a relationship. Train staff members to be mindful of important dates. If a client or client contact is promoted, do more than send an e-mail. Call his or her assistant and ask whether he or she has a hobby you do not know about or a favorite musical group. A colleague of mine once referred a client to me and I found out that he is an avid collector of Beatles CDs and records. This was before they were on iTunes so I scoured eBay and found a rare collector's disc from early in their musical career. I really wanted to demonstrate gratitude by matching my effort with his interest.

Today, the call doesn't necessarily need to be made. One can ask common friends on Facebook or connections on LinkedIn for assistance. In addition, most people reveal much more than they realize in the social media groups they enjoy, including religious beliefs, sports team admiration, regional affiliations, charitable endeavors, and others. Ask audience members about their interests for future use. After all, you will eventually want to follow up with them for personal or professional reasons. Understanding your audience helps you tailor your communication.

Before every training program I conduct, I prepare a survey using Zoomerang.com to ask about the concerns, challenges, and triumphs of the prospective attendees. I want to know as much as I can about them before I enter the room. Consider what more there is to know about your clients and patients. What are they looking forward to in the New Year or for the holidays or as the fiscal year closes? What would they like to accomplish? Are they meeting internal milestones? What kind of support do they need that is different from what you provide?

Asking questions like these will provide a remarkable level of insight that most professionals do not ask. These tools are traditionally used for sales and marketing, which experts have always viewed as incongruous with their roles. Professional schools do not typically provide education on techniques beyond basic interaction. Once in practice, newly minted doctors, lawyers, accountants, and others tend to be so busy doing the work that they forget even the basic ideas about getting more of it.

For that reason, consider experimenting every single day with something. Visit a survey site, many of which offer basic capabilities for free, and create a three-question survey. Simply distribute an e-mail poll with one or two questions. The benefit of using a tool designed for this effort is that it automatically aggregates the data to show percentages and patterns. Then study the results and identify trends.

Pay closer attention to what the potential market is talking about by following lists of different users on Twitter. For instance, to pay attention to the conversation about accounting on Twitter, visit Listorious.com and simply type "accounting" into the search box. The results will reveal numerous Twitter users that are associated with that industry (as well as a few that have some connection to the field, but probably are not sharing the type of commentary on which you would like to focus).

Like surveys, this simple act will provide a glimpse into the concerns and considerations of your market. That knowledge will help you determine what type of information you should share on your preferred social media platform. It will also provide guidance on which blog topics might be most appealing, what webinars could attract participants, and the types of issues you can raise in your newsletters.

Technology is meant to support the relationship that professionals create through genuine means. Those who remember are remembered in return. In order to remember, ask. Many tools give you the chance to ask, and our cultural norms have shifted to a place where people are typically less guarded about revealing their answers. After all, if they don't, Google will.

Pay Attention to the Pitfalls of Participation

Early in 2001, an editor asked me to write a periodic column about the convergence of the law and technology for *eWEEK*. Given its prominence, I was very excited and proud to be writing for this print magazine. In response to many columns, I received e-mail comments from my readers. Some offered compliments and others simply shared a personal experience that related to the article. One note asked for my opinion on a legal problem, but as a general rule, since I was practicing law at the time, I did not provide advice in response.

Students seem comfortable posting without consequence and entrepreneurs are always trying to bring new ideas to market, but licensed experts are often conservative distributors of content. They want to stay far away from providing advice, but close to conveying their knowledge and experience. As the conversation online is becoming increasingly free, with others adding comments to blog posts, and messages to your Facebook page, or even retweeting your initial notes with additional comments, professionals are understandably cautious.

After all, unlike many authors and users of social media, licensed individuals have ethical obligations and privacy rules that specifically prohibit them from sharing certain information, and even creating any type of relationship that mimics the one they have with clients. They also have malpractice concerns, which, in an increasingly litigious environment, are critical considerations.

Think of it as "techn-ethics," a term that attorney Stuart Teicher uses in teaching lawyers about the intersection between technology and their ethical obligations. A lawyer for almost two decades, including as in-house counsel for a real estate-development company, a municipal prosecutor, and a public defender, he teaches ethics at Rutgers School of Law in Camden, New Jersey.

Although most of the questions professionals ask him are about social networking, he reminds them that similar rules apply to the use of cloud computing, smart phones, and flash drives, among others. "As I started to research the issues, I realized how intertwined we are with the ethics rules," Teicher says. "The existing rules don't fit so well into this new medium." In fact, soon after amending its model codes to reflect the increased use of technology by lawyers, the American Bar Association established its Commission on Ethics 20/20 to develop rules on operating in an even newer digital environment.

While the tools change, the guideposts remain the same. Lawyers, doctors, accountants, financial advisors, and other professionals have a similar duty to respect the views of clients and colleagues. They need to be accurate in the advice they provide and the manner in which they provide it. "I am more like a hitting instructor," says Teicher. "I don't teach them something new, I just help them understand it better."

Confidentiality Is Critical, So Know When to Keep Quiet

The idea of preserving a client's confidential information is not new. Even non-licensed professionals with no formal obligation to do so follow this practice because it is just good business. Today, however, in an era of waning personal privacy, the expectations have changed. As more people are communicating in open or more public social media environments, they may not consider the risk of repeated revelations of previously confidential information. Professionals, however, often do not have that luxury even if the client is initiating the discussion. Teicher cites stories of judges and lawyers having conversations about cases, and there are certainly other professionals and clients or patients engaging in a similar dialogue.

For medical professionals, the privacy and security rules promulgated under the Health Insurance Portability and Accountability Act of 1996, known as HIPAA, are very strict. In fact, most readers have probably signed more than one "Notice of Privacy Practices" in their lifetimes. And, while the restrictions seem obvious, most individuals interpret them through the lens of a live conversation or a formal document. They are not viewed in the context of a tweet or a Facebook update.

I have met professionals who refuse to join LinkedIn groups because they think it provides competitors with an unfair advantage since the communication in those groups can be open for public scrutiny. "When you consider the fact that we have the Internet as a buffer, we let our guard down," cautions Teicher. "Things that may seem obvious to us when we're talking in the real world don't have the same urgency in the social media world."

When Dr. Anas Younes of MD Anderson Cancer Center, who was discussed in Chapter 2, receives a query via Twitter from a prospective patient or specific questions from fans on Facebook, he encourages the individual to call his office directly. He is aware that once the discussion becomes specific, taking it offline is probably the most cautious approach. While there is a lowered expectation

> When you consider the fact that we have the Internet as a buffer, we let our guard down. Things that may seem obvious to us when we're talking in the real world don't have the same urgency in the social media world.
>
> *Stuart Teicher, ethics instructor, Rutgers School of Law, Camden, New Jersey*

of privacy in a social networking environment, if any, some level of caution is still wise.

Variations in privacy policies and evolving rules on particular personal settings make confidentiality and even doctor-patient or attorney-client privilege an increasing issue for consideration. Those professionals who violate confidentiality are typically subject to certain industry ethics rules. "We go ahead and take this action and people think that we are only talking to our friends, but there is no limit to the audience to which we are speaking," advises Teicher. "The ramifications are much broader."

For instance, if you post something to your Facebook page, and your "friends" share that post, you are inadvertently perpetuating it far beyond your network. Always assume that anything shared will be resent in ways that you cannot typically anticipate. The foundation of Twitter is also in many ways the ability to retweet what someone else has written.

Privilege, on the other hand, is something that a client can actually waive, either knowingly or otherwise, warns Teicher. If a client involved in a pending personal injury case discusses the details of a strategy session he or she had with his or her attorney on a public blog, or posts a comment on his or her Facebook page where he or she reveals points A, B, and C that the lawyer made during a confidential conversation preparing for trial, those revelations are now at issue. "Our clients like to vent on social networking and as a result it creates the very real danger that they could blow the attorney-client privilege inadvertently," warns Teicher.

Be Careful Creating Professional Relationships Online

The same is true for creating relationships. If a random person walked into a professional's office and asked him or her to explain everything the expert knows about a particular issue, the professional would suggest that he or she make an appointment, fill out an intake form, and return at another time. This was true decades ago and it is true for in-person meetings today.

Add the buffer of the Internet that Teicher describes and professionals are perfectly happy to provide some level of guidance and engage in some conversation with complete strangers. After all, consumers demand it and there has been a dramatic shift in the nature of modern communication. Of course, continue to engage the audience in some fashion using all of the tools and strategies discussed in this book.

There is a gray line, however, where someone seeks advice and information is provided on which he or she relies. Consider the example of a professional providing a response to a generic query on LinkedIn, such as "Where can I find a corporate tax form online?" or "What is required to evict a tenant in New Mexico?"

The initial response may or may not create a relationship, but if they continue to follow up with a direct message or e-mail, take note of the resulting interaction, advises Teicher. "If you don't have a heightened state of awareness, you will not see that happening," he says. Consider appropriate disclaimers as well as knowing when to discontinue the communication or recommend a more formal follow-up.

Occasionally, social media "friends" may be on different sides of a transaction, Teicher explains. A lawyer may represent someone adverse to a social media contact, or an accountant, with "friends" in government agencies, may be forensically reviewing the books and records for a company accused of inflating its earnings. The variations of these situations are large, as are the potential consequences. Give careful thought to whether and when there is a duty to disengage from a passive association with a layperson friend.

Advantages of the Cautious Approach

Absolutely engage in conversation with clients and prospects where they reside online. Use tools that are comfortable and freely share resources. While doing so, however, "Keep your big laptop shut," recommends Teicher.

The comments that are inappropriate in person are similarly improper online, whether they are sent by e-mail, text, blog post, or tweet. Those professionals who guide their online interactions in the same manner they monitor their personal behavior will generally be on fair ground.

Focus on maintaining your sense of professional credibility and your reputation while conveying your expertise. "The people you do business with are watching," says Teicher, noting that the list includes potential clients and employers. Also, be careful about the authenticity of those with whom you are participating in social media. "You don't really know who is on the other line there and it is almost impossible for you to really verify it," remarks Teicher.

In addition, while professionals are able to dramatically expand their networks and increase their business prospects, they have less control about what others say about them. As a result, "We've got to be diligent in asking others to take down postings that damage us," says Teicher, who encourages careful management of your reputation and credibility online.

RECAP

- There is a meaningful difference in doing something digitally and engaging in a more traditional form of human contact.
- The Internet often masks itself as a fictitious buffer, which prompts individuals to let their guard down in their online communication. Things that may seem obvious to us when we're talking in the real world don't have the same urgency in the social media world.
- Delivering superior work product and honoring the concerns of clients is an ever-present balance. The key today is to achieve that equilibrium by leveraging technology to enhance the client experience.

14

The Foundation for Follow-Up Is Easy to Establish

Many professionals believe that the initial contact is the most valuable, but often, the first meeting is not nearly as fruitful as the second and third. Most relationships begin with that primary inter-action, but they are built on subsequent communication. For that reason, follow-up tends to challenge the creativity of even experi-enced experts. This chapter will reveal proven strategies for follow-ing up and remaining in touch with new and long-time colleagues.

■ ■ ■

Before the rise of Facebook and its useful reminders, I tried to make recalling the birthdays of my contacts a signature. I would not remember everyone I met, but I did recollect many for enough consec-utive years that people would come to appreciate the gesture. I found it so effective that I recommended that the readers of my first book utilize BirthDatabase.com to help them find the birthdays of their contacts.

This is, however, an imperfect science because the site provides multiple birthdates for those people with the same name and you have to choose wisely. In one instance, I identified the birthday of a colleague and on the appropriate date sent her a message. She thanked me for my thoughtfulness and politely let me know that her birthday was actually in six months. Embarrassed, but unde-terred, I wrote back and let her know that I would be in touch later in the year. I had set the foundation for genuine follow-up.

My effort highlights a variety of the principles I have tried to convey in this book. Connecting with others is not an exact process. It requires an honest approach and a willingness to falter. It also requires a target on which to coordinate follow-up efforts and a type of communication for which the community can come to know a practitioner. That could be a birthday, an e-mail newsletter, a Facebook or LinkedIn update, a regular blog post, a video report, or other items.

The rise of social media has changed the way individuals share messages, both personal and professional. "In the old days, you had to buy your attention and now you have to earn it," says Michael Port, the *New York Times* bestselling author of numerous books, including *Book Yourself Solid* (Wiley, 2006).

A black belt in Aikido and blue belt in Brazilian Jiu-Jitsu, Port compares the need for professionals to innovate with the study of martial arts. "When something is not working, you don't try to become fancier. You go back to basics," he says, noting that students must ask whether they are holding their hands correctly or properly positioning their feet. "You might have been training for 20 years, but you are still learning."

Port proposes choosing a target market when departing from a known communication routine to set the foundation for a new one. This is important in the digital world, where is it so much easier now to market to and follow-up with great numbers of people, but not necessarily effective to do so.

Taking that step of choosing a target market will identify where to market, convey dedication to that field, and grant access to an established network of communication, advises Port. When one sets that target and understands how the market communicates, one can leverage that with the communication, follow-up, and social networking tool preferred. But, one must first make that initial commitment, which is a decision rather than an action. "Identify a community that already exists and bring them a derivative of a community," recommends Port.

Date-specific events are often easiest to follow up on because they have a natural connection to the lives of the audience and they are something to which all of us can relate—going back to basics, as Port points out. Birthdays, anniversaries (personal and professional), and certain milestones (including winning a case, receiving an award, and retaining a new client, among others) are great opportunities to reconnect with a colleague, client, or prospect.

Professionals struggle with following up, not due to fear, but because they are unsure of the reason for their second contact. By timing follow-up efforts to coincide with an event or time of year, you can easily make the seamless reconnection. For instance, many people send holiday cards annually and it is often the only interaction he or she might have with that contact all year.

Timing Your Tidings to Connect with Colleagues

The end of the calendar year provides an ideal opportunity to engage a network through charity because individuals are generally forthcoming with certain types of information during holidays. Take advantage of that inclination to learn about clients, prospects, and friends. That genuine interaction will be a fundamental element of creating opportunity throughout the year.

Consider asking others about a favorite social cause. Most people will have a reason why its mission is important to them. One of the keys to creating opportunity is to build relationships, not just networks. Philanthropy gives one a window into the personal philosophy of others that does not often arise in professional conversation, but defines their character.

Naturally, once their preferences are known, consider donating to those organizations in their honor (which is, of course, tax deductible). Visit CharityNavigator.org or Give.org for more information about charitable giving.

I conducted an experiment once for an article I was writing about business development during the holidays. I had a sense based on prior discussions with colleagues about their charitable interests that if I asked people about their favorite causes that they would reveal them to me. I created a survey using Zoomerang.com, a free Web-based tool (the Resources section at the end of this book lists a variety of similar sites) that permits a user to create an online questionnaire and analyze the results.

What surprised me about that experiment was not the identification of the charities by my clients, colleagues, and prospects, but the level of detail each individual shared about why that particular institution had meaning to him or her. It provided tremendous insight, and my donations to those charities influenced our relationships throughout the year. The survey took minutes to create and review.

Learning about what is meaningful to people is especially important now because we often gather with others online, where we know little about them of a personal nature. When we meet others socially, we have a greater opportunity to ascertain what is important to them. As Port points out, before the Internet, people physically met at social clubs, many of which still exist today, such as Rotary International and the Harvard Club, among others. Port leveraged the power of Ning.com (which ranges in its monthly subscription fees depending on features) to create his own social network at ThinkBigRevolution.com, which boasts more than 4,500 members.

He uses that group as much to listen as to speak. "It is not just about being the one with the megaphone," he says. "Create a place where they have almost as much potential to speak as you," he adds, highlighting that people want to join something that is bigger than them, but also they hope to express themselves through it.

"Build trust over time and allow people in the community to raise their hand," suggests Port. "People buy when they're compelled to buy, not because you did some great self-promotion," he advises, then warns that if a quid pro quo approach is taken, an opportunity to build trust will be missed.

> It is not just about being the one with the megaphone. Create a place where they have almost as much potential to speak as you. Build trust over time and allow people in the community to raise their hand.
>
> *Michael Port,* New York Times *bestselling author,* Book Yourself Solid *(Wiley, 2006)*

Just as Phil Strassler, the accountant from Chapter 3, suggested that professionals make five calls each day for proactive networking, Port recommends, "Do one or two really smart marketing things every day." Create a single community to invite people into and find ways to engage them, but bear in mind that "consistency is the key to credibility building," notes Port.

That type of consistency used to take time. After seeing the same advertisement in the phone book for a few years, one would come to recognize a particular company. "Now you can speed up that kind of credibility building through the Internet by being in so many places simultaneously," Port says. "Plan it into your calendar the way you plan your client work because one doesn't exist without the other," he adds.

Or, poll ideal vacation spots and holiday plans. Collect New Year's resolutions and offer to remind contacts about their commitments to themselves over the course of the next year. Everyone struggles with maintaining professional and even personal resolutions. Engage them in a less formal setting like a Facebook or LinkedIn group about fueling progress in the next 12 months. It connects one to one's audience in a much richer way and is a genuine effort at building the foundation for a relationship. In addition to creating online questionnaires, one can use a variety of free resources to automatically tally the responses for future use.

Beyond research, take 20 minutes out of vacation time, whether it is during the holidays or over the summer, and find someone to meet for coffee.

During a trip to Walt Disney World, I met Bruce Jones, the remarkable programming director for the Disney Institute cited in this book's Introduction, early one morning before storming the theme park with my kids. My daughter did, however, require that I wear the Mickey Mouse sticker we all received when we arrived at our hotel. Jones actually appreciated the gesture, given his employer and the venue. Port echoes my daughter's wisdom. "Try to do all of the things that are an expression of your personality, but make selling the last thing you do in those environments," he recommends.

The meeting does not have to be with a client prospect or even a professional, but it should be someone with whom you are genuinely interested in connecting. Individuals interact differently outside the corporate setting. There is often a more relaxed tone when having coffee while on vacation, than before going into work for a typical day. People listen, learn, and retain more effectively, which helps set the foundation for a stronger long-term relationship.

Prior to the next trip, business or otherwise, conduct this experiment: Visit LinkedIn.com, log in, and conduct an advanced search for one's college or professional school as well as the city being visited. Study the results and select a few people who look interesting and with whom you would like to have a conversation.

Alumni tend to be remarkably receptive to meeting one another. In fact, one feeling particularly positive about the experiment, who enjoys writing (more about that later in this chapter), should contact the alumni office and ask if they would be interested in a profile of the person being met for the alumni e-mail newsletter that every school periodically distributes. If the conversation goes well, perhaps it can be shared with others.

Hosting Events Is for Everyone

Given that sharing is the essence of the communication revolution and a great form of engagement, the only variable is how. There was a time when the only way to gather an audience and address the members was to speak live at an industry conference. Today, one can create an event associated with any point of discussion in his or her industry. There are free conference call services from FreeConferenceCall.com or FreeConferencePro.com, which offer registered users a personal conference call number and a fairly large number of participants (96 and 200, respectively).

Their revenue models are interesting in that ConferenceCallPro. com, for instance, claims on its web site to make money "in the form of a rebate that we receive from the phone company who hosts our conference servers." You can create a customized greeting through FreeConferencePro.com and both services offer access 24 hours per day seven days per week. They also allow recording and generous call durations (about six hours per call).

So the next time there is a desire to share thoughts on the latest federal regulation, a new cancer drug trial, an energy-efficient new building design, or another item of interest to a particular community of professionals, consider a free conference call that can easily be recorded for later distribution.

In order to show as well as tell, host a webinar. It sounds very complicated, but is really as easy as logging into a web site, assuming that the computer has a microphone and speakers. There are a variety of tools listed in the Resources section of this book that are completely free and fully accessible, including Join.me and AnyMeeting.com.

The value of a webinar is in its replay, as much as it is in the initial live broadcast. If I meet someone interested in creative ideas on repurposing content, I offer to send him or her a 30-minute webinar on the subject. If he or she is interested in something else, and I do not have a webinar available, I add it to my list of suggested topics for the future. To show, tell, and be on camera, Skype.com allows live broadcast by video call.

All of these tools offer savvy professionals the chance to gather their target market into a virtual room and address an issue that is of critical concern to them at any given moment in time. The key is to determine what that issue may be and then immediately work to attract an audience to listen to the discussion. This requires a captivating theme and a dynamic speaker. It is possible to provide both by asking the audience who it thinks meets those requirements. By asking for advice, a natural opportunity to follow up is created, and those who responded can be shown how their advice was used by including an invitation to the event.

Social media platforms offer a variety of ways to achieve the distribution necessary for these events. For instance, Twitter allows one to listen to the discussions of audience members to determine what interests them most. It also provides a network far greater than that of the average microblogging site's user through which to broadcast. Colleagues within a particular profession and beyond are often happy to retweet a webinar or tele-seminar announcement if they think it offers value to their followers.

Consider that if one has 1,000 followers, but five contacts with 2,000 followers each share a link to register for a live webinar or to access a recording, he or she exponentially increases his or her reach. Expanding that to include friends on Facebook, contacts on LinkedIn, as well as others from various networks, creates a massive distribution channel.

Before attempting to access it, however, credibility and trust must be built with others in those sectors, just as with clients and prospects. To do so, retweet their information and share their links on other platforms. It is not complicated, but it must be done before asking for something in return. It simply applies traditional marketing principles to a variety of new techniques.

Thoughtful Follow-Up Is Favorable

Reaching out to someone after meeting him or her is not only the essence of business and career development, it ultimately sets the foundation for opportunity, particularly when done in the most genuine form. For example, on any given day, a connection on LinkedIn changes his or her status. That person may note a few details about a business trip or he might highlight his status from employed to something else.

Whenever I see this, I follow up and ask my contact if I can make any introductions. After all, connecting two colleagues is as simple as typing a few words on my computer for me, but it could have a material effect on the job search of someone else. At its core, follow-up is about thoughtfulness. It requires a proactive approach to considering goals and those of others.

If one can help others achieve their objectives, perhaps by sharing their webinar announcement on Twitter, showcasing their work in a LinkedIn group, or quoting them in a white paper to raise their profile before their audience, it will set the foundation for trust and future opportunity.

Everyone has a story about his or her first client or first job. It always seems like serendipity in hindsight, where the stars aligned and someone caught a very lucky break. In fact, there is often additional detail that reveals the coordinated long-term effort required to create that opportunity and others like it.

That effort might come in the form of networking or it might manifest itself in one's dedication to improving his or her community. Ultimately, it is demonstrated in ways that individuals can easily tailor to their own strengths and personalities. It is the modern hustle for longevity and client service recognition. Each of us can take a common sense approach with our own branding, which reflects our character and capability.

Writing and Its Spinoffs as Marketing Are Remarkably Effective

Creative marketing is about engagement, and written products that allow organizations to tell a story by enlisting ideas from their target audience are more likely to find success. White papers, for example, provide a vehicle to conduct surveys, promote polls, and characterize products and services most effectively. They can also provide the foundation for dynamic audio and video, as well as invitational events for those they are trying to reach. Research statistics inform and provide benchmarking.

White papers are increasingly effective in an information-driven economy because they promote thought leadership, and offer flexibility in the ways white paper authors can distribute content. Those who are first, different, and creative, as well as understand their audience or the market, are most likely to find distinction. Ultimately, they enhance the brand of an individual or an organization while creating direct relationships.

Leveraging the credibility of a white paper is ideal for a professional because it can be used to organically promote a variety of ideas, ranging from business thought leadership (e.g., how the medical industry is changing and what can be done to prepare oneself) to technical guidance (e.g., five ways to use the next generation of 3D CAD tools), and political/regulatory insights (e.g., how Sarbanes-Oxley can actually help a small business).

A white paper can be under 1,000 words or many thousands of words, depending on the subject and the amount of time available to conduct the research, and interview sources and how the paper will ultimately be used. A single white paper can be broken into a series of blog posts. Then create an instructional video series using Skype.com and record those videos. Host webinars or teleseminars to discuss the topics, recording those efforts as well. Create a LinkedIn or Facebook group associating the audience with that content for long-term follow-up.

For instance, I created an experimental LinkedIn group called "Lawyers and Other Professionals Interested in Getting Published for Business Development," to see if I could create a community of people interested in this aspect of my work. I did so by simply clicking on the "groups" tab and following a few very simple prompts to create the group.

I started by inviting two colleagues to join, yet only one thought it was a good idea. And, then people just started to find the group. Some joined after getting a notification that another contact joined (LinkedIn tells everyone in a network when someone has an update, which is either an action he or she has taken, such as joining a group, or connecting up with someone new), clicking on the links in my e-mail signature, newsletter, or web site, and by simply searching for groups featuring content and keywords similar to mine.

Once content is created, it can be used in extensive ways. Worry less about the type of technology mastered and more about the information it is helping to share. This is particularly important as most issues have a lifecycle that repeats depending on the time of year, current events, or movements in the market. Converting the form of media also transforms an audience as well as how people receive the information. Similarly, using it to host a seminar, webinar, or free conference call offers a fresh interpretation.

Don't be afraid to pull out a smart phone and interview someone at a conference. Use video or audio to record their responses to a few questions (with permission, of course). The quality is not always as important as the content and the enthusiasm it conveys. In the early stages, the key is to simply make the attempt.

Consider referencing the insight received in a published article as a way of further valuing the skill of a network. It is a clear benefit to the individual being quoted, but it will also enhance one's reputation as the writer. In fact, effective writing can shape standing in the community and naturally expand a network. Writers tend to meet more interesting people, develop stronger relationships with them, and find continued reasons to interact. They master the fundamental techniques that are associated with business and career development by concentrating on a couple of key points that contribute to their publishing success.

First, they tell a story about their work and incorporate their peers as characters. Connect individuals of interest to the work enjoyed most. Brainstorm with them and study the items that appeal to trade publications in the field. Those periodicals will help offer guidance on identifying the proper venue for an idea, gauging the level of exposure to the target demographic, and determining the type of flexibility for future use of the piece. Try to maintain copyright so it can be repurposed and posted to a web site.

Second, they focus on their niche to foster sharing within the community, both online and off. By incorporating individuals specific to his or her industry into one's work, he or she will organically enhance its appeal.

Every individual encountered has a unique outlook on some aspect of business and the marketplace. Capturing those insights in a tangible form, either written, audio, or video, and sharing them with others highlights appreciation for their ideas and allows reflection on them through distribution. Instead of or in addition to a traditional publishing format, post those ideas to a blog as the author or guest, offer them through Twitter, or create a group to convey them.

Regardless of the venue, recognition will occur for appreciating the expertise of peers. It will also provide a memorable foundation on which to follow-up.

Getting published is more about motivation than mechanics. Professionals do not write just to see their name in a byline or send their article to others. They write to inspire. Ironically, in the process, they are the ones who become inspired.

RECAP

- Create a place where those you meet can interact with one another. Grouping functions on LinkedIn, Facebook, and other sites provide this opportunity.
- Worry less about the type of technology you master and more about the information it is helping you share.
- Writing for publication gives you the opportunity to spotlight individuals that you have just met and others you have known for years.
- Host a webinar or tele-seminar and invite guests to share the virtual stage with you.

Conclusion

Cultivating Community

I am an Eagle Scout. Among other requirements for achieving this goal, one needs to plan and perform a public service project. I always had the impression that most Eagle Scouts built bridges over rural ravines by weaving a complex series of knots out of vines. My friends and I, however, grew up in Brooklyn, New York, and there was a much greater need for neighborhood safety patrols than forestry projects (valuable as they are).

For my service effort, I led a team of uniformed Boy Scouts through an area of the borough that was experiencing higher than normal crime. We approached storeowners and asked if they would consider placing a sticker in their front windows and commit to being part of the security effort. The sticker alerted people who thought that they were being followed or felt in danger of being assaulted that they could enter the store and find a safe haven to make a phone call.

I tried to build a community to help the community.

Today, the proliferation of professional services is about harnessing the power of community. While the last generation could rely on the model that existed in their specific industries, the next generation needs to be more dynamic. Professionals must consider how their fields are currently organized and adapt to that organization. Those who excel dynamically modify the way they approach clients or connect with colleagues when appropriate.

Yet there are limitations to that approach if the professional does not fully embrace the underlying idea of the new way technology has connected us to each other—and hence fundamentally changed professional practices. Like entrepreneurs and innovators, they need to create a new world and then take action to support their updated ideas for greater results.

Judge Randall R. Rader is in many ways the arbiter of innovation. As the Chief Judge of the U.S. Court of Appeals for the Federal Circuit, he leads an elite group of jurists that decide cases related to intellectual property and other issues associated with invention, technology, and ingenuity. A federal judge for more than two decades, he notes that the shift in professional services is a human problem as well as a technology problem. "We have to almost change psychologically," he says. "We have to adjust our thinking to new ways of doing things and to new ways of competing." The path to success for experts requires an innovation in lifestyle as well as surroundings.

Once you set that target and understand how your audience communicates, you can leverage whatever communication, follow-up, and social networking tool you like. But, you must first make that initial commitment, which is a decision rather than an action.

A blog generates a public conversation for any reader to review and upon which he or she can comment. The same is true for discussion in a LinkedIn group or on a Facebook fan page. Twitter similarly offers an open forum for engagement. It is not self-promotion or marketing that ultimately secures new opportunities; it is the trust created from that interaction.

From trust, community follows. Instead of focusing on yourself, find ways to invite people to a free community that appeals to their interest. Share links to sites and encourage others to do the same.

In terms of the platform, despite all of the discussion about blogging, Facebook, Twitter, and LinkedIn, as well as the variety of other tools that are available, engage your audience where they interact. It may not be obvious where that is. For instance, the Pew Research Center's Internet & American Life Project conducted a survey of 2,257 adult Internet users in November 2010 and found that only 8 percent of adults who use the Internet in the United States were using Twitter and less than half of those users check it daily.[1] While that is still a large number and Twitter continues to gain prominence, "Innovation is unique to every discipline as it requires attention to the people whom you are serving," says Rader.

In a few years there may be another set of tools, or you may be focusing your professional services on another aspect of your industry. Consider your own character as well as that of your audience. Determine where you are most comfortable.

Strategies for how to get started abound. At your next industry conference or professional education course, ask your peers what they are doing and share ideas. Search for professionals in your area on Facebook and LinkedIn. Identify those people in your area of expertise who are on a Twitter list and begin following the conversation.

On the subject of lists, make a note of the topics on which to create content. Use the Dragon Dictation iPhone or BlackBerry application, which can be downloaded free from your smart phone's application store. It will allow you to transcribe those lists on the run and let you e-mail the transcribed text to yourself for future reference. Your phone likely has an audio recorder as well to use for brainstorming ideas.

Consider searching for blogs that focus on your industry or area of expertise. Identify a few that appeal to you and contact the owner to express your interest in guest posting. Test yourself. Call someone in your LinkedIn network and offer to profile him or her for the blog post.

Here is my guarantee: Failure will occur.

I am certain that some effort will not bear fruit. It could be the approach, the timing, or just bad luck. And, the pursuit will simply end. After all, a licensed professional has good advice to give and people should respect that. Period. If there was a desire to make cold calls or spend days selling, why waste time on earning that diploma or certification?

But that attitude is not good enough anymore. It limits you. It denies you all of the potential opportunity that awaits.

[1.] Lance Whitney, Survey: 8 percent of online Americans use Twitter, CNET.com, December 9, 2010 (http://news.cnet.com/8301-1023_3-20025144-93.html).

The night we moved into our new suburban home from our apartment in the city, I stood in the unlit dining room and looked out the window. It was dark and I stared out into the moonlight. I imagined the exact same view, but from the vantage point of myself 30 years older, the night before selling the home after our grown children had moved out. I wondered what memories that man would have had of his life, of dreams realized and hopes dashed, of triumphs and failures, of raising children and living a worthy life.

Imagine yourself in the future, looking back to where you are now. Think of the simple tasks that challenge you and how obvious they will seem in the future. Your goal is not to become popular, generate millions of fans, or attain celebrity status in the world of social media. It is simply to engage.

Ultimately, says Craig Newmark, the visionary founder of craigslist, who started the web site using volunteers, "the technology is secondary; treat people as you would like to be treated." It is that philosophy that has helped him and his team to create one of the world's largest networks of communities, serving 570 cities in 50 countries.

Just start by serving one.

Resources

Like the issues noted in this book, the information in this section is meant to serve as a foundational resource. Each site is a potential starting point. I have not listed any one as an endorsement of its value or verification of its content. Instead, I encourage you to explore, experiment, and evaluate. Most offer some level of interaction for free, and all may help you engage with your audience or community. That engagement is the goal and I hope that these tools help you achieve it.

Conference Calling

FreeConference.com

FreeConferenceCall.com

FreeConferencePro.com

Domain Names

1and1.com

GoDaddy.com

NetworkSolutions.com

Register.com

Newsletters

BenchMarkEmail.com

CampaignMonitor.com

ConstantContact.com

GetResponse.com

iContact.com

MailChimp.com

MyEmma.com

SendLoop.com

StreamSend.com

VerticalResponse.com

Podcasting

Audacity.sourceforge.net

Epnweb.org

Ipodder.org

Juicereceiver.sourceforge.net

Podbean.com

Podcastalley.com

Podcastpickle.com

Podcast.tv

Press Releases

1888PressRelease.com

eCommWire.com

Express-Press-Release.com

Free-News-Release.com

Free-Press-Release.com

FreePressIndex.com

FreePressReleases.co.uk

i-Newswire.com

IndiaPRWire.com

NewswireToday.com

PageRelease.com

PressAbout.com

PressBox.co.uk

PressFlow.co.uk

PressMethod.com

PressReleasePoint.com

Publications

CrainsNY.com
FastCompany.com
Inc.com
Wired.com

Social Networks

Academia.edu (academics/researchers)
Athlinks.com (athletes)
Audimated.com (independent music)
Bebo.com (general)
Blogster.com (bloggers)
CafeMom.com (mothers)
Care2.com (volunteers)
Classmates.com (alumni)
Eons.com (baby boomers)
Exploroo.com (travel)
Flixster.com (cinema)
Flickr.com (photography)
Facebook.com (general)
FledgeWing.com (student entrepreneurs)
Focus.com (business)
Folkdirect.com (general)
Fotolog.com (photoblogging)
Foursquare.com (location-based)
Friendster.com (general)
Geni.com (genealogy)
Goodreads.com (literature)
Google.com/Buzz (general)
GovLoop.com (government)
IndabaMusic.com (music)
italki.com (language)

InterNations.com (international)

Lafango.com (entertainment)

Last.fm (music)

LibraryThing.com (literature)

LinkedIn.com (professional)

LinkExpats.com (expatriates)

Livemocha (language)

Meetup.com (offline meetings)

MySpace.com (general)

Ning.com (create social networks)

Ravelry.com (knitters; crocheters)

ResearchGate.net (scientific researchers)

Ryze.com (business)

Scispace.net (scientists)

SocialVibe.com (charity)

StumbleUpon.com (general)

TeachStreet.com (education)

TravBuddy.com (travel)

Tumblr.com (general)

Twitter.com (general)

WeeWorld.com (teens)

Yammer.com (office colleagues)

Yelp.com (local reviews)

Surveys

eSurveysPro.com

FreeOnlineSurveys.com

KwikSurveys.com

LimeSurvey.org

PollDaddy.com

SurveyGizmo.com

SurveyMonkey.com

Zoomerang.com

Webinar/Collaboration Tools

AnyMeeting.com

DimDim.com

GoToWebinar.com

Join.Me

Mikogo.com

ShowDocument.com

Vyew.com

WebEx.com

Yugma.com

Acknowledgments

After someone close to me passed away 16 years ago, I started keeping a journal on New Year's Eve. I was bothered, among many things, by the fact that she would never again have the opportunity to reflect on the past or dream about the future. In the pages of this personal record, I note my frustrations and my hopes. I share triumphs and failures. I relate events and set goals.

At the beginning of 2010, I challenged myself to write a second book. I had been touring the country discussing *The Opportunity Maker*, and had encountered thousands of professionals with remarkable insights. I engaged them in conversation and the themes in this book are the direct result of that dialogue. I am particularly grateful to everyone who shared his or her perspective and experience in its pages. Each interview inspired me to seek out another.

I was fortunate to meet Paul Dinas of Alpha Books at the American Society of Journalists and Authors conference, and am indebted to him for referring me to Debby Englander at Wiley. I am also lucky to work with a talented group of colleagues, who not only give me the tremendous opportunity to collaborate with them, but also encourage me on a regular basis. They include: Sharon Abrahams, Cinnamon Baker, Larry Bodine, Jennifer Bluestein, Steve Butterworth, JeanMarie Campbell, Bari Chase, Kendall Coffey, Richard Demb, Sean Doherty, Gabe Galanda, Steve Harber, Jonathan Hayter, Paula Holderman, Kate Andrejack Holmes, Nakia Humphrey, Kerstin Isaacs, Rebecca James, Serena Josephs, Mike Kinnaman, Heather Milke, Mark Moran, Christine Musil, Paula Nailon, Kay Nash, Molly Peckman, Meg Reuter, Jane Rhee, Maria Rutkin, David Schnurman, David Snow, Allison Stegich, Mark Weber, and, of course, my mentor, Lisa Linsky. Thank you also to my friends, both cool and almost cool; my editors, Emilie Herman and Carla Main; and my excellent assistant, Michael Cummo.

My parents, Felice and Mike, my uncle, Jeff, my sister, Bonni, and my Nana instilled in me a sincere interest in others and a quirky sense of humor. Those characteristics define who I am and they deserve a lifetime of loyalty for helping me develop them. My appreciation for humor may be why I often remember the distinct sound of someone's laugh long after they are gone. Richie and Bubby had two of the best. Their lightness echoes in the wonderful chuckles of Emory and Hannah, my inspiration for living fully and authentically. Esther, Shari, and David, thank you for laughing with me. And, as always, to Lauren, for joining me on this journey.

About the Author

Ari Kaplan is a consultant who offers guidance on transforming one's perspective, profile, and practice. He spent nearly nine years with large law firms in New York City and has interviewed hundreds of authorities on topics related to innovation in career and business development. He is the founder of the Innovative Professionals Initiative, an interdisciplinary endeavor to create parallels and partnerships between licensed experts worldwide.

In addition to being the author of *The Opportunity Maker: Strategies for Inspiring Your Legal Career Through Creative Networking and Business Development* (Thomson-West, 2008), which is about how students and professionals can stand out in a stagnant economy, Kaplan has also written for *Wired*, *The Daily Telegraph*, *eWeek*, *Crain's New York Business*, *CIO Today*, *The Journal of Commerce*, *ComputerWorld*, and *The Star Ledger*, among others.

Kaplan has been recognized in *The Wall Street Journal*'s Law Blog, the *Houston Chronicle*, the *Miami Herald*, the *New York Post*, and other publications. As the principal of Ari Kaplan Advisors, he provides ghostwriting and industry research services, personal coaching, and training for students and professionals on publishing, communications, career enhancement, business development, and networking.

He established the Ari Kaplan Advisors charitable book collection through the Intergenerational Literacy Project in Chelsea, Massachusetts, and has served on the board of editors for various publications. Kaplan was a regular commentator for CNET Radio and has been interviewed on CNN. He received Apex Awards in 2010, 2008, and 2007 for feature writing.

Admitted to the bar in New York, New Jersey, and Washington, D.C., he earned his J.D. from George Washington University Law School and his B.A., magna cum laude, from Boston University. He enjoys playing catch with his kids, juggling, strumming a lefty guitar, and participating in triathlons.

Learn more at AriKaplanAdvisors.com.

Index

A

Accelerant
  creation, 147
  engagement letter, 146–147
  launch, 145–146
Accelerant Preferred, 146
Accountability, importance, 51–54
Accountants
  business development skills,
    testing, 36
  client borrowing, 79
  hustling, foreignness, 38
  information product, provision, 82
  numbers, focus, 98
  reactive life, 42–43
  regulatory shift, impact, 35–36
  skill, improvement, 40–41
  technology, usage, 63–64
Accounting, Sarbanes-Oxley Act
  (impact), 79
a-connect, creation, 118
Active Rain, usage (increase), 17–18
Adaptive reuse, 92
Adelphia, scandal, 36
Advantage Performance Group,
  111–116
Aladdin (system), 171–172
Alignment, usage, 39–43
Al Odah v. United States oral arguments,
  coverage, 4
American Donut Shoppe, growth,
  13–14
Architects
  budget/marketing, focus, 98
  creativity, perception, 98
  models, experimentation, 114–115

Arthur Andersen, downfall, 116
Art of Non-Conformity, The
  (Guillebeau), 109
Asset allocation, advice, 67
Attendees, engagement, 128
Audacity.sourceforge.net, 166
Audience
  focus, 102–103
  time, 110
  tools, 103–104
Avvo.com (online doctor/lawyer
  location/rating service), 2
Axiom
  baseline benefits, 77
  engagements, legal opt-out, 76–77
  functions, client outsourcing, 76

B

Bank foreclosures, processing, 24–25
Bank-owner property portfolio, trust
  (increase), 20
Barton, Rich, 102–106
Benchmarking, 910
Beta testing, continuation, 1
Bet-the-franchise multi-jurisdictional
  matters, 75
BirthDatabase.com, usage, 183
BlackBerry, usage, 197
BlackRock Solutions, 171–173
  creation, 172
  marketing, 173
Blog
  consistency/failure, 109
  distribution source, 9
  public conversation generation, 196
Blogger (Google), 10

Blogging
  benefits, 107–108
  FeedBlitz.com, usage, 157
  posts, pre-writing, 108
  usage, decision, 107–109
BlogTalkRadio, 91
Bookkeeping services, increase, 63
Book Yourself Solid (Port), 184
Boumediene v. Bush oral arguments,
    coverage, 4
Britton, Mark, 2
Brogan, Chris, 109
Brokerage model, guidance, 71
Broker Price Opinion (BPO), 25
Brunner, Frédéric, 118–119
Budget, architect concern, 98
Building codes, complexity
    (increase), 96
Building-information modeling trend,
    requirements, 96
Bukzin, David, 98, 135–138
  mailing list, power (leveraging), 138
  referral sources, value (addition), 138
Business
  cards, collection (networking), 102
  consumer, power shift, 44
  development, 111, 158–159
    skills, impact, 36
  evolution, 144
  fan page, creation (consideration),
    107
  growth
    demand, impact, 79
    technology, impact, 65
  operation, risk/realities, 36
  prospects, approach, 38
  revenue, 112–113
  technology, usage, 144
  traditional notions, constancy, 131–132
Business-development initiatives,
    increase, 51

C

Callahan, Michael, 133
Call Recorder (Ecamm), 165
CamStudio, usage, 166
Cancerwise.com, guest blog posts, 29

Candito, Lauren, 17–18
Candito Group, 17–20
  blog, creation, 18
  business, problems, 18
  goals, 19
  online efforts, 20
  public communication, usage, 22
  referrals, sharing, 25
Capital, usage, 99
Career
  overview, development, 126
  placement office, contact, 105
  success, basis, 49–50
Carnegie, Dale, 154
Carr, Jeffrey, 36–39, 97–98
Center for Medicare and Medicaid
    Services (CMMS), 121–122
Certifications, receiving
    (advertisement), 34
Cetra, John, 91–93
CetraRuddy, 91–93
  client marketing, 94
  recognition, pursuit, 94
CharityNavigator.org, usage, 185
Chat systems, usage, 83
Chronicle.com, email alerts, 57
Client-centric environment, expertise, 69
Clients
  accountant borrowing, 79
  CetraRuddy marketing, 94
  connection, usefulness, 39
  consulting organizations, impact,
    85–86
  conversation, caution (advantages),
    180–181
  direct meeting, 141
  experience, impact, 40
  grouping, 42
  hustle, 50
  ideas, conveyance, 116–117
  interaction, modernization, 81–82
  knowledge, 61
  privileges, waiver, 179
  questions, answering, 66–70, 83
  relationships
    alignment, 39–43
    management, 74

secret shopper status, 131–132
self-reliance, increase, 150
servicing, 41
success
    human talent, excitement, 12
    measurement, 41
    support, provision, 84–85
Clinical trials
    patient awareness/participation,
        increase, 28–29
    promotion, 29
Co-authoring industry, 95
Colic Solved (Vartabedian), 26
Collaboration
    impact, 95
    tools, resources, 203
Colleagues, connection (timing),
    185–188
Comfort level, provision, 39
Comfort zone, exit, 9
Commissions, decrease, 69
Commoditization, 49–50
Communication
    direct form, emergence, 82–83
    improvement, technology (usage),
        43–45
    seamlessness, 43–44
    tools, variety, 49
Community, building, 110, 195
Company
    acquisition, 112
    budgets, purchase information, 78
    development, time (necessity),
        145–146
Complete Guide to Game Audio (Marks),
    142
Complexity (simplification),
    technology (usage), 157
Computer-aided architectural design
    (CAAD), self-service programs, 6
Conference calling, resources, 199
ConferenceCallPro.com, 188
Confidentiality, importance, 177–179
Connections (finding)
    social media, usage, 62
    speed, 62
Consultants, information (sharing), 64

Consulting model, 118
Consulting organizations, client
    attraction, 85–86
Consumers
    empowerment, 103
    informed decisions, 66
    professionals, community
        interaction, 2
    questions, answering, 112
Contacts
    birthdays, usage, 174
    details, print publication
        provision, 159
    focus, 56–58
    followup, 58–59
    issues, discussions, 51
    location, 159–160
    making, reason (development), 53
    speed, 55–56
Content, creation, 27–28, 44, 191–192
Continuous positive airway pressure
    (CPAP) machine, usage, 122
Conversation
    caution, advantages, 180–181
    dates, calendaring, 174
    simplicity, 162
Corporate office space, downsizing, 92
Cost conversations, 36–39
Counsel-client relationship,
    existence, 66
Courtesy, usage, 40
Cozen O'Connor Trial Academy/
    Deposition Program,
    creation, 15
Crain, Janet, 33–35
Creating Rainmakers (Harding), 43
Credentials, advertising, 34
Credibility, building, 189
    Internet, usage, 186–187
Criticism (attack), content (usage), 27
Cross-border public mergers and
    acquisitions, 75
Customers, knowledge, 62
Customer Service (Shankman), 163
Cyberspace, information
    (sending), 154
Cyber-visibility, increase, 106–107

D

Data-analysis capabilities, 80
Data distribution model, 45
Date-specific events, follow-up, 184–185
Davies, Gareth, 35–39
  business prospect approach, 38
  people, meeting (necessity), 37
  Sarbanes-Oxley Act, impact, 37
Dealbuilder.wsgr.com (tool), 148
Decision-making process, trust
    (reliance), 71
Defined metrics, creation, 41
Demand
  confluence, 79
  rigorous segmentation, 77
Dentists
  advertisement, necessity, 34
  certifications, press releases, 34
  models, experimentation, 114–115
  practice, changes, 34–35
Desk Set (1957), 149
Digital footprint, physician
    understanding, 27
Discipline, importance, 51–54
Discount brokerage firms, planning
    tools (usage), 68
Displacement anxiety, 149–152
Distribution lists, usage, 54
Doctors
  advertisement, necessity, 34
  networking, focus (absence), 27
  patients, disconnection, 26
Documents, digitization (impact), 3
Do-It-Yourself (DIY) online document-
    assembly services, 147
Domain name
  registration, 55, 134
  resources, 199
Dow Jones Industrial Average (DJIA),
    drop, 100
Dragon Dictation iPhone, usage, 197
Due diligence, conducting, 41, 62
Duffin, Lawrence, 24
Dwyer, Mike, 144–145

E

Earning multiples, 74
Economic downturn, impact, 52

Eco-system, service firm location
    (determination), 78
Eden, Liann, 83–86
Eden McCallum, talents (leveraging),
    83–86
Elance.com, usage, 65
Electronic data room, usage, 132
Email
  effectiveness, 172
  responses, generation, 54
  sample, 161
Email newsletters
  benefits, leveraging, 156
  message, conveyance, 158
  sending, 158
Emotional intelligence, 69
EmploySecure.com, usage, 66
Enron, scandal, 36
Enthusiasm
  importance, 11–14
  level, conveyance, 12–13
Escrow companies, online presence,
    25–26
ESPlanner, calculators, 68
Estate planning techniques, 70–71
Estate planning topics, lawyer
    proposal, 72
Ethics rules, 177
Events
  hosting, 188–189
  philosophy (Korff), 129
Expectations, setting, 133–135
Expedia.com, Britton (impact), 2
Expert, enthusiasm (importance), 5–6
Expertise
  conveyance, ease, 14–16
  elusiveness, 14
  sharing, 57, 162

F

Facebook
  assistance, 175
  birthdays, usage, 174
  discussion, comfort, 105
  exploration, 107
  growth, 183
  popularity, 151–152
  profile, 49

public communication, usage, 22
updates, 62
Facebook-style platforms, growth, 26
Failures
necessity, 153
occurrence, 52, 197
sharing, 54–55
Fair Credit Reporting Act, compliance,
65–66
Falk Harrison, 7, 9
Fan page, creation (consideration), 107
Feedback forms, 131
FeedBlitz.com, usage
(consideration), 157
Ferguson, Karen, 78–82
Ferriss, Timothy, 165
Financial meltdown, 67
Financial service, information-
processing industry, 172
Financial services firms, online service
transition, 118–119
Financing, raising, 41
Finley II, Edward J., 69–71
Flip video recorder, usage, 9, 164
Follow-up
foundation, establishment, 183
thoughtfulness, 189–190
4-Hour Workweek, The (Ferriss), 165
Fox, Nancy, 2
FreeConferenceCall.com, 188
FreeConferencePro.com, 188
registration, 53
Free information, availability, 3
Free services, examples, 163
Friendster, impact, 151–152
Future, focus, 78–80

G

Garland, David Siteman, 53, 108–109,
164
video success, Skype (usage), 165
Geek
location, 104–105
pairing, 105
General Securities Representative
Examination (Series 7), 89
Geographic markets, broadening, 93
Give.org, usage, 185

Glassdoor.com, growth, 104
*Global Email Deliverability Benchmark
Report* (Return Path, Inc.), 155
Globalization, impact, 173
Godin, Seth, 165
Goldstein, Robert L., 171–174
Google
analytics, incorporation, 151–152
keywords, indexing, 9–10
Google Earth, usage, 22
Grass roots media, 26–30
Guettel, Alec, 74–76
Guillebeau, Chris, 109
Guinea pig profile, misperception, 29

H

Harding, Ford, 43–45
Harrell, Katrina, 63–64, 67–68
Harris, Mark, 73–77
Headaches.com, domain name
registration, 134
Health Insurance Portability and
Accountability Act of 1996
(HIPAA), 178
Hedge Fund Hotel, 90
Hedge funds, catering, 99
HelloHealth.com, impact, 26–27
HelpAReporter.com, usage, 163
Hepburn, Katharine, 149
High-frequency traders, attraction
(strategy), 90
Hourly valuations, legal focus, 75
Housing focus, broadening, 93
Hsieh, Tony, 165
Huggies Little Movers Diaper
Race, 128
Hunt, Hayes, 15–16
links, sharing, 16
marketing efforts, 15–16

I

iGlasses (Ecamm), usage, 165
iMovie, usage, 166
Inbound marketing leads
generation, 10
Inbox, attention, 155
Incentive, necessity, 50
Independence trend, 119

Independent professionals (IPs),
  expertise/experience, 118
Individuals
  interaction, technology (impact), 91
  interviews, productivity, 51
  understanding, 126
Industry-driven information database,
  Web usage, 106
Industry value (potency dilution),
  collaboration (impact), 95
Inefficiency, elements (impact),
  75–77
Information
  accessibility, 106
  availability, increase (impact), 117
  communication/management, 173
  delivery market, 62
  gathering, model, 45
  migration, advantages, 24
  processing, 172–173
  sending, 154
  sharing, 64
In-house attorneys, control, 36
Initial public offerings, 75
Initiatives, starting, 81–86
Innovation
  ability, 81
  adaptation, 26
Innovation-driven market, 73
Innovators, adaptation, 17
Insecurity, fighting, 58
InstyMeds.com, pharmaceutical
  dispensers, 149
Intensive care, on-call physician
  interpretation, 120
Internet
  buffer, addition, 179–180
  impact, 79
  investment, continuation, 3
  service provider, impact, 84–85
Investment bankers, referral network
  (construction), 135
Iordanishvili, Levan, 142–145
  credibility, building, 144–145
  LinkedIn success, 143–144
  links, sharing, 144
  web site, updates, 143

J
Jamaica Underwear Run, 127–128
Janus Financial Executive Challenge, 128
Jobs, change (frequency), 91
Johnson, Rodney, 20–23
  presence, improvement, 21
Join.me, recommendation, 106
Jomati Consultants, 116–117
  reports, 117
Jones, Bruce, 187
Jones, Butch, 90
Junior lawyers, project management/
  research tasks, 74

K
Kapadia, Tejas, 13
  enthusiasm, leverage, 14
  market creation, 13–14
Kaplan, Robins (legal resources
  development), 146
Kaufman, Brad, 127, 129–133
  responsibility, acceptance, 131
Key words, identification, 107
King, Billie Jean, 125–126
Klemons, Ira, 23, 33–35, 133–135
  domain name, registration, 134
  patients, number, 134
  report writing, 134–135
Know, like, and trust formula, 9
Knowledge
  availability, increase, 25
  development, 128
  leakage, prevention, 119
Kooldocs.com (Web-based service), 148
Korff, John, 125–129, 164
  creative philosophy, 128
  responsibility, acceptance, 131

L
Law, technology (convergence), 176
Law firms
  chairpersons, contact
    (maintenance), 117
  corporate client attraction
    methods, 11
  industry, transformation, 137–138
  leverage ratio, 75

permanent associates, hiring, 74
talent-driven services, completion, 76
Lawyers
baseline benefits (Axiom), 77
engagements, opt-out, 76–77
evolution, 70–71
hustling, foreignness, 38
information
product, provision, 82
sharing, 64
models, experimentation, 114–115
self-determination, consequences
(absence), 76–77
self-perception, 73
Leads
improvement, 45
review, 163
Lee, R. Randy, 150
Legal documents, drafting, 6
Legal resources, development, 146
LexisNexis, change, 62
Licensed professionals, success
strategy, 5
Licenses, advertising, 34
Life-impacting situations, on-call
physician interpretation, 120
LinkedIn
advanced search, usage, 141–142
Answers tool, usage, 105
assistance, 175
discussion, comfort, 105
preference, 28
professionals, joining refusals, 178
profile, cyber-visibility (increase),
106–107
questions, answering, 103–104
success, 143–144
usage, 104–105, 162
work, showcasing, 190
Liquidity risk, client concern, 173
Liss, David, 121–123

M
MailChimp.com, newsletter tool, 154
Mailing list, 153
members, interaction, 154
power, leveraging, 138

Marketing
approach, 151
architect focus, 98
evolution, 116–119
forgiveness, 8
Marketing, spinoff effectiveness,
190–193
Marketplace, transformations, 118
Market research, data-analysis
capabilities, 80
Marks, Aaron, 142–145
Martindale-Hubbell guide, 126
McCallum, Dena, 83–86
McCarthy, Mary Ellen, 66–70
McLaughlin, Charles E., 65–66
Meal-time events, productivity, 51
Media, 153, 164–165
access, 162
meeting, 159–160
Media relations
experience, absence, 160
management, 50
Medical records, 119–123
Medicare.gov, long-term-care cost
calculator, 68
Medu Vada, 13–14
Mentor, assistance, 58–59
Message
conveyance, 158
energy/creativity, 39
Metri, Sam, 24–25
Metrics, creation, 41
MF Global, commission, 99
Microblogging site, network ability, 189
Miest, Ryan, 145–149
Miller, Stephanie, 155, 157
Milligan, Graham, 11–12
Mistakes, making, 153
Mobile medicine, phenomenon, 121
Mobile phone
applications, usage (determination),
103
leverage, 106
Modative in Los Angeles (Timschell),
98
Modeling technology, 95–96
Mohler-Erickson, Leisa, 111–116

MondoTimes.com, resource, 159
Money managers, advice (provision), 66
Monthly newsletter, usage
    (consideration), 156
Moore, Gordon, 99
Morningstar.com, portfolio
    management tools, 68
Motivation, importance, 97–98
Multex Systems, 66–67
Multi-family offices, emergence, 70
Multi-jurisdictional matters, 75
Multiple Listing Service, usage, 22
Multi-purpose conference usage,
    study, 92
MySpace, impact, 15–152

N
Neighbors, befriending, 89
Networking
    approach, 56
    business cards, collection, 102
    capabilities reach (increase), social
        media (usage), 19
    challenge, 101
    description, 49
    myths, 50–51
    showcasing, 42
Newmark, Craig, 198
Newsletters
    provision, 156
    resources, 199–200
New Year's resolutions, collections, 187
Ning.com, power (leverage), 186
Non-compete agreement, breach
    (handling), 129–130
Nye, Dan, 156–157

O
Off-hour emergency room, on-call
    physician interpretation, 120
Offline relationships, online
    cultivation, 21–23
Olympic Games, NYC bid, 126
OpeningDesign.com, development, 104
Opportunity
    creation, 5–6
    generation, 83

maximization, 92–93
    protocol, 53–54
    Sarbanes-Oxley Act, impact, 79
    seizing, 35–36
Organizations
    familiarity, list (making), 128–129
    profitability, focus, 77
Overhead, accounting, 74

P
Pain treatment, 133–134
Paper newsletter, replacement, 30
Parkinson, Jay, 26–27
Participation, problems, 176–177
Patience, collective level
    (reduction), 117
Patients
    direct meeting, 141
    insurance company control, 37
    knowledge, 61
    over-the-counter remedy,
        recommendation, 149
    report, writing (Klemons), 134–135
    success, human talent
        (excitement), 12
    symptoms, review, 148–149
Pattern-matching, 45
People
    connection, usefulness, 39
    meaningfulness, understanding, 186
    meeting, focus, 37
    personal pressures/stresses/goals,
        consideration, 130–131
    sales/speaking, holistic process, 116
Perseverance level, demonstration,
    39–40
Personality, public/private aspects
    (convergence), 3
Personal marketing, challenge, 1
Phone book, replacement, 2
Physicians, online community (Sermo.
    com), 26–27
Pivawer, Gabriel, 119–121
Podcasting, resources, 200
Port, Michael, 184–187
Posts (blogs), pre-writing, 108
Potential, realization, 6–11

Practice, 73
    promotion, tools (leveraging),
        65–66
    staffing models, experimentation,
        114
Press releases, resources, 200
Pre-venture capital stage, 146
Print publications, contact details
    (provision), 159
Privacy
    policies, variations, 179
    settings, control, 107
Private equity fund managers, referral
    network (construction), 135
Privileges, client waiver, 179
Proactive professionals, attention, 111
Problem solving, 40
Professional advice, necessity, 3
Professional relationships, online
    creation, 179–180
Professionals
    consistency, ensuring, 153
    relationship support, technology
        usage, 176
    self-determination, consequences
        (absence), 76–77
    technology, impact, 115–116
    types, 137
Professional services
    advantages, 81
    flexibility, absence, 81
    focus, 130
    marketing, 99
    proliferation, 195
Profitability, organizational focus, 77
Profit model, cost savings basis, 97–98
Profit-sharing pool, 74
Progress, proactive professional
    attention, 111
Prospects
    conversation, caution (advantage),
        180–181
    counsel, reason, 103
    questions, answering, 112–113
Prosperity, path, 93–95
Prozes, Andrew, 61–63
Publications, resources, 201

Public company accounting reform/
    auditing responsibility, Sarbanes-
    Oxley Act (impact), 35–36
Public conversation (generation), blog
    (usage), 196
Public domain, details, 45
Public information, scarcity, 126
Puddle, Tim, 113–115
Purple Cow, The (Godin), 165

Q
Qureshi, Sajeel, 81–83

R
Rader, Randall R., 196
Rainmakers, motion, 43
Recession, impact, 92
References, guarantees, 42
Referrals
    art, 135–138
    cultivation, 117
    network, power (leveraging), 135
    sources, value (addition), 138
Referral sources, network
    (cultivation), 85
Regulatory shift, impact, 35–36
Reimer, Chris, 11
    career, discovery, 11
    inbound marketing leads
        generation, 10
    Twitter usage, 6–7, 9
Relationships
    building, 112–113, 169
    creation, 180
    development, 3–4
    establishment, knowledge (usage), 10
    intersection, 42
    management, traditional notions
        (constancy), 131–132
    online creation, 179–180
    technology, balance, 170–171
    tracking, technology (usage), 43–44
    usage, 127–129
Reminder programs, usage, 83
ReporterConnection.com, usage, 163
Reporters, direct access (free
        services), 163

Research statistics, usage, 190
Resiliency revolution, 33
Resource, offering, 56–58
Resources Global Professionals, 78–80
  variable model, usage, 80–81
Responsibility, acceptance
    (philosophy), 131
Revenues, origination (change), 38
Risk
  aversion, 49
  value, relationships, 36
Rizzo Tees LLC
  Twitter usage, 6–7
Ruddy, Nancy, 91–97
Rutter, Jolienne/Scott E., 119–120

S
Sales, 93–95
  activities, necessity, 37
  euphemisms, 43
  evolution, 116–119
  strategies, improvement, 45
Sarbanes-Oxley Act (2002)
  enactment, 38
  impact, 35–37
  opportunities, 79
Savage, Charlie, 5
Schedules, coordination, 103
Schonfeld, Steven, 89–91
Securities lawyers, referral network
    (construction), 135
Self-diagnosis problem, impact, 112
Self-image, change (avoidance), 95–97
Self-knowledge, importance, 91–93
Self-marketing, usage, 51
Self-reliance, trend (increase), 150
Self-sufficiency, 137
Senior lawyers, client relationship
    management, 74
Senior professionals, model
    reconfiguration, 149
Seniors Club, 116
Sermo.com, 26–27
Service firms, eco-system location, 78
Service providers
  results, delivery (efficiency), 77
Service providers, feedback, 2

Services
  consumers, responsibility, 44
  continuation, 77
  delivery, demand, 133
  demand bucket, identification, 77
  sale, Sarbanes-Oxley restrictions, 38
  value chain, disaggregation, 44
  value identification, 85
Shankman, Peter, 163
Shatz, Matthew, 69–70, 89–91, 94,
    99–100
Single electronic records,
    integration, 26
Skechers Shape-ups Go Mommy Go
    race, 128
Skype, usage, 164, 165
SlideShare, usage, 145
Small discussion groups,
    productivity, 51
Small groups, comfort, 51
Smarter, Faster, Cheaper (Garland), 53
SnapzProX, usage, 166
Social cause, enquiry, 185
Social media
  connections, 62
  engagement, 9
  environments, communication, 178
  goals, 19–21
  grass roots media, 30
  platforms
    rise, 101
    usage, 189
  power, leveraging, 57–58
  space, doctors (absence), 27
  usage, 19, 62, 103
Social networking, popularity, 150
Social networks, resources, 201–202
Specialness, treatment, 40–41
Specificity, goal, 157
Spreng, Kevin, 145–149
Staff augmentation, 79
Staffing models, experimentation, 114
Strassler, Phil, 40–43, 186
  due diligence, usage, 41
Strengths, weaknesses, opportunities,
    and threats (SWOT), 92–93
  analysis, 93

Students
  networking, 56–58
  polls, 49
  recruitment, 105
  white collar hustle, 47
Success
  architect measurement, 41
  effort, requirement, 127
  failure, necessity, 153
  profits, connection, 97–98
  sharing, 54–55
Super transparent world, 104
Support, provision, 84–85
Surveys
  preparation/creation, Zoomerang.
      com (usage), 175, 185
  resources, 202–203
  responses, 117–118
  usage, 83
  web site, examination, 175–176

T
Talent-driven services, completion, 76
Talents, merging, 70–72
Target market, selection, 184
Techn-ethics, 177
Technology
  accountants, connection, 63–64
  avoidance, 169
  deficiency, 170
  emergence, 96
  impact, 176
  integral role, 63
  landscape, navigation, 50
  law, convergence, 176
  professional reliance, problems,
      115–116
  relationships, balance, 170–171
  role, increase, 63–64
  transformational difference, 173
  usage, 43–45, 144, 157
    extension, 174–176
Teicher, Stuart, 177–181
Teleradiology, 120
  contracts, Valor Network
      bidding, 120
  initiation, 121

10e20, creation, 150
Term, search (user preference), 23
Text messages, usage, 174
TheRisetotheTop.com, 164
ThinkBigRevolution.com,
      creation, 186
30-Minute Thursdays, webinar
      series, 8
Timekeeping, legal focus, 75
Timschell, Oscia, 96–97
Tip$ter, financial planner, 68
Title issuers, online presence, 25–26
Top-tier consultancies, access, 83–84
Tracy, Spencer, 149
Trade publication, experience, 161
Trade speed, focus, 99–100
Transactions, software (impact),
      24–25
Transparency, usage, 24–26
Triathlon, potential, 127
True worth, discovery, 80–81
Trulia, usage (increase), 17–18
Trust
  building, 97–98
  requirement, 100
Trust Agents (Brogan), 109
Twitter
  commercial usage, 6–7
  discussion, comfort, 105
  following, 7–8
  popularity, 151–152
  preference, 28
  public communication usage, 22
  transparency, 9
  webinar announcement, 190
Tyco International, scandal, 36
Typepad.com, usage, 108

U
Umbrella salesman, 154–157

V
Valor Network, 119–121
  military treatment facilities,
      continuity, 121
  Veterans Administration (VA)
      hospitals, connection, 120

Value
  chain, disaggregation, 44
  perception, importance, 38
  proposition, defining, 78–80
  risk, relationship, 36
Vartabedian, Bryan, 26–30
Veterinarians
  economy, impact, 114
  information, sharing, 64
  partnerships, 113
  pet wellness promotion, newsletter
    usage, 156
  practices, consolidation, 113
  Seniors Club, 116
Veterinary instruction, rote
    memorization (focus), 12
Virtual introduction, 42
Virtualization, downside, 150
Virtual offices, concept, 48
Virtual practices, creation, 174
Virtual spaces, global roots, 132–133
Visibility, increase, 6–11
Voicemail, simplicity, 162

W
Wall Street, interconnectedness, 91
Wealth, splitting, 71
Web 2.0 interactivity, 2
Web-based interview, 148
Web-based meetings tools, 106
Web-based pre-employment
    screening, 65
Webinar
  announcement, Twitter (usage), 190
  tools, resources, 203
  value, 188
Web sites
  efforts, integration, 105–107
  engagement, 104
  power, leverage, 23

  updates, 143
  work repository, 55
White collar hustle, 47
White papers
  credibility, leveraging, 191
  effectiveness, 190–191
Williams, Tony, 116–119
Windows Video Player, usage, 166
Winfield, Chris, 150–151
Wordpress.org, usage, 108
Workflow, concern, 143
Workstation sharing, study, 92
WorldCom, scandal, 36
World Wide Web (Web)
  information migration,
    advantages, 24
  practice profile, advantage/
    disadvantage, 33–34
Writing, spinoff effectiveness, 190–193

Y
Yelp.com, growth, 104
Yes business, 129–131
Younes, Anas, 28–30, 178–179
  Twitter, impact, 30
  Twitter query, receipt, 178–179
"Your Wealthy Business" (Harrell), 64
YouTube, usage, 165–166

Z
Zeve, Brian D., 44
Zillow
  database, usage, 106
  usage, 22
    increase, 17–18
  visitors, 102
Zipnosis (Web-based medical
    services), 148
Zolve, usage (increase), 17–18
Zoomerang.com, usage, 175